"*Christianity and Psychoanalysis* catapults a once languishing interdisciplinary dialogue to previously unattained levels. Through impeccably organized contributions by leading authors, Bland and Strawn have accomplished a substantive theoretical and clinical comparison of major psychoanalytic perspectives, all in nuanced dialogue with multiple traditions in Christian theology. This is a remarkable book whose time has come, a 'must read' for all with interest in this dialogue, and an essential text for educational programs in psychology, counseling and theology."

Marie T. Hoffman, assistant professor in the New York University Postdoctoral Program in Psychotherapy and Psychoanalysis

Bring → regulate my emotions
perceive, measure/label
sense of intensity,

realize, deal it down, how to soothe myself

my affect back to order

may require mirroring)

CAPS
INTERNATIONAL

An Association for Christian Psychologists,
Therapists, Counselors and Academicians

CAPS is a vibrant Christian organization with a rich tradition. Founded in 1956 by a small group of Christian mental health professionals, chaplains and pastors, CAPS has grown to more than 2,100 members in the U.S., Canada and more than 25 other countries.

CAPS encourages in-depth consideration of therapeutic, research, theoretical and theological issues. The association is a forum for creative new ideas. In fact, their publications and conferences are the birthplace for many of the formative concepts in our field today.

CAPS members represent a variety of denominations, professional groups and theoretical orientations; yet all are united in their commitment to Christ and to professional excellence.

CAPS is a non-profit, member-supported organization. It is led by a fully functioning board of directors, and the membership has a voice in the direction of CAPS.

CAPS is more than a professional association. It is a fellowship, and in addition to national and international activities, the organization strongly encourages regional, local and area activities which provide networking and fellowship opportunities as well as professional enrichment.

To learn more about CAPS, visit www.caps.net.

CAPS BOOKS
from IVP Academic

The joint publishing venture between IVP Academic and CAPS aims to promote the understanding of the relationship between Christianity and the behavioral sciences at both the clinical/counseling and the theoretical/research levels. These books will be of particular value for students and practitioners, teachers and researchers.

For more information about CAPS Books, visit InterVarsity Press's website at www.ivpress.com/cgi-ivpress/book.pl/code=2801.

CHRISTIANITY & PSYCHOANALYSIS

A NEW CONVERSATION

Edited by

EARL D. BLAND and BRAD D. STRAWN

IVP Academic

An imprint of InterVarsity Press
Downers Grove, Illinois

InterVarsity Press
P.O. Box 1400, Downers Grove, IL 60515-1426
World Wide Web: www.ivpress.com
E-mail: email@ivpress.com

InterVarsity Press® is the book-publishing division of InterVarsity Christian Fellowship/USA®, a movement of
students and faculty active on campus at hundreds of universities, colleges and schools of nursing in the United
States of America, and a member movement of the International Fellowship of Evangelical Students. For
information about local and regional activities, write Public Relations Dept., InterVarsity Christian
Fellowship/USA, 6400 Schroeder Rd., P.O. Box 7895, Madison, WI 53707-7895, or visit the IVCF website at
<www.intervarsity.org>.

All Scripture quotations, unless otherwise indicated, are taken from the Holy Bible, Today's New International
Version™, Copyright © 2001 by International Bible Society. Used by permission. All rights reserved.

While all stories in this book are true, some names and identifying information in this book have been changed
to protect the privacy of the individuals involved.

Cover design: Cindy Kiple
Interior design: Beth Hagenberg
Images: spxChrome/Getty Images

ISBN 978-0-8308-2856-2 (print)
ISBN 978-0-8308-9588-5 (digital)

Printed in the United States of America ∞

Library of Congress Cataloging-in-Publication Data
Christianity and psychoanalysis : a new conversation / edited by Earl D.
Bland and Brad D. Strawn.
      pages cm
Includes bibliographical references and index.
ISBN 978-0-8308-2856-2 (pbk. : alk. paper)
1. Christianity--Psychology. 2. Psychoanalysis and religion. I. Bland,
Earl D., 1963-, editor of compilation
BR110.C463 2014
261.5'15--dc23
                                                                                2014004274

P   20   19   18   17   16   15   14   13   12   11   10   9   8   7   6   5   4   3   2   1
Y   31   30   29   28   27   26   25   24   23   22   21   20   19   18   17   16   15   14

For Beth Brokaw,

who enlivened our hearts

Contents

Acknowledgments

By way of confession, Earl and I both grew up in fairly conservative Christian environments. For that reason it has been a long journey for us, first to psychology and then to psychoanalysis. This journey has been full of challenges, bumps and bruises, and some criticisms by fellow Christians and psychologists. It has included sacrifices of time and money spent in training above and beyond our doctoral programs. Nevertheless we would not trade any of it for the world. We believe that our journey into psychoanalysis has not only made us better psychotherapists but also better integrators (Christianity and theology) and even better followers of Christ.

Just as humans need others in order to develop and form, books also don't come into being in a vacuum. This book might not have come to fruition were it not for the stimulating environment that has developed in the last few years through the Society for the Exploration of Psychoanalytic Therapies and Theology (SEPTT). SEPTT was the brainchild of Marie Hoffman and Lowell Hoffman (both trained psychoanalysts from NYU) who developed a psychoanalytic track as a part of the yearly conference of the Christian Association for Psychological Studies (CAPS).

This track began to grow while the Hoffmans were strategizing the development of the first and only psychoanalytic training institute with a distinctly Christian emphasis. From this dream the Brookhaven Institute for Psychoanalysis and Christian Theology (BIPACT) was born. Earl and I were both lucky enough to be invited to be early contributors and board members. We will always be grateful for this honor and for the amazingly enriching experiences of sitting in the Hoffmans' home over the past few years, fellowshiping, dreaming, worshiping, praying together and listening to world-renowned psychoanalysts.

We would be remiss if we didn't also thank other early contributing members to SEPTT and BIPACT, such as Mitchell Hicks, Natalia Yangarber-Hicks, Shawn Hoffer, Paula Hamm, John Carter, Linda Barnhurst, Roy Barsness and BIPACT's pastor and spiritual director in residence, Beth Brokaw. All these individuals have further challenged us, loved us, supported us and enriched our thinking and work. And to BIPACT's first graduating class of psychoanalytic candidates (Scott Hickman, Philip Hudson, Angela Allen-Peck, Adrianne Sequeira and Nancy Thurston) we say we are terribly proud of you and delighted to call you colleagues and friends.

I (Brad) would also like to first thank my parents who "allowed" me to change my major in college to psychology. I'd like to thank my wife, Suzanne, and my two boys, Evan and Keaton, for putting up with their psychologist husband and dad (i.e., "doctor of feelings"). Thanks for letting me visit bookstores, travel to strange conferences across the country and for reminding me at home just to be Dad. Thanks also to the San Diego Psychoanalytic Society and Institute for the hospitality they showed to me during my training. They warmly welcomed an overt Christian in their midst. And thanks to my colleagues, students and patients in San Diego (Point Loma Nazarene University), Bethany, Oklahoma (Southern Nazarene University), and Pasadena (Fuller Theological Seminary, School of Psychology) for all they have taught me. Finally, thanks for individuals who have graciously read portions of this manuscript and given their feedback: Ron W. Wright, Brent A. Strawn,

George Horton, Lowell Hoffman, Paula. J. Hamm and Alvin Dueck. I would be remiss if I did not point out our gratitude for the substantial assistance provided by Nathaniel Strenger in the preparation of this book for publication.

Echoing Brad, I (Earl) am very grateful for the SEPTT community and the many treasured encounters I have enjoyed with those who desire to deeply explore the love of Christ and the transformative nature of psychoanalytic treatment. In addition to Marie Hoffman and Lowell Hoffman, and all those in the SEPPT community, I want to extend my appreciation to colleagues and instructors at the Greater Kansas City Psychoanalytic Institute who not only provided me with training but continue to be a source of learning and professional growth. To my colleagues at MidAmerica Nazarene University I am grateful for the support and encouragement you have provided during this project. A special thanks to my administrative assistant, Shawnda Kahl, for her willingness to keep me organized so that I could find time to write in the midst of a busy academic schedule. Much gratitude also goes to the many students and patients I have had the privilege of working with over the last twenty-five years of my professional life. It has been an honor to learn with you and from you. On a more personal note, much love and thanks to my wife, Cayla, and my children, Alexandra and Austin, for their encouragement and support through this project.

Thanks to all those who were willing to read various chapter drafts and provide valuable critiques—Eric Johnson, John Carter, Beth Russell, Jim Olthuis, Scott Koeneman—many thanks. In particular I want to thank Rich Zeitner, whose influence on my professional and personal life has been substantial. His thoughtful and careful reading of chapter drafts was particularly useful. Finally we both want to thank InterVarsity Press and our tag-team editors Gary Deddo and David Congdon for the opportunity to write this book as part of a partnership between IVP and CAPS.

representation of God as normative, his argument would lose much of
its force. (p. 17)

The important implication of Jones's argument is that as theology shifts,
such as the contemporary view of relationality within the Trinity as a
template for human-divine engagement (Grenz, 2001; Holmes, 2012;
Shults, 2003), Freud's construction of the psychoanalytic meaning of religious experience based on an exalted paternal figure declines in its explanatory value.

By the time of Freud's writings, science had a fairly robust methodology for seeking knowledge and explaining its findings. With the diminishment of God and theological knowledge as essential for compre-
hending the natural world and human development, movements in
science looked for universal certainties that would allow for confident
predictability of the natural order (Murphy, 1997; Toulmin, 1990).
Through methods of inquiry that searched for regularities in sensory data
and material proofs, science built its knowledge edifice founded on empirical observations that presumed either naturalism or at least a value-
free metaphysic. With the development of representative language that
differentiated fact from value, scientific knowledge attempted to divorce
itself from traditional knowledge that had for so long set the agenda for
discovery and understanding. As Toulmin (1990) states, "one aim of 17th
century philosophers was to frame all their questions in terms that ren-
dered them *independent of context*" (p. 21). Metaphysical assumptions
presumed the supremacy of the material realm and focused on explanations that could be reduced to understanding the world through the different properties of physics, chemistry, biology, physiology or other
natural processes. This ill-fated, pervasive reductionism was perhaps
most rabid in the logical positivists, who sought to base all knowledge on
physics. From this reductive intellectual bent, values, ethics, culture and
religion were not unimportant but became unverifiable domains of
knowledge and thereby of little consequence to science. Also, given that
science was investigating only natural phenomena, no value or ethical
tradition could be extracted from its processes. Science was neutral, a

technology useful for the advancement of human society.

In a mirror of this process, psychoanalysis adopted a systematic methodology for seeking knowledge and understanding of the human mind and behavior. Careful theoretical proofs were proposed using the case study method and concepts of human nature based on drive instincts, which flowed from the original Freudian understandings of Darwinian evolutionary theory, Lamarckian principles, and nineteenth-century progress in biology and neurology. Freud was an empiricist and conceived psychoanalysis within an organic causal frame wherein psychological processes were reduced to instinctual drives. While some have argued that standard English translations of Freud portray a rabid scientism that is not evident in his original writings (Bettelheim, 1982), others point out that overly structuralized images of Freud's concepts such as id, ego and superego take away from Freud's more flexible, immediate and personal style that is meant to portray varying degrees of complexity and open-endedness to his concepts (Ornston, 1982, 1985).[1] Nonetheless, despite the psychological/relational nature of psychoanalytic technique, Freud never abandoned his convictions regarding the biological foundations of his metatheory (Sulloway, 1979). Freud's ambition to explain complex psychological and relational dynamics via reductionist biological categories was in step with the scientific zeitgeist of the late nineteenth and early twentieth centuries. Although his singularity put him at odds with some of his contemporaries, in its early years Freud's psychoanalysis flourished, especially in postwar America, where psychoanalytic constructs infused the modern cultural imagination.

AFTER MODERNITY: CONTEMPORARY CHANGES IN SCIENCE, PHILOSOPHY AND PSYCHOANALYSIS

Assuming that all psychological theory is embedded in cultural contexts and reflects temporal philosophical and scientific assumptions, any contemporary critique of psychoanalysis must acknowledge the considerable intellectual shifts that have developed in the post-Freudian era. The well-

---

[1]For a review of several works discussing translations of Freud's writing see Coen (1988).

known turn from what has been called modern to postmodern or post-critical thought has arrested much of the objective certitude modernity promised. While the hard sciences of physics, chemistry and to some extent biology continue to thrive with a largely reductive methodology, the human sciences of psychology, sociology and anthropology have found reductionist principles to be as constraining as they were enlightening. Thankfully new language has emerged to help scaffold our understanding in ways that are not antithetical to processes of reductionism, foundationalism and universality. While there is certainly room for the scientific discovery of universals and regularities, the value-neutral position of science has been soundly refuted. Naturalism and its scientific methodology are not value-neutral (Polanyi, 1958; Jones, 1994), tend to reflect a pervasive utilitarian ethic (Taylor, 2007) and reveal a context-dependent social knowledge that pursues particular goals emanating from background assumptions that are not always articulated (Longino, 1990). In other words, psychoanalytic knowledge, or knowledge of any type, is unavoidably shaped by forces of constructivism and hermeneutics. All therapeutic knowledge reveals a particular narrative structure that situates the clinical exchange as meaningful within a given relational matrix, culture, intellectual tradition and religious or ethical configuration. Knowledge is not detachable from the knower. It matters where one is from, one's gender and race, the economic pressures faced, one's cultural and religious traditions, the familial structure present during development, and the presence or absence of unique or traumatic life events. As these factors conspire with given biological and genetic potentials, human life at once becomes universal and particular. Our full understanding of a person is not complete until we have told the story of this life as understood not just in the distant categories of empirical classification but also in the intimate narratives of self-in-relationship, and with any story it matters who is telling the story and who is listening (McAdams, 2001, 2011).

With strong implications for the practice of psychoanalysis, theorists began to see how psychological experience was irreducibly embedded in a relational matrix, including the treatment relationship (Aron, 1996; Greenberg & Mitchell, 1983; Mitchell, 1988; Wachtel, 2008). Further, as science in general has moved to a place more comfortable with the ways that its truths are situated within certain value structures and tell the story of a particular culture or tradition, we are able to reevaluate the reductionist inclination regarding causal relationships. If explanations of human behavior cannot be reduced to biology and physics alone, how does one make sense of human functioning that accounts for nuanced and complex relationships between multiple levels of explanation? The critical nature of this question becomes evident in our current discussion because as soon as we attempt to explain human functioning in psychoanalytic or theological frames we move toward abstract, complex categories that may not link directly to physical or material substance. The ante goes up further when we attempt to develop a meaningful conversation between these two forms of dialogue. No longer are we looking for language of justification, trying to get each discipline to consider the truth claims of the other. Rather, the muting of the modern objectivist frame invites a new rapprochement between psychoanalysis and Christian theology. Distinct theological and psychoanalytic explanations of human behavior and functioning can share constructive explanatory space, operating within a framework that does not contend fundamental evidence from other domains of knowledge, most particular for our purposes, biology and neuroscience. At the same time we recognize that theological and psychoanalytic explanatory concepts are capturing particular qualities or domains of human functioning that are not fully explainable using the language of biology and neuroscience.

To clarify our point, science has attempted to explain complex phenomena, like human biological or psychological functioning using reductive methods, by looking for the smallest units of causation—explaining the whole by understanding its component parts. In psychology this has taken various forms, most popular being behavioral learning theories and psychoanalytic drive theory. While some important gains were achieved via this reductive model, almost from the beginning there have been voices complaining about how complex dynamic systems such as human behavior and mental processes cannot be fully reduced to component parts. In the last fifty years or so these voices have risen to a crescendo, claiming loudly that human psychological functioning is more complex and dynamic than the component parts can explain (Nagel, 2012; Plantinga, 2011; Searle, 2008). The rise of systems theory and the linking of causal factors within complex systemic interactions have greatly increased our understanding of human psychological and relational functioning.

In addition to systems theorists who see relationship and individual psychological development contextualized within concentric levels of influence (Barton & Haslett, 2007; Stanton & Welsh, 2012), others see individual psychological development as firmly embedded within dynamic relational systems (e.g., the child-caretaker dyad) that mutually influence and regulate developmental processes (Beebe & Lachman, 1988, 1998; Siegel, 2012). In their seminal work on development from a nonlinear dynamic systems perspective, Thelen and Smith (1994) argue that human perception, cognition and motor systems develop within a self-organizing system. Knowledge and action emerge from a continuous dynamic exchange of sensory input, action and categorization of experience. In other words, psychological capacities such as thought, emotion, memory and self-reflective functioning, to name a few, emerge from biologically rooted and embodied developmental processes that continually organize and interact with perceptual and sensory input in a mutually regulating dynamic system. Complex human capacities are relationally derived and not reducible to their component parts. Reductive explanatory frameworks simply fail to account for many complex psychological phenomena.

Arising in this discussion is the concept of emergence, which can be defined as the tendency for complex systems to operate in a manner that produces higher-order properties, organization or ways of being that cannot be sufficiently predicted or explained by an analysis of their component parts (Brown, Murphy & Malony, 1998; Clayton & Davies, 2006; Peacocke, 2007). Because theology and psychoanalysis operate with immaterial concepts and hypothesize the existence of structures, functions and processes (e.g., self, soul, relationality) that exert causal influence that cannot be reduced to their biological or neurochemical correlates, we think of these constructs as verifiable emergent phenomena. For example, one of the most self-evident emergent phenomena is consciousness (Koch, 2004; Pinker, 1997). Because the exact neurobiological process of consciousness cannot be accounted for by neuroanatomy and neurophysiology, we can refer to consciousness as an emergent property of a sufficiently ordered human brain. Consciousness is not an epiphenomenon; it emerges from neurophysiological processes and also exerts a causal influence on these neurophysiological processes. The bidirectional nature of causal influence is, of course, not equal; one must have a brain to have consciousness, but there are aspects of consciousness that influence the structure and nature of neurophysiological processes, what Peacocke (2007) has called "whole-part influence" (p. 27).

Similarly, psychoanalytic and theological concepts involve higher-order (meaning more complex and inclusive) levels of explanation that emerge from our correctly functioning neuroanatomical structures. One possible way of avoiding a layered model of reality is to think of what Silberstein (2006) called "systemic causation" (p. 204), where mental properties exert a causal influence on neurochemical operations because both are bounded within a human system. Silberstein elaborates:

> The universe is not ordered as a hierarchy of closed autonomous levels such as atoms, molecules, cells, and the like. Rather, the universe is intrinsically nested and entangled. The so-called physical, chemical, biological, mental, and social domains of existence are in fact mutually embedded and inextricably interconnected. (p. 204)

Moreover, although each discipline's conceptual language is an attempt to capture core human experiences in grammatical or verbal form so as to increase understanding, important psychoanalytic and theological concepts are not merely metaphors used to explain human behavioral tendencies, psychological processes or spiritual forces. We argue that many psychoanalytic and theological concepts can be considered ontologically *real* in that they have causal efficacy. This is considered to be a strong emergent position, which makes it possible to conceptualize emergent processes as having some causal impact on physical or biological substances (Gregersen, 2006). For example, one might consider relational or self-processes as influencing one's biological or neurochemical functioning in a real way. At the same time we recognize "an antecedent bottom-up influence from the constituent physico-chemical level which has led to the emergence of biological, psychological, and social levels of organization" (p. 285). Psychoanalytic phenomena such as the unconscious, self, object representation and relational schemas involve real neurochemical traces and patterns that have their root in the natural system of neurophysiology. Parallel to nonreductive physicalist notions of soul (Brown et al., 1998) many psychoanalytic processes (e.g., object relations, transference reactions, enactments, identifications, attachment states) are complex emergent phenomena directly tied to affective motivations emanating from neurobiologically rooted need states evoked and shaped by developmental contexts (Lichtenberg, Lachman & Fosshage, 2011; Schore, 2009; Fosha, Siegel & Solomon, 2009). These affective states reflect neurophysiological processes but also function in a manner that alters and shapes cognition and behavior, which can exert a systemic influence on the same neurophysiological processes that give rise to affect, cognition and behavior.

In a similar manner, we can think of divine causation and creative activity as an immanent systemic potentiality in which new realities can emerge within sufficiently complex physical material (Clayton, 2006; Peacocke, 2007). Important to our consideration of integrating psychoanalytic and theological perspectives, we are not suggesting that divine action arises from brain processes. Rather we suggest that the essential transcendent, wholly Other, ontological status of God is in mutual harmony and in noncontradictory existence with his immanence. Happel (2002) discuses the notion of "transcendence within immanence" wherein God has chosen to "cooperate with human agency" (p. 304). We agree and argue for an immanental cosmology in which God is present and at work within the very nature of the material world (Lodahl, 1997). Aspects of divine action that have influence on individual humans somehow arise from the material brain's complex processes, which exist because of God's immanent creative qualities and by the very nature of God's creative action. In other words this transcendent God who is "over all creation" is concurrently immanently present: "in him all things hold together" (Col 1:15, 17). As Paul says in Acts 17:28, "For in him we live and move and have our being." He has created the potentiality for real communion with him, and we assert that the integration of theological understandings and psychoanalytic processes may provide a helpful model for conceptualizing this action.

THEOLOGY, RELATION AND INTEGRATION

If the divine-human relationship and human relatedness in general are as important as we are proposing, then we need to understand how this squares with recent developments in theology. Human relatedness includes and is dependent on such capacities as language, a theory of mind, episodic memory, conscious top-down agency, future orientation and emotional modulation (Brown, 1998). In fact it may be these capacities that create the condition for relatedness as an emergent property. While other animal species are capable of relatedness, the human capacity far surpasses and distinctly separates humans from other animals. The growing emphasis on relatedness in psychology resonates with a similar emphasis in contemporary theology.

For example, in recent years theologians have come to conceptualize the triune God in relational terms. This relational turn (Shults, 2003) in theology has subsequently led to a reconceptualization of the *imago Dei* in humans. Early understandings of *imago Dei* were conceptualized in substantive terms, which emphasized characteristics or capacities that humans and God shared, such as reason or will. As the triune God was conceptualized as a being of three persons in ever and constant self-emptying relatedness marked both by particularity and unity (Balswick, King & Reimer, 2005), theological anthropology concurrently changed. It

grative task at a philosophical and theoretical level, but in short, we believe that a relational approach to integration must recognize the tension between unique perspectives and a collective goal. We believe this is a kind of practiced hospitality with a postmodern sensibility that respects the self and other. To this end we hope we are successful.

CASE STUDY: TONY

The following case acts as the main channel for our conversation and comparison of contemporary psychoanalytic perspectives. We hope to illustrate the power of unified diversity as various authors engage the case from a particular theoretical perspective and theological tradition.

Tony, a twenty-three-year-old Caucasian college graduate, sought therapy for a number of vague but perplexing difficulties. Tony reported a general inability to maintain connection in relationships with both men and women, and a troubling lethargy regarding vocational aspirations. Although he regularly dated, Tony had been unable to sustain a romantic relationship for more than a month or two. He would become bored and passive, slowly letting the relationship die. The girls he dated typically found his lack of interest and initiative frustrating, and they would end up being the originators of the breakup. He reported no close male friends; male relationships were marked by competition and distrust. Tony couldn't decide whether he should pursue graduate school or stick with his current job till something better came along. At the time of intake Tony was a part-time caregiver for an adult male with Down syndrome.

Tony was a thinly built, average-height male who looked his age. He was talkative, engaging and appropriately groomed, but presented with slightly depressed affect. He entered once-weekly psychoanalytic psychotherapy and quickly wanted to lie on the couch. He reported that he wanted to use the couch so that he could focus more on his own internal experiences and spend less time monitoring the reactions of his male therapist. Tony quickly took to free association on the couch and let his mind wander widely.

History revealed that Tony was the older of two children (one younger sister) from an intact family. He reported a warm but somewhat ambivalent relationship with his mother and a highly conflicted relationship with his father. As the primary homemaker, his mother was present and available for him during childhood, but he often experienced her as overly intrusive, both when he was a child and now as a young adult. During adolescence he resented being asked personal questions and having to give an account of his whereabouts and activities to her. When feeling intruded upon, Tony would become quiet and avoidant. On the other hand, he would frequently seek refuge with her from his father. With his father Tony felt that he could never measure up—especially as a man. He experienced his father as frequently disappointed in him, leaving Tony with feelings of shame and anger. For example, Tony reported that his father regularly challenged him by asking him questions at the dinner table that Tony couldn't answer. His father would also push him to excel in sports or academics, and when Tony began normal adolescent separation from his father in terms of ideologies (e.g., political differences) his father would argue with Tony vehemently. Subsequently, Tony vacillated in his feelings toward his father, one moment desperately wanting his approval and the next minute belittling him as being uneducated and old-fashioned. Tony had a conscious fantasy that his father somehow held the key to his own manhood and that his father had never given it to him.

In addition to Tony's concerns about closeness, he also was disturbed about his compulsive masturbation. Indeed, Tony could be obsessive and ruminative around a number of issues and behaviors (e.g., new ideas he was learning, whether he should ask out a particular girl, how he should go about applying for a job), but his sexual preoccupation and behaviors were especially distressing. Tony reported that he would engage in masturbation in almost any location where he could find some privacy (e.g., public bathroom, his car). He found these experiences to have a "driven quality," which were regularly triggered by stress or "boredom," and always self-soothing yet guilt inducing.

In summary, Tony was a young man suffering from a number of anxiety and depressive symptoms. His primary complaint was a sense of disconnection from friends and romantic relationships. In relationship to others he reported high levels of anxiety as he wondered if he fit in and was acceptable, or whether he was being taken for granted. He regularly felt competitive with others and had a vague sense that sometimes he might be driving others away due to this competitive stance. Ultimately he would collapse into depression and a vague sense of hopelessness.

Last, Tony was raised in a highly religious home. His parents, and especially his father, could be described as fundamentalists who practiced a literal interpretation of the Bible. Tony attended a Christian university. When his own religious perspectives were challenged, considerable tension and competition with his father ensued. Although Tony described himself as a Christian, he was not sure whether this influenced his daily life. For example, his beliefs about behavioral constraints of Christianity differed widely from his parents (e.g., alcohol consumption, premarital sex). Tony felt spiritually empty; he remained academically interested in theology, but any connection to or involvement with a personal God was absent.

enment and, as such, have proposed solutions that are perhaps not as effective as they could be due to a still-too-broad, or "thin," particularity. As such we will both propose and model a way to think in "thick" ways about the practice of integrating psychology and religious subtraditions.

Our third and final argument is based on contemporary psychoanalytic literature that argues that the subjectivity of the analyst cannot be reduced and must be taken more seriously in clinical practice. That is, integration is not just something that takes place on a theoretical level, but there is also a need to understand the place of the particularities of both the therapist and client in clinical practice. Taking seriously the subjectivities of both the patient and analyst provides room for the particularities of each, including religious subtraditions, to be part of the therapeutic process. As such, we are asking the participants of this book to take seriously their own particularity and subjectivity by considering how their own tradition-specific theologies and moralities influence their psychological theory and practice. We are asking our participants to join us in the practice of confession.

Integration as Moral Discourse

We begin our argument with a critique of the philosophical presuppositions that have led the social sciences, and subsequently psychological theorists and practitioners, to assume a stance of value or moral neutrality. In many ways this premise can be linked back to Freud. In *An Outline of Psychoanalysis*, Freud (1940/1989) states

> It may be that there are still undreamt-of possibilities of therapy. But for the moment we have nothing better at our disposal than the technique of psycho-analysis, and for that reason, in spite of its limitations, it should not be despised. (p. 62)

Freud was apparently willing to accept that something other than psychoanalysis could be therapeutic; however, he was convinced that such an alternative, at least among his contemporaries, did not exist. Least impressive were the existing religious traditions that offered, in his mind, only the illusion of solace from a threatening external world. While Freud could not grant the solace that religions offered, he did offer an alternative of less misery. For this reason Freud's psychoanalysis became attractive because, for so many modern persons, the religious traditions of the past had failed humanity and left people with only their internal psychological resources to survive the misery of life (Rieff, 1966). Freud's task was to reinforce and shore up these internal psychological resources in order for people to circumvent their primitive impulses that might have destroyed civilization and to navigate the guilt and shame that derived from the demands of society. The purpose of strengthening the ego and giving it mastery over mental life, according to Freud (1940/1989), was to help the patient "behave as normally as possible outside the treatment" (p. 56). Psychoanalysis took the neurotic individual and transformed that person into a well-adjusted and functioning individual for the purpose of contributing to society.

Yet Freud had no alternative ethical system to propose as a replacement for the religious traditions that he rejected as illusion. He offered no ethical solution for everyday human life and gave no justification for what is healthy or normal living, and thus, in this way, gave the appearance of moral neutrality. He was not offering an alternative belief system; rather, he was offering assistance in a modern world of unbelief. Strengthening the ego was Freud's answer to a world of misery. Though he proposed no new standard for living, he nevertheless proposed psychological norms that defined the healthy or normal life. In this way Freud was offering an implicit standard of living. As such, because Freud's psychoanalysis sought to transform the human person, it had an ethic. "[Freud's] psychology not only studies the conduct of life but seeks also to affect it. For that reason alone, it is just to call Freud's a moral psychology, whatever one's judgment as to its scientific merits" (Rieff, 1966, p. 39).

Since Freud, all subsequent psychoanalytic theories, and all psychotherapeutic theories for that matter, have sought a route to understanding the human person. These routes may have differed in perspective on human life and conduct, yet most psychoanalytic (or psychotherapeutic) theories have remained true to the modern influence of Freud by prological practices "theologically laden" disciplines (p. 26). As a result, psychoanalysts must explore how their own personal theological ideals and moral values influence their selected theoretical frameworks. But in order to do this psychoanalysts must show how their theories make moral and theological claims. However, what is so often ignored in this endeavor is the notion of pluralities within both psychoanalysis and theology. Both psychoanalysis and theology consist of a vast number of accounts of human nature and human flourishing. To assume a largely unified or generic understanding of both psychoanalysis and theology misrepresents the nature of both psychoanalysis and theology where differences in subtraditions have led to varying and sometimes contradictory views of human flourishing.

Murphy (2005b) suggests:

> We need to resist the desire to find a generic Christian answer to questions of human flourishing. Different subtraditions organize their theological systems around different core theories, and these cores, along with the doctrinal elaboration that concretizes them, lead to strikingly different accounts of human nature and the human good. (p. 28)

The task is therefore to be particularistic from both the side of psychoanalysis and of theology. Psychoanalysts must be able to demonstrate the presence of moral and theological claims within specific psychoanalytic theories and traditions while investigating how their tradition-specific theologies and moralities influence those psychological theories.

INTEGRATION AND PARTICULARITY

Perhaps the greatest myth of the "Enlightenment Project" (MacIntyre, 1984) was the belief that "pure reason," untainted by subjectivity and tradition, could lead to the discovery of universal truths. To enter into this search for "Truth" one needed to strip off everything that had made one who one was (e.g., think of Descartes alone in his room attempting to think his way to a foundational truth and how his *cogito ergo sum* reflected, in his mind, a nonsubjective, a-traditioned, a-historical ground for ultimate knowledge). This belief in "neutrality," the realm where subjectivity does not exist, permeates the psychological scientific enterprise, the majority of psychotherapeutic orientations and much of the literature on the integration of psychology and theology. This last claim might come as a surprise to many, given that the integration literature is based on the premise that theology is a separate (and legitimate) field that can be integrated with psychology, and the focus of theology as the study of God is perhaps the paradigm case for *not* being neutral. Perhaps this is an overstatement, but the problem we are attempting to illuminate in the integration literature is that much of it reflects a thin, generic and primarily rationalistic Christianity where the particularity and subjectivity of the author's own subtradition within Christianity is not explicated or brought to light. We think the literature on the relationship between theology and psychoanalysis can be furthered and deepened by owning and explicating one's theological particularity and subjectivity. Of course, this perspective stems out of our experiences.

In many ways we are conflicted about our graduate education in psychology at Fuller Theological Seminary. Each of us (Brad, Paul and Ron) came to Fuller after graduating from a Nazarene undergraduate institution and having been raised in the Church of the Nazarene for our entire lives. Each of us went to Fuller because of deep desires to make meaning out of how Christianity and psychology might be integrated, and we threw ourselves wholeheartedly into the integrative endeavor. We deeply appreciated and are forever grateful for the rich, intellectual frameworks we were taught, mainly from a Reformed Christian perspective, which helped us articulate a system and approach to how we might think through the task of integration. At the same time, we also faced what might have been akin to the experience of learning a second language. Many of the assumptions and convictions of the Reformed perspectives we were learning were different from the assumptions and convictions of our Wesleyan Holiness "first language," and this created tension and confusion for us that became important for us to resolve. Perhaps this experience at Fuller overly sensitized us to these theological differences, but as we read more and more of the integration literature, we couldn't help but notice the manner in which a generic and thin Reformed perspective was often assumed as *the* model for a Christian perspective in this discussion. (We hasten to add that these generic Reformed perspectives often do not do justice to the rich, deep and thick Reformed perspectives and practices we were taught at Fuller!)

This type of thin evangelical Christian approach can be seen in three important, popular and highly influential integration books: Jones and Butman's (1991) *Modern Psychotherapies: A Comprehensive Christian Approach*, Yarhouse and Sells's (2008) *Family Therapies: A Comprehensive Christian Appraisal*, and Johnson's (2010) *Psychology and Christianity: Five Views*. In each book the various authors and contributors refer to "Christianity" or to "evangelical Christianity" in ways that seem to treat Christianity as monolithic. For example, in the introduction of *Modern Psychotherapies*, Jones and Butman (1991) write, "This book attempts to appraise each of the current major psychotherapy theories in the mental-health field from the perspective of *evangelical Christianity*" (p. 9, italics added), while Yarhouse and Sells (2008) desire to reflect and engage "various models of family therapy from a *Christian worldview*" (p. 9, italics added). The contributors to *Psychology and Christianity: Five Views* never address their denominational backgrounds or affiliations and how those might influence each of the five views presented in the book. Instead, it is left for the reader to presume that the contributors are all "Christian" and thus similar in their theological assumptions, which only leaves individual subjective differences in understanding how psychology might then be integrated with Christianity.

While the terms *evangelical Christianity* and *Christian worldview* are meant to point to broad, doctrinal agreement within Christianity, this language often hides the many areas of difference or uniqueness that denominational subtraditions have on these understandings. To use one quick example, Jones and Butman (1991), as well as Yarhouse and Sells (2008), focus on the sovereignty of God in ways that reflect a Reformed worldview, but which ring somewhat foreign for the Wesleyan Holiness tradition where the sovereignty of God is understood within and tempered by the larger context of the loving nature of the character of God (Maddox, 1994; Wynkoop, 1967). We would argue that something as seemingly simple as emphasizing God's sovereignty or God's love has major implications for how the relationship between theology and psychology might be understood and that might be fruitfully examined if the people engaged in this dialogue were asked to enter it with a focus on their theological particularity and uniqueness. We believe that this is one unique aspect of the present volume, as the editors have asked the contributors to reflect on how their theological particularity and subjectivity affects their dialogue with various psychoanalytic theories and their clinical work.

To be fair, the intent behind each of the three books just noted reflects an attempt to focus on the *unity* of the Christian tradition and how broad, unified models might then be built for understanding the relationship with the field of psychology. We want to affirm these types of moves, as well as to draw upon trinitarian theology, to suggest that *uniqueness* has a place as well. Within the Christian tradition the Trinity is understood as three unique persons who are unified in their love for one another. Perhaps the Trinity can provide a model for integration as well, as sometimes moves toward unity are necessary for larger theory building, and sometimes moves toward uniqueness are necessary to explore and deepen current understandings. We would argue that the current integration literature could do with a dose of Pentecost, where the task is to speak our unique theological languages and begin to explore how that opens up or contributes to common understandings of integration.

For example, according to Johnson (2010) one of the issues at work in the differing perspectives of the five views is the question of what "counts" as a source of psychological knowledge. We think that this is an important issue as well and would go further by also arguing that how one understands the relationship between the various sources or authorities (e.g., psychological, theological) also matters a great deal. Within the Wesleyan tradition there are four sources of authority that make up what has come to be known as the "Wesleyan quadrilateral" (Outler, 1985). These authorities are Scripture, reason, tradition and experience (with

Scripture traditionally viewed as the highest authority). Putting these various authorities in dialogue with one another has resulted in Wesleyans using metaphors such as "living tension" (McAdoo, 1965), "resonance" (Brown, 2004), "symbiosis" (Oord, 2004) or "dance" (Wright, 2010). Common to each of these Wesleyan approaches is a conviction that the dialogue between these authorities needs to be as holistic as possible. While these four sources of authority never stand totally independent of one another, attempting to put all of them into dialogue with one another allows for a perspective where the scriptural, communal, contextual/historical, subjective/experiential, scientific (natural and social) and philosophical are all held together in an attempt to understand more completely. It is a deep Wesleyan conviction in God's prevenient grace that undergirds the use of the quadrilateral as a broad hermeneutical method. These convictions allow the three of us to take seriously psychoanalytic theories, even though they are often antagonistic to religious understandings. Despite the potential for antagonism, psychoanalytic theories are given a voice in the dialogue as aspects of what reason and experience may have to contribute to an understanding of human nature and what it means to be human. Within the Wesleyan tradition, this is understood to be a dynamic process where humility reigns and understanding is seen as partial, never fully complete, and open to new dialogue.

A second conviction seen in these Wesleyan approaches is the commitment to reciprocity in the dialogue between the four authorities. This can be especially seen at junctures where implications from one source may have repercussions for another source. Reciprocity of this type allows for the differing sources to mutually illuminate or "problematize" aspects of each other. This means that sometimes Wesleyans are in uncomfortable positions of allowing scientific understandings to speak to scriptural interpretations or of allowing scriptural interpretations and theological understandings to speak to scientific perspectives. Wesleyans live in those tensions! Using trinitarian language, ideally each of the authorities makes room for the other, not in an effort to extinguish particularity but with the hope that in this dialogue or dance the unique sources may each become more complete and together create something new. This Wesleyan emphasis on the mutuality between theology and psychology is a central methodological (and theological) conviction for our perspective and argument in this chapter (for further examples see Armistead, Strawn & Wright, 2010; and the special issues of the *Journal of Psychology and Christianity*, Strawn, 2004).

THE IRREDUCIBILITY OF THE INTEGRATOR'S SUBJECTIVITY

In light of the previous discussion we can move into our final argument for taking the particularity of the integrator's theology seriously. This argument stems from the changing realm of psychoanalysis itself. In the history of psychotherapy there has always been a dialectic between practice and theory. Theory development informed clinical practice, and practice informed further theoretical development. In a similar vein we believe it is now time for the advances in clinical theory and practice to inform Christian integrative theory development and integrative practice. This is highly consistent with the "language" of our Wesleyan tradition, which conceives practice (orthopraxis) and theory/theology (orthodoxy) as mutually influencing each other.

The field of relational psychoanalysis has been particularly influential in clinical theory and practice by utilizing hermeneutics, narrative theory, continental philosophy and social construction. Relational psychoanalysis, which has been shaped by advances in object relations, self-psychology and interpersonal psychoanalysis, has not only introduced a shift from Freud's biological drive model to a relational model, but also introduced a transition from a one-person psychology to a two-person or systems psychology (Sorenson, 2004a). This created an alteration in psychoanalytic understanding from a positivist to a constructivist stance. This means, among other things, that clinical knowledge/reality is *created*, not only *discovered*, and that the therapist is not an objective archaeologist/ scientist mining the psyche of the patient, but that the patient and therapist together cocreate meaning and understanding in an intersubjective matrix (Orange, 1995).

This change led to "a revised psychoanalytic epistemology" (Sorenson, 2004a, p. 54). Gone was the idea that therapy was a search for historical truth and that the analyst's task was to sit back and function as an objective, neutral mirror or blank screen (Hoffman, 1983). Transference is therefore not simply a distortion on the part of the patient projected on a neutral therapist, but is rather the patient interacting with something *real* in the therapist. Based on these theoretical changes, Hoffman posited that patients would become interpreters of their analyst's experiences (i.e., thoughts and feelings the therapist may have). Therefore, transference, and all of therapy, is actually cocreated by patient and therapist. Again, clinical understanding is not (only) unearthing an objective reality found inside the patient (one-person psychology), but is a dialogue that occurs between this *particular* patient and this *particular* therapist (two-person psychology).

A few years after Hoffman's (1983) influential paper, Lew Aron (1991) suggested that while there was a growing acceptance of the influence of the therapist's subjectivity in therapy, not enough had been done via clinical technique. Aron suggested that since transference is not solely distortion but also interacting with the real therapist, clients would be capable of intuiting things about their therapists of which even the therapists might be unaware. For this reason therapy must include the client's experience of the therapist's experience as part of its exploration. This two-person psychology becomes the dialogue in which to explore transference-countertransference. Clients bring their unique psychological configurations (as do therapists!), and they can and do distort in the transference, but they also interact with the real person of the therapist.

Owen Renik (1993) eventually named the therapist's continual and unavoidable participation in therapy "the therapist's irreducible subjectivity" (p. 408). The implication was that the subjectivity of the therapist could not be, nor should it have been, partitioned off or dismissed; it just was—irreducibly. Renik's goal, as was Aron's (1991), was to further reconceptualize technique in light of this changing understanding of therapy. He advocated acknowledging it and studying its effects.

According to Renik (1993) this way of conceptualizing the therapist's participation in therapy forces therapists to give up the belief that transference-countertransference enactments can be avoided. Therapists' unconscious motivations are a necessary part of the therapy and are what allows transference-countertransference analysis. He subsequently suggested that we change our metaphors for therapy. Instead of thinking of ourselves as surgeons (classical metaphor) or even reflecting mirrors (object relational metaphor) who understand transference and then interpret it, we see ourselves as skiers or surfers interacting with powerful forces of transference-countertransference which are to be harnessed but never fully controlled (p. 417).

Therefore, Renik (1993) sees no reason for therapists to try to keep themselves out of the therapy (i.e., be objective), but to fully acknowledge their participation (i.e., own their subjectivity). Later he coined the term "playing one's cards face up" (2006, p. 53) to describe this approach. While there is always the possibility that this could lead to therapist domination and gratification, Renik argues that by owning their subjectivity therapists reduce the likelihood that therapy will become covertly coercive. Analysts have long feared that when a therapist inserts his or her subjectivity, it will lead to therapy becoming nothing more than "suggestion." Again Renik advocates that rather than being afraid of suggestion, therapists need to study its effective use.

The bottom line for Renik (1993) is that therapists need not be afraid of their irreducible subjectivity but should rather learn how to use it therapeutically. For if therapy is a dialogue, even a moral one, then both parties must own their part in it. To this end we quote Renik (1993):

> Sometimes the best way to facilitate a patient's self-exploration can be for an analyst to present his or her own, different interpretation of reality for the patient's consideration—even to present it as persuasively as possible, in order to be sure that the patient has taken full account of it. When an analyst feels constrained against doing this, an important tool is lost. (p. 429)

When we don't own our subjective component of the dialogue, we risk covertly influencing the patient. Rather than believing we can maintain some sort of objective neutrality, as promised in the Enlightenment project, and bracket ourselves to be blank screens, what really protects our patients is our honesty. Again, we quote Renik (1993):

> It seems to me a fundamental principle of analytic collaboration that an analyst's aim in offering an interpretation is not to have it accepted by the patient, but rather to have the patient consider it in making up his or her own mind. If the analyst is clear about this, then respect for the patient's autonomy—we might even say insistence on the patient's autonomy—comes through, and it can be useful for the analyst to communicate a definite point of view, even a sense of conviction about his or her own inferences. (p. 419)

We see a kind of parallel process here in the field of crosscultural competence. Dueck and Reimer (2009) have argued in *A Peaceable Psychology: Christian Therapy in a World of Many Cultures* that when therapists do not respect the thick cultures of their patients' first languages, they may unwittingly engage in violence toward them by forcing a secondary language on them. One way to respect a client's culture is for the therapist to own his or her own thick culture (i.e., irreducible subjectivity) or what we have called "tradition." But all too frequently therapists present as neutral, objective providers, what Dueck and Reimer call thin therapy. Dueck and Reimer (2009) state, "The danger in so-called value-neutral therapy is that thin therapies mask a thick tradition that is unconsciously imposed on clients" (p. 221). This is the exact warning made by Renik and Aron.

We are suggesting that there is a similar violence done in the task of integration when integrators do not own, acknowledge or even consciously utilize the subjectivity of their thick traditions. This is the violence that we have felt when reading Christian integrators who were speaking a language they called Christianity but that was not consistent with our primary Wesleyan language. Therefore we call for Christian integrators of psychology and theology to own their subjectivity and use it in their theory development, and ultimately to inform clinical practice. We will then ask each of our subsequent authors to participate in this process by confessing their own particularities and subjectivities that influence each of their respective ventures into integrating psychoanalysis with their respective Christian subtraditions.

3

Contemporary Freudian
Psychoanalysis

Brad D. Strawn

I n the beginning was Freud. This is undoubtedly how the history of psychoanalysis must begin. While this book will demonstrate that psychoanalysis
is no longer primarily the work of one man, and that it has developed con-
siderably in the last one hundred years, it is still true that many of Freud's
key concepts so permeate the psychotherapeutic landscape that it wouldn't
be a misnomer to say we are all Freudians (Mitchell & Black, 1995).

Today it is increasingly difficult to find a pure or classical Freudian who
subscribes solely to a tripartite view of the mind, dual instincts of sex and
aggression, and the Oedipal complex. It is possible, however, to find what
might be called a *contemporary Freudian*, a *neo-Freudian* or a *contemporary structural psychoanalyst*. In fact, there is so much psychoanalytic
diversity in the literature that some writers refer to psychoanalytic *pluralism* (McWilliams, 2004). While this book will highlight several distinct
schools of psychoanalysis, which are often presented as mutually exclusive,

the present chapter will focus on what might be called a "total composite psychoanalytic theory" (Rangell, 2004, p. 8). Theologian Robert Webber (1999) coined the term *ancient-future* to capture the growing dialogue surrounding emerging patterns of church structure and worship. Webber used this term to describe a growing ecclesiological tendency to recover and retradition ancient forms and practices of worship while integrating them within a changing postmodern culture. This aptly describes the goal of this chapter as it relates to psychoanalytic theory.

ONE THEORY OR MANY?

In his riveting memoir, *My Life in Theory*, Leo Rangell (2004), a classically trained psychoanalyst, argues that the development of new theory has as much to do with relational and group dynamics as it does with actual clinical advances.[1] Rangell does not eschew theoretical developments but suggests that, in the history of psychoanalysis, group dynamics and personality conflicts have led to theoretical splintering and sequestering of models. Rangell's concern is that model building that is oppositional and even hostile eventually hurts the cause and advancement of psychoanalysis. He argues for a cumulative theory of psychoanalysis where new developments are incorporated while older concepts are challenged to change without necessarily being jettisoned. Rangell's primary concern is not what is added when theory develops but what is left behind. For example, while contemporary theories have made excellent use of advances in philosophy and developmental psychology, Rangell wonders whether it is necessary to completely abandon concepts such as drives and conflict.

A slightly different approach to a composite theory could be found in those theoreticians who suggest that all theories contain some truth and subsequently are useful in *particular* situations. Lawrence Hedges (1991) advocates for theoretical *listening perspectives* based on a patient's psychodynamic development. His central argument is that different psycho-

---

[1]Marie Hoffman (2011) has demonstrated a similar process at work in Freud and early psychoanalytic theorists in that particular sociological pressures of being Jewish led to the subsequent denial of a Judeo-Christian narrative that underlies psychoanalysis.

analytic theories are applicable based on each patient's specific historical experiences and subsequent developmental needs. It is not that one theory is better than another, but that different theories are beneficial for *particular* patients. The choice of theory—that is, which theory to listen with—is dictated by the developmental needs of the patient.

Fred Pine (1998) takes a slightly different approach. He too suggests that different psychoanalytic theories are useful for different patients but believes that psychoanalytic dynamics such as drive, ego, object relations and self-experience (roughly paralleling classic, ego psychology, object relations and self psychology theories) are operative in hierarchical ways within the same patient. He prefers to speak of these theories as the "four psychologies of psychoanalysis" (p. 38). The goal of therapy is then in meeting patients where they are and working toward higher levels of psychological integration and development.

While it may be true that theory development, or at least splintering and sequestering of theories, is influenced by political and psychological dynamics (Rangell, 2004), it does not follow that advances in theory may provide nothing new. Atwood and Stolorow (1993) demonstrated that theory development could be understood as autobiographical. Each theory is in some sense true for that particular theorist (and their cultural period) and subsequently true for particular patients. Of course all of life is culturally influenced, including psychopathologies, and therefore new theories must arise to understand and treat the new challenges that a changing culture creates (McWilliams, 2004). While theoretical pluralism should not be conceptualized as a theory but as a way of practicing, and while one may naively attempt to integrate theories that at times may be mutually exclusive, the question remains, is it necessary to swear absolute allegiance to one theory?

This chapter concurs with McWilliams (2004) that psychoanalytic therapists should offer to various theories the same kind of respect they offer their patients. While it may be presumptuous to suggest, as some have, that all advances in theory can be found within Freud (this would be to ignore the impact of culture and tradition), it is also ridiculous to throw out the baby with the bathwater. So instead of offering an exaggerated caricature of a strict classical Freudian psychoanalysis, we will attempt to explicate an integrative approach to theory that respects the best of ancient practices (roughly late Freud and ego psychology) while incorporating newer developments (object relations and following). And while this project runs the risk of errors in over simplification, it is offered as a model of clinical utility and flexibility. It is also presented as a challenge to other clinicians to do the same.

LEADING THEORISTS

Most readers of this volume will be moderately familiar with Freud and his most enduring contributions. Perhaps Freud's greatest and most lasting offering was the concept of the unconscious and his conceptualization of the topographical model of the mind. He conceptualized the mind as layered, made up of the conscious mind (ideas, thoughts and feelings that were acceptable to the person and therefore knowable), the preconscious mind (primarily acceptable concepts that could become conscious to the person) and the unconscious mind (containing unacceptable wishes/desires that could only become conscious obliquely). The methods of discerning the unconscious included dreams, parapraxis (e.g., slips of the tongue) and transference (the process of the patient experiencing and interacting with the therapist as someone from their past). The concept of the unconscious was, and in some ways remains, a highly controversial and disturbing concept to many, for it implies that much of how we think, what we feel and how we behave is driven by forces outside rational and conscious control. While this may be troubling, this concept has now been fairly substantiated in the field of cognitive psychology through concepts such as procedural memory and automaticity (Damasio, 2005; Wilson, 2002).[2]

---

[2]Research has demonstrated that when it comes to the unconscious, Freud was right and wrong. Evidence indicates that human feeling, perception, thought and behavior are directed in a number of ways outside consciousness; however, this unconscious is not the seething cauldron of bestial desires as Freud conceptualized it. This new adaptive unconscious (Wilson, 2002) is the accumulation of experiences that are encoded through interpersonal experiences unlike Freud's id.

Some of the Freudian contributions that have remained controversial in psychoanalysis include the theory of infantile sexuality and the stages (i.e., oral, anal, genital, latency, phallic), the dual drive instinct theory (i.e., sex and aggression) and the Oedipus complex (see the later section on development). But perhaps the most disturbing idea remains Freud's claim that much of what humans desire, and what drives their thoughts, feelings and behavior cannot be admitted to the conscious mind because these are dangerous in some way. Because of the danger, defense mechanisms are employed as compromises in order to obtain some aspect of the wish, while at the same time protecting oneself from knowing what one is really up to (S. Freud, 1923). This internal and unconscious battle is what Freud described as intrapsychic conflict and is the bedrock of Freudian metapsychology.

Over time Freud realized his topographical model couldn't explain the complexity of the data he was experiencing in the consulting room, so he developed the structural model of the mind (1923). The structural model conceives of the mind as made up of not only three levels of consciousness but of three distinct structures: id (it), ego (I) and superego (over I). The id was conceived of as the source of biological motivation and operated on the pleasure principle. The pleasure principle states that humans strive for pleasure while attempting to avoid displeasure. As parents and culture socialize children, children internalize prohibitions against certain biologically driven wishes. This internalization is the source of the structure that Freud called the superego (the over I). It was the job of the ego to mediate the biological desires of the id and the socially internalized prohibitions of the superego (S. Freud, 1920).

In 1920 Freud also hypothesized another force at work in the human personality. His drive theory now moved to a dual-instinct theory containing both sex and aggression as the driving forces in persons. Humans don't just strive for pleasure and have to repress socially inappropriate sexual wishes, but actually have powerful destructive longings deriving from a death instinct. He came to believe that this drive was stronger than the pleasure principle and helped explain previously unexplainable behavior such as the repetition compulsion, which he perceived to be the human tendency to repeat an unhappy scenario over and over.

Sigmund Freud (1920) placed all three structures of the mind in the unconscious. He did this because he believed that persons were not conscious of their conflicts, and he came to realize that symptom removal was not possible by simply making the unconscious conscious (see the following pathology section). It is important to understand that Freud did not conceptualize these structures as reified objects that resided somewhere in the brain like little homunculi, but as processes of the mind. Bettelheim (1982) has persuasively argued that much of the humanism of Freud has been lost in the English translation of Freud's writing, and subsequently the metaphorical and personal aspects as well. Bettelheim argues that, particularly in America, the English translations have led to a rigid, scientific, distant kind of psychoanalysis that was never Freud's intent.

After Freud's death a group of theorists lead by his daughter, Anna, came to be known as ego psychologists. While they did not abandon the instinctual biological drives of the id, they placed much greater emphasis on the role, function and development of the ego. Anna established the ego as an object worthy of study in and of itself. While subjective feelings of guilt and anxiety (some conscious but much unconscious) arose from the conflict between id and superego, Anna was acutely interested in the ego defenses that developed to deal with these conflicts. If the ego was well developed (i.e., high in strength), an individual could develop adaptive or mature defense mechanisms to manage conflict. However, some individuals had low ego strength due to constitutional or environmental damage and were incapable of managing intrapsychic conflict in adaptive ways. Subsequently, they developed immature defense mechanisms. While Freud believed that anxiety from unconscious conflict triggered defenses, Anna demonstrated that defenses could also arise from fear of displeasure coming from the external world (A. Freud, 1936).

Later Heinz Hartmann (1939) made an important contribution when he conceptualized the ego as adaptive, by which he meant that it was actually shaped by the individual's environment. He also hypothesized that the ego did not always develop in conflictual ways. The possibility of conflict depended on the type of interactions between a child and his or her caregivers. Hartman posited conflict-free capacities of the ego such as perception, language, thinking, feeling and so forth. Ego developmental researchers Rene Spitz and Margaret Mahler, who directly observed infants, furthered this work (Mitchell & Black, 1995). While Spitz and Mahler did not jettison all of Freud's teachings, their work suggested that rather than babies being seen as "beasts in the nursery" (Phillips, 1998) prewired from the beginning, caregivers had a profound role on the shaping of the child's ego development (Tyson & Tyson, 1990).

These developments advanced core issues in Freudian metapsychology and opened the door to later object relations theorizing, but it was Edith Jacobson (1964) who pushed and reworked the understanding of drives. She suggested that the drives themselves were in fact biological *potentialities* that were actually shaped by the environment. This meant that sex and aggression (or any other biological motivation, for that matter) did not have a predetermined form and did not *have* to become conflictual. Rather it was the environment's response to the child's drives (e.g., pleasure seeking) that laid the groundwork for possible intrapsychic conflict.

Since these early theorists, contemporary thinkers have advanced Freud's work by both incorporating new ideas and rethinking older ones. Many of these theorists have been bridges between ancient and future ways of thinking. They have built paths between structural Freudian thinking and more relational models such as object relations and others. Space does not permit an exploration of these important contributors, but interested readers are directed to the work of such seminal figures as Melanie Klein, Hans Loewald, Otto Kernberg, Roy Schaeffer, Charles Brenner, Paul Gray, W. W. Meissner and Christopher Bollas, to name a few. These theorists, both past and present, have had great respect for Freud and have maintained much of his theorizing, but have not been afraid to incorporate new developments as they have experienced them in their clinical work.

PERSPECTIVES ON MOTIVATION

In advancing the dual drive theory (i.e., sex and aggression), Freud was attempting to explicate a model of motivation. Contemporary Freudians may still subscribe to sex and aggression as important biological motivators while not limiting themselves to these being synonymous with sexual intercourse and death (nor simply a response to environmental frustration). Contemporary Freudian analysts may also subscribe to multiple human motivations (Lichtenberg, Lachman & Fosshage, 2011) including the relational. But what must be retained for a theory to be truly psychoanalytic is the concept that humans are motivated primarily in what they feel, think, perceive and do by forces residing in the unconscious. From a contemporary Freudian perspective, these forces must be understood as embodied (i.e., rooted in the actual physicality of the person) *and* embedded/relational (i.e., rooted in the interplay between self and other). In fact, it may be argued that it is problematic to dichotomize these two concepts. While some contemporary theorists posit that all experience is relationally constructed, it would be just as true to say that all of experience is bodily constructed, for relationality can only be experienced and internalized through the medium of the body. Humans are not disembodied or isolated minds (Stolorow & Atwood, 1992). Recent work in embodied cognition demonstrates that even internal, private, abstract cognitions, such as time, can be understood as embodied as "defined by systematic mappings from body-based, sensorimotor source domains" (Johnson, 2007, p. 177). For this reason, human beings are best conceptualized as whole-embodied-persons-embedded-in-the-world of relationships (Brown & Strawn, 2012). Humans are bodies in relationship to other bodies. Sigmund Freud himself said it well when he wrote, "the ego is first and foremost a body-ego" (1923, p. 20).

PERSPECTIVES ON DEVELOPMENT

Even those who have only been exposed to Freud in cursory ways are familiar with his psychosexual developmental stages, which located sources of pleasure at various body locations (e.g., oral, anal, phallic) based on chronological age. The central issue was how the libidinal (sexual) drive navigated through these stages, the inevitable conflicts and defenses that arose, and ultimately the resolution of the Oedipal constellation. But psychoanalytic developmental theory did not end there. Later theorists and infant observational researchers began to amend developmental understandings.

In their text *Psychoanalytic Theories of Development: An Integration*, Tyson and Tyson (1990) attempt "to present a synthesis of psychoanalytic developmental theory" (p. 1) as a means of making sense of the disparity between analytic theories. While they integrate contemporary work in development that focuses more on interpersonal processes, their central focus remains the intrapsychic mind. Their approach is fundamentally a systems model.

> We have come to a perspective that development is a continuous and discontinuous process involving a large number of interacting, intertwining systems (or structures), each with its own developmental sequence that must be considered in relation to the development of the others. We describe a developmental sequence for each of the major, simultaneously evolving systems that make up the human personality. In describing them, we maintain that no one developmental phase holds a central position in relation to the final outcome and that no one system is superordinate to the others. (p. 2)

In this way they are able to emphasize process rather than "psychosexual or libidinal phase specificity" (p. 3).

A central tenet of psychoanalytic developmental theory is the genetic or psychogenetic viewpoint. Simply stated, this model hypothesizes and explores how early experiences in an individual's past have influenced their personality and current behavior (i.e., symptoms and character). Clearly Freud's model was psychogenetic, but even Freud realized that if one attempted to make meaning of adult behavior solely in relation to suspected past experiences, one could be found guilty of what has been called the genetic fallacy (Tyson & Tyson, 1990). On the other hand, psychoanalytic theory cannot be completely developed through child observation alone, because the meaning and impact of childhood experiences are really only determined later in adulthood. When Freud introduced his stages of sexual development, he was not only proposing universal innate sequences (as some have accused him of) but also their interaction with experience/ environment. This is why his theory became known as *psycho*sexual.

A contemporary Freudian approach to development will emphasize innate aspects as well as experiential. As the Tysons point out (1990), this will include data gathered from the clinical setting (i.e., child analysis, naturalistic observation including longitudinal) and scientifically designed experiments. Both are important to avoid the genetic fallacy— simplistically finding the child in the adult and vice versa. A systems approach recognizes that development is not rigidly epigenetic and that the complexity of tasks functioning at any one time (as well as back and forth in terms of time) leads to continuity and discontinuity (Tyson & Tyson, 1990).

The Tysons (1990), who could be classified as contemporary Freudians, maintain a structural model of the mind (i.e., id, ego, superego) because they believe that it "can be employed at several levels of abstraction and that it is sufficiently elastic to accommodate an integration of many models" (p. 20). For example, they integrate contemporary experimental research on infant innate abilities for activity (i.e., infant shapes the environment), predisposition toward human relating, self-regulation, resiliency, capacity to distinguish between pleasure and displeasure, and adaptation. The experiential aspect of development adds to a systems model in that it proposes that innate capacities "provide the limits within which later developing psychic structures can operate. And so, in addition to the infant's innately determined developmental potential, we have come to appreciate individual experiences as having a crucial developmental impact" (p. 25).

Over time the innate capacities and experiential moments come to form what can be called psychic structures (Tyson & Tyson, 1990). This structuralization not only leads to the development and adaptation of psychic structures such as the id, ego and superego, but mental representations of self, other and self-and-other interactions. Sometimes these interactions become conflicted and pathological, but not always. Conflicts are first external and then become internalized over time, and compromises developed by the ego may or may not resolve them. Therefore, not all developmental conflicts are pathological. Some conflict, even if it includes temporary or transient symptoms, can be understood as a function of normal development (Tyson & Tyson, 1990). However, the Tysons hypothesize that internalized conflicts can be superimposed over Oedipal conflicts and become neurotic, affecting further development negatively.

In summary, a contemporary Freudian psychoanalytic developmental model is characterized by movements forward and backward, by multiple systems interacting with one another, by innate processes being influenced by and influencing environmental experiences, and all of this building psychic structures that include object relational configurations. This dynamic, open system does not replace Freud's model but describes it in greater detail (Tyson & Tyson, 1990). The complexity of this approach allows for some level of pattern predictability as well as unpredictability (p. 33) and the recognition that the human organism is continually evolving (p. 37).

PERSPECTIVES ON PSYCHOPATHOLOGY

A contemporary Freudian approach to psychoanalysis will conceptualize pathology as a combination of unconscious conflicts and their subsequent defense mechanisms arising between naturally occurring (embodied and relational) drive derivatives/motivations (e.g., sex, aggression, safety, relational, self-efficacy, etc.) and prohibitions imposed by caregivers and the larger culture, and experiential events such as trauma or external conflicts that disrupt development and healthy structural formation.

Intrapsychic conflicts lead to compromise formations (Brenner, 1982). Stated simply, if a drive derivative (as conceptualized to include more than simply sex and aggression), which is conceptualized as a wish/desire (e.g., motivation for closeness or sexual attraction), arouses too much anxiety or other unpleasurable affect (e.g., depressive), ego defenses are initiated. The ego must either find a way to satisfy the wish (or partial satisfaction) or if this is not possible it must find a way to ward it off. To reiterate and make perfectly clear, intrapsychic conflict arises from innate processes and interpersonal experiences. Thus all intrapsychic conflict can be understood as interpersonal. Interpersonal conflicts may be comprehended in terms of a developmental-arrest model (i.e., client did not receive something they developmentally needed) or a more pure relational-conflict model (i.e., conflict between what the client wants and what he or she has internalized; Mitchell, 1988, pp. 9-10). But whatever the source of the conflict, the subsequent pathology can be conceptualized as a compromise formation (Brenner, 1982).

As stated earlier, personality structure is developed through the combination of innate potentialities and acute and prolonged (traumatic and nontraumatic) interactions with the environment. If the ego cannot find a way to satisfy the wish, and defenses are initiated to protect the person from becoming aware of the wish, problems may ensue (e.g., affect disorders or personality disorders). It should be noted, if not already clear, that not all compromise formations are pathological in the same way that not all defenses are pathological. A compromise formation becomes pathological when there is

> too much inhibition of functional capacity, too much unpleasure—i.e., too much conscious anxiety, depressive affect, or both—too great a tendency to injure or to destroy oneself, or too great conflict with one's environment—i.e., usually with the people one comes into contact with. (Brenner, 1982)

A contemporary Freudian perspective validates the reality of childhood experience and trauma and subsequent structural/ego deficits. So pathology is always related to conflict, and the source of conflict is the interaction between innate processes (embodied motivational systems) and interpersonal interactions.

Process of Therapeutic Change

For Freud the primary process of the pleasure principle, fueled by the id, must become conscious so that the patient can begin to engage in secondary processes—a metacognitive process. The battle cry was "where id was, ego shall be" (S. Freud, 1923, p. 100). Therefore, the goal of psychoanalysis for Freud is self-knowledge (Bettelheim, 1982). Essentially the patient develops the ego capacity to choose differently. The compromise formation takes on new, more mature and flexible forms. Freedom and determinism are not static concepts but are dynamic. As a person gains more insight, he or she has more degrees of freedom with which to choose (Wheelis, 1973). Individuals can give up their infantile wishes and move into adulthood. This understanding of therapeutic action was initially conceptualized as being accomplished through the analyst's correct interpretation of the patient's unconscious wish. However, Freud began to recognize that the unconscious defenses fought to keep this knowledge outside of awareness, so no amount of clever interpretation could overcome this resistance. Therefore, psychoanalysis began to move more toward the interpretation of defense (Brenner, 1982; Gray, 2005) as the first line of attack. Instead of interpreting unconscious wishes lying behind a conflict, the analyst would interpret defenses against *knowing* the wish, with the goal that over time the defenses would loosen and the wish would become available to the patient. Defenses could manifest themselves in numerous ways, but to treat a patient psychoanalytically was to watch for them primarily in the transference. This therapeutic action was essentially a cognitive task aimed at a high-functioning ego. Because early psychoanalysis required a fairly healthy ego, it was determined that not all patients were analyzable. Patients with poor ego strength (i.e., the psychotic and many persons with serious character disorders) would not be able to do the intellectual work of analysis.

Many contemporary psychoanalytic theories espouse versions of intrapsychic conflict, usually organized around relational needs and wishes, but divergence with classical Freudian theory occurs at the point of understanding therapeutic change. While recent theories have provided an important service by incorporating changes in culture and its impact on patients, they may have jettisoned important elements of early theory as they have strived for originality. This is where the work of integrationists such as Rangell (2004) and the Tysons (1990) may be helpful. For example, are there ways to integrate biological motivations, compromise formations and structures of the mind while still maintaining a relational sensibility? Can the intrapsychic mind of the patient still be considered important while also making room for the real impact of experience?

For the ego psychologists, such as Anna Freud, who believed the ego could be damaged by interaction with the environment, the therapeutic goal became, in part, the strengthening of the ego. This included assessing the psychic structure of the patient and developing more mature defense mechanisms rather than simply uncovering an unconscious conflict (Mitchell & Black, 1995). This was the beginning of an idea that therapy was not just an intellectual pursuit (where id was ego shall be), but that there was something therapeutically mutative that occurred *between* the patient and the therapist that brought about structural change to the patient's psychic world (Meissner, 1992).

But it also remains true that much of what needs to happen or be understood is not consciously available to the patient, so defense analysis continues to be an important aspect of therapeutic change. At times defense analysis may be overlooked or deemphasized in contemporary versions of analysis where the focus may reside more on the therapeutic action of the therapist providing developmental needs or second chances to the patient (e.g., in object relations or self psychology). Or the defense analysis may be limited to those defenses that are protecting a patient from some relational conflict/wish rather than embodied motivations.

In the contemporary Freudian psychoanalytic therapy advocated in this chapter, the therapist must point out to patients when and how they are protecting themselves from something unpleasant. This source of displeasure may be a repressed desire/wish of biological significance or it may be relational in nature (often both). But as hinted to earlier, all of life is embodied, so relational and biological motivations must be understood in light of each other and not set up as a false dichotomy. This is why many therapists who practice from the perspective outlined in this chapter will speak of practicing psychoanalysis with a "relational sensibility" (P. Hamm, personal communication, July 2012).

Space dictates that this chapter be a cursory introduction to what might be called a contemporary Freudian psychoanalysis, but in summary I am suggesting the following:

1. Contemporary Freudian psychoanalysis consists of an embodied understanding of persons that allows for such classical concepts as sex and aggression being two of many embodied, and at times unconscious, biological motivations that drive human behavior.

2. The theory espouses that drives, structures of the mind (processes) and ego capacities are shaped by one's environment and may or may not become conflicted. Development relies on numerous systems (innate and environmental) working simultaneously in complex ways leading to developmental spurts forward and backward.

3. Because some conflict is an inevitable aspect of human development, defenses arise and must be analyzed as part of the therapeutic process. Compromise formation is the shorthand way to talk about psychic conflict.

4. Insight to unconscious conflict, however, is not the only mutative aspect of therapy, for patients also suffer from deficits and developmental derailments (leading to structural deficits and conflicts) that are often mended in the *between* of the therapeutic relationship.

5. In short, contemporary Freudian psychoanalysis is a type of unified process theory (i.e., always in flux and flow) where newer theoretical concepts are incorporated (such as deficit and relational models) while older concepts are not necessarily jettisoned (e.g., retraditioned Oedipal constellation).[3]

---

[3]Contemporary psychoanalytic authors have retraditioned the Oedipal issue to involve sexuality and relationality (see Kohut, 1984; Pappenheim & Papiasvili, 2010). The general crux of the argument is that sexuality is an important developing edge for children, but it is the response of the primary caregivers to that emerging sexuality which may or may not lead to pathology (see Mitchell, 1988).

TRADITIONING

I begin by traditioning myself within the Wesleyan-Arminian branch of theology. While I have been an active member in several different denominations during my adult life, I grew up in the Church of the Nazarene (a Wesleyan denomination), attended a Nazarene university, have worked at two Nazarene universities and am an ordained elder in the denomination.

There are several distinctives of the Wesleyan tradition that have important implications for psychotherapy. First, John Wesley worked diligently to maintain a tension between human freedom and responsibility while retaining the sovereignty of God as Creator. Human freedom was essential for Wesley's understanding of God's grace as freely given and freely chosen. Human freedom to choose grace or to reject God was so important to Wesley that one theologian has coined it "response-able grace" (Maddox, 1994). Therefore, Wesleyans subscribe to salvation by faith, but believe that it is resistible and can be rejected even after accepting Christ.

Second, Wesleyans have a high respect for Scripture, holding to an inspired understanding but not an inerrant view (Lodahl, 2004). Third, a Wesleyan emphasis on holiness demonstrates the importance of the lived life in the body (Powell & Lodahl, 1999). In some contemporary Wesleyan communities, issues of orthopraxis (right behavior) are as important as orthodoxy (Oord & Lodahl, 2005). Fourth, Wesleyans are trinitarian and understand God's nature as reciprocal, self-emptying love (Oord & Lodahl, 2005). God loves humanity so much that God will not force Godself on humanity, and for this reason Wesleyans are often comfortable with theologies that fall within the open theism (Pinnock, 2001) or even process traditions (Stone & Oord, 2001). Finally, a true Wesleyan theology does not dichotomize nature and grace, and therefore holds that God's hand is at work even in theories and science developed outside Christian settings (Guntor, Jones, Campbell, Miles & Maddox, 1997). Wesleyans can interact with and utilize the theorizing of even a devout atheist such as Sigmund Freud. It is from this theological specificity that I will interact with the psychoanalysis I have outlined.

CHRISTIAN CRITIQUE

Sigmund Freud conceptualized religion through the lens of his system of psychoanalysis. Religion, and particularly God, was to be understood as a projection of the Oedipal father (1913) with whom the child has an ambivalent relationship. He hypothesized that humanity needed this projected God image (i.e., religion) to protect itself from the fear of the capriciousness of nature and fate (1927). This relationship with God was ambivalent, so humanity also feared God and therefore sought to appease him through obsessional rituals (S. Freud, 2001). Freud believed that just as the healthy child eventually grows out of his Oedipal neurosis, society could also outgrow its need for religion and replace it with the more mature system of science and reason (S. Freud, 1927).

Many excellent writers have interacted with and critiqued Freud's views on religion. It has been argued that it was not so much that Freud was wrong but that he was limited by his understanding of religious experience (Symington, 1994), his own psychology (Rizzuto, 1998) and the sociopolitical pressures of being Jewish (Hoffman, 2011). What Freud described as religion was really only one form of religious experience that might have been best understood as primitive (Symington, 1994). He seemed incapable of conceptualizing of a mature form of religion that was not based on anxiety, fear and ambivalence. This was true in spite of the fact that he had warm and meaningful relationships with strong, mature Christians (Hoffman, 2011). Because Freud saw all of religion through the lens of the Oedipal complex, he had no mechanisms to understand illusion, paradox, fantasy or even surrender in a psychologically positive light (Ghent, 1990). Later, theorists with relational sensibilities (some whom could be categorized as contemporary Freudians) further opened up the way for religious analysts (Jones, 1996; Meissner, 1984; Rizzuto, 1979; Sorenson, 2004a) to move beyond Freud's reductionist metapsychology and conceive of religious experience that was not necessarily pathological.

The Wesleyan tradition can easily place theology in dialogue with psychoanalysis by way of the Wesleyan quadrilateral (Outler, 1985). The

quadrilateral, which consists of Scripture, tradition, reason and experience, is a kind of theological epistemology. When attempting to understand a subject, a Wesleyan should consider what Scripture has to say (if
anything), as well as tradition (e.g., church history), reason (e.g., philosophy, logic) and experience (e.g., personal and accumulated observation). Brown (2004) adds empirical science as a fifth element to the
quadrilateral to incorporate the unique methodology of empiricism.
Where these five factors are in resonance with one another, issues of truth
become clearer. If they are out of resonance, truth will be fuzzy, and one
or more of the five areas will need to be fine-tuned. Of course not every
area has something to say to every issue or even carries equal weight in
the dialogue.[4] Nevertheless, this model provides a process for dialogue
(or what some might call "integration") between issues such as theology
and psychotherapeutic theory (Strawn, 2004).

The following are some examples where the theory from contemporary Freudian psychoanalysis (as already outlined) and theology (a
specific Wesleyan theology) would find resonance. It could be argued
that both contemporary Freudian psychoanalysis and Scripture portray
humans as having a narcissistic bent toward self-seeking, which may lead
to self-delusion and sinful behavior.[5] Because persons are motivated to
action by the unconscious, they are deluded in thinking, perceiving,
feeling and behavior. Therefore, they are in need of something, or
someone, outside themselves to help free them from this prison. Wesley
believed that all human capacities are corrupted by what he called "in-
being sin" and subsequently he believed that persons were in need of
healing of their sin-diseased natures. This healing was ultimately understood to come from God and was available for both the *pardon* of sin and
for the healing or release from the *power* of ongoing sin (Maddox, 1994).

---

[4]Scripture has nothing to say about the structure of the human brain, while neuropsychology
has nothing to say about the meaning of life. This does not mean there may not be important
dialogues between the two on issues of human behavior, but in some situations certain elements of the new pentagon may have more to say than others.

[5]Contemporary psychoanalysis that is relationally configured would most likely argue that
early or primary narcissism is ethically neutral and will only become pathological if the child
experiences some kind of developmental failure.

So while psychoanalysis and Wesleyan theology would suggest that much of human behavior is overdetermined (i.e., shaped by sin theologically, and shaped by experiences outside of conscious awareness psychoanalytically), Wesleyan theology would assert that God has provided the liberty or freedom to *not* enact one's sinful proclivities, which is possible through the restoration of the moral image of God within the human person (Runyon, 1998). As mentioned earlier, both psychoanalysis and theology would posit that something is needed from outside the individual to bring about increased freedom and subsequent change. For psychoanalysis it is the work occurring between the analyst and patient. For Wesleyans this "something" is undoubtedly the grace of God at work through the Holy Spirit wooing the person toward the ultimate telos of love. For Wesley this also included the grace of God mediated through physical means or human actions—what he called the *means of grace*. So while sacraments of the church, such as Eucharist, may be a means of grace, so may ordinary activities such as love feasts, covenant renewal services and class meetings (Maddox, 1994). So a Wesleyan may understand psychotherapy as a means of grace in which the grace of God is mediated to the patient through the therapeutic situation (Strawn, 2004), wooing them toward love of self, other, God and all of creation.

Wesleyans would also resonate with the psychoanalytic understanding of the person as embodied, as long as it is not a reductionism that leads to materialism (a more Freudian perspective). Wesleyans would not have a problem with the idea that humans are in part a product of their innate biology and early bodily experiences, and that these unconsciously influence thoughts, feelings, perception and behavior. John Wesley himself posited an *affectional* psychology (Maddox, 2010) based on the British empiricism of his day. He posited that persons developed motivating dispositions, which were affect states that had been habituated into enduring *tempers*. An affect was transient, but a *temper* was characterological. These tempers may not be consciously experienced but nevertheless affect a person's thinking, feeling, perception and behavior. These tempers (along with some biological givens) are the deep structures of unconscious motivation. These are developed through both biology and relational experiences, and therefore are embodied in physicality and embedded in the world of the person. Because the psychoanalysis previously outlined suggests that relationality and even biology cannot be simply reduced to "nothing but" physicalism, this approach avoids reductionism (Brown, Murphy & Malony, 1998).

In summary, the areas of dissonance between Wesleyan theology and aspects of a more Freudian psychoanalysis (some of this has been touched on earlier) would be (1) rigid materialistic reductionism, (2) God as "nothing but" psychological projection, (3) an overly deterministic understanding of persons, (4) a motivational system that doesn't allow for something like a benevolent love for others and (5) an overly individualistic understanding of human persons and human change. While the more contemporary Freudian perspective outlined here is more resonant with a Wesleyan theology on the first three points, it is still worthy of a critique on the last.

Even contemporary psychoanalysis has been criticized for its tendencies toward individualism, narcissism, isolation and disconnection (Rubin, 1997; Cushman, 1995). Ultimately the primary subject of study is the individual, and psychoanalysis has no ethical tradition on which to argue for an ethic of love of the other (Wright & Strawn, 2010). And yet there are other voices that argue that love is exactly what psychoanalysis is about. Rubin (1997) argues that within psychoanalysis is the possibility of what he calls "non-self centricism" (p. 87). Winnicott and Klien argued that psychoanalysis might move individuals from a state of self-preoccupation to concern for others and the world (Symington, 1994). The work on how psychoanalysis can develop a theory of mind (Siegel, 2012) suggests that psychoanalysis can help people move from an egocentric view to a recognition of the other. Jessica Benjamin (1995) and Marie Hoffman's (2011) work raises the development of mutually recognizing the other as a central ethic of psychoanalysis. There have been others such as Guntrip, Fromm and even Freud himself who recognized that love was an essential aspect of the therapeutic work. I have argued elsewhere that the central telos of psychoanalysis, and one of the central aims of religion, is the restoration and development of the person's capacity to love and accept love (Strawn, 2004). But the point still remains: Because psychoanalysis has disconnected itself from any particular tradition, this "love" remains defined and enacted in highly individualized ways (Wright & Strawn, 2010). On the other hand, a Wesleyan theology has been called a "theology of love" (Wynkoop, 1972) and understands the work of God (and I argue that one of these works of God can be understood as the means of grace that is psychotherapy) to be restoring an individual's capacity for love of God, neighbor (including creation) and self in self-renunciating ways (Phil 2:1-11). In the end, a contemporary Freudian perspective, as processed through a specific Wesleyan theology, must include love of God, neighbor (including creation) and self as its ultimate telos.

However, none of this denies that fact that a person's religious experience is greatly shaped and even misshaped by their environment. For this reason a patient's religious experience is fair game for analysis, not to be analyzed away—via Freud—but in hopes of moving from a more primitive religious experience to a more mature one (Symington, 1994).

CASE STUDY: TONY

From a contemporary Freudian perspective, Tony can be conceptualized as within the neurotic range of functioning.[6] The case material indicates no evidence of reality testing difficulties or serious problems in affect tolerance or regulation, which would suggest borderline functioning. His primary affective complaints are in the realm of anxiety and depression, and his interpersonal problems, which seem to include a high level of passivity and competitiveness, are also consistent with neurosis (McWilliams, 1994).

Because Tony is being conceptualized in the neurotic range of functioning, his problems would be understood not in terms of ego damage

---

[6]The diagnostic approach used here is derived from both McWilliams (1994) and Mitchell (1988). This is a dimensional model as opposed to a categorical one. Throughout the lifespan all humans must cope with the same central vicissitudes of life (e.g., connection versus differentiation) but in different dimensional ways.

but rather in terms of relational conflicts as captured by the metaphor of the Oedipal complex (including sex and aggression, but retraditioned from Freud) leading to an overly harsh superego and conflicts in self-and-other structures.[7] Tony is ambivalent toward his "warm" mother and highly conflicted with his father. It could be hypothesized that because of Tony's (probable) narcissistic father, he never truly identified with him or separated from his mother. Because the environment did not empower him to effectively navigate this highly emotional and biologically tinged period, Tony is also highly conflicted regarding his own sexuality (and possibly his gender). This may be due to his parents' difficulty accepting Tony's developmentally appropriate sexuality. Tony appears heterosexually oriented and expresses a desire for a relationship with a woman, but he continually self-sabotages. It is possible that he has confusing feelings and wishes related to his mother and his own sexuality, and for these reasons he is unconsciously anxious about sex. He defends against this fear of sexuality by becoming "bored" in relationships or acting passively till the woman he is involved with is forced to break off the relationship. These behaviors, as well as his compulsive masturbation, may be understood as compromise formations to get some of his sexual needs and wishes fulfilled while defending himself against the fear of being in a real intimate sexual relationship with a woman (either because of fear of rejection like he experienced from his parents and/or fear of his own sexual urges).

Tony's father appears to have had great difficulty letting his son compete with him without shame. Subsequently, Tony struggles with shame and anger, but defends against this anger by avoiding relationships with men where he might feel competitive. In fact he reports that he has few if any male friends, probably because he fears becoming competitive, which might lead to either shame and self-loathing or some form of aggression that frightens him. Again, he defends through avoidance and passivity.

It would be anticipated that, in the transference, Tony would become competitive with his therapist, maybe belittling him, disagreeing with him just to see what would happen, or vacillating in his feelings toward

---

[7]See the earlier discussion regarding contemporary views on Oedipus.

idealization of the therapist and shame of himself. Tony would be working out his conflicted feelings toward his father as well as working out his aggression. Of course he would defend against these, and it would be the therapist's role to interpret his defenses against both anger and feelings of warmth, and longing for a meaningful relationship with a male figure. If Tony were able to have warm feelings toward his therapist, this too could become frighteningly sexual at times. He may feel these warm feelings as sexual and fear that he is homosexual (possibly related to some of the gender confusion that was not totally resolved in relationships with mother and father). Were the therapist to interpret Tony's defenses against these feelings and tolerate them, the therapist would be running interference between Tony's ego and his overly harsh superego. Over time this relational intervention would help reconfigure Tony's superego and allow him to desire and understand his conflicts. This should free him to not be afraid of his sexual strivings or his anger, and allow him to develop a different self-and-other configuration than idealizing the other and shaming the self.

Tony's neurosis concretizes itself in his religious experience. He projects his unresolved relationship with his Oedipal father onto his heavenly Father so that he is "intellectually interested in theology" but can't feel close to a God who intimately cares about him. He may be anxious to fully embrace his newfound theology, as he may unconsciously fear punishment from his earthly father as well as his heavenly one. He wants to push against (be aggressive) the rules and regulations he grew up with (i.e., morals about drinking and sex), but this area has become conflicted due to his parents' inability to provide space for him to differ-entiate without it being a threat to their sense of self and worldview. Again, we see the effects of an overly harsh superego.

The therapist would need to analyze Tony's religious experience in the same manner that his family experience would be analyzed. What un-conscious wishes are defended against, and what superego retaliations does he fear if those wishes were owned? All this difficult and time-intensive work would be in the service of freeing Tony from debilitating compromise formations so that he would become capable of forming more conflict-free relationships with self, others and God. And these conflict-free (or more free) areas of functioning would enable Tony to enlarge his capacity to love and be loved.

4

Ecumenical Spirituality, Catholic Theology and Object Relations Theory

A Threefold Cord Holding Sacred Space

Theresa Tisdale

I was drawn to this project by the hope and prospect of enlarging the within-and-between group conversations about Christianity and psychoanalysis. Some years ago Douglas Jacobsen and Rhonda Jacobsen wrote *Scholarship and Christian Faith: Enlarging the Conversation* (2004) and hosted a conference, Faith in the Academy, at Messiah College. In both contexts Christian academics were invited to locate and articulate themselves within their Christian tradition and to consider the ways their tradition-based theology and spirituality informed their academic work and vice versa. What the Jacobsens pioneered for higher education at that time, Earl and Brad are seeking to do at this time; this current project reflects a similarly ecumenical spirit of openness, hospitality and inclusivity in the conversation between psychoanalysis and Christianity.

In declaring religion an illusion, Sigmund Freud (1927) cast a long, dark shadow over the notion of faith as positive and adaptive. In the last several decades a growing body of theoretical (McDargh, 1983; Sorenson, 2004a), clinical (Finn & Gartner, 1992; Tisdale et al., 1997) and empirical (Brokaw & Edwards, 1994; Hall & Brokaw, 1995; Lawrence, 1997; Tisdale, 1998) literature has helped reduce the size and intensity of the shadow. Ana-Maria Rizzuto's (1979) *The Birth of the Living God* is considered a seminal contribution to an enlarged and enlightened conversation between psychoanalysis and religion.

Added to these considerations are discussions of the religious or spiritual tradition of key psychoanalytic theorists and how cultural and personal context may have influenced the development and evolution of theory (Dobbs, 2009; Hoffman, 2004, 2011; Parker, 2012; Rizzuto, 1998). Adding to these biographical considerations are personal reflections by analysts regarding the ways in which their religious or spiritual commitments influence, inform and affect their analytic work and vice versa (Rizzuto, 2004; Aron, 2004; Fayek, 2004; Sorenson, 2004b). Through this book and a related CAPS symposium (Bland, Strawn, Tisdale, Hicks & Hoffman, 2012) the editors are inaugurating tradition-specific dialogue and discourse.

FROM BIOLOGY TO RELATIONSHIP:
THE OBJECT RELATIONS MOVEMENT

Object relations theory represented a paradigmatic shift within psychoanalysis from a focus on drives to a focus on relationship as the fundamental human motivation. This tectonic shift in theory, with attendant shifts in clinical practice, was also manifested in an organizational split (in the early 1940s) within the British Psychoanalytic Society between those who remained loyal to Freud (with Anna Freud leading this movement) and those who aligned with Melanie Klein. Between these two camps emerged the British Middle School, later referred to as the British Independents. Those most influential within this group were W. R. D. Fairbairn, D. W. Winnicott and H. Guntrip; John Bowlby (1969,

(4)

1973, 1980) and Michael Balint (1968) were other quite prominent members. For more detailed explications and summaries of the work of these influential contributors to the movement, readers are referred to Greenberg and Mitchell (1983), Rayner (1991), Summers (1994), and Mitchell and Black (1995).

Greenberg and Mitchell (1983) have noted that the concept of object relations originated from within Freud's drive theory. Freud's use of the word *object* follows the use of the word in everyday English, which refers to both a thing and a goal or target. In object relations theory the object is a representation of a person (external or internal other) and is sought for itself rather than as the means to an end (gratification and drive satisfaction). However, these are not static or independent objects, these are object *relations*. The object (other) is always experienced in relation to the self with some associated affect. These complex affective and associational links between real and imagined internal and external relationships become extremely significant when understanding personality, psychopathology and treatment.

Summers (1994) observed that object relations theories were developed by clinicians who had become dissatisfied with the presuppositions and limitations of classical theory and practice. As the movement evolved it was never entirely clear whether these ideas were an amendment or replacement for classical views (at times the theorists themselves were still wrestling with this notion). Whether amendment or replacement, object relations theory is most meaningfully understood within the historical and theoretical context in which it evolved.

Providing a summary of the object relations movement is a formidable task because of the theoretical breadth represented and because there is not widespread agreement about who should be included in this branch of psychoanalysis (Greenberg & Mitchell, 1983; Summers, 1994; Mitchell & Black, 1995). For reasons of time, space and (admittedly) personal preference, I have chosen to focus my discussion on those who most scholars agree represent the key figures within the British independent movement: Fairbairn, Winnicott and Guntrip.

BIOGRAPHICAL BACKDROP OF KEY THEORISTS

Theories are not created in a vacuum; they are the fruit of the intraper-
sonal, interpersonal and environmental context in which the theorist has
evolved. Some broad brush strokes will be used to paint a backdrop for
the theoretical review. Historically, the relevance of religion in the life of
Fairbairn, Winnicott and Guntrip has been minimized or ignored; thanks
to the work of Hoffman (2004, 2011), Dobbs (2009) and Parker (2012) the
oversight is being remediated.

William Ronald Dodds Fairbairn (1889–1964) was born in Edinburgh.
He was the only child of a Presbyterian father and Anglican mother. He
had a strict Calvinist upbringing that reportedly he did not mind, and
though his mother wanted him to enter the Presbyterian clergy, in his
adult years Fairbairn embraced Anglicanism. He obtained an MA degree
in philosophy and spent three years postgraduate study in divinity. There
is substantial evidence of the influence of these academic and personal
experiences; in *Psychoanalytic Studies of the Personality* (1952) Fairbairn
often uses religious terminology to describe psychological phenomena.
After service in WWI, Fairbairn completed a four-year course in medicine
followed by a yearlong specialty in psychiatry. He underwent analysis with
Ernest Henry Connell, a devout Christian (M. T. Hoffman, personal
communication, November 7, 2012). Because of his unconventional
training path, Fairbairn's credentials were viewed by some in the British
Psychoanalytical Society as questionable. During WWII he worked with
soldiers and veterans who experienced shell shock, what today we know
as post-traumatic stress and traumatic brain injury. Because he was located in Scotland rather than London, Fairbairn worked in relative isolation, which may have enhanced his creativity but hindered his connection to and warm reception within the British Psychoanalytical Society.
Recently, Clarke (2011) has explored the likely significant influence of Ian
Suttie on Fairbairn's thinking and theory. Fairbairn's writing is largely
theoretical, and it was the concerted effort of two of his analysands, Harry
Guntrip and John D. Sutherland, that made Fairbairn's work more accessible to the wider analytic community. Fairbairn died from complications

of depression, alcoholism and Parkinson's disease. These biographical details were taken from Sutherland (1989) and Hughes (1990).

Donald Woods Winnicott (1896–1971) was born in Plymouth, England;
his father was knighted and twice mayor of Plymouth. His premed
studies were interrupted by WWI, in which he served as a medical tech-
nician in the Navy. He completed his medical training in 1920 and in 1923
began a forty-year post at the Paddington Green Children's Hospital.
Also in 1923 he began a ten-year analysis with James Strachey (authorized
translator of Freud's works) followed by a five-year analysis with Joan
Riviere, a collaborator of Melanie Klein. Winnicott was supervised by
Klein for five years. During WWII, Winnicott treated many children who
were separated from their families due to wartime evacuation. Although
raised Methodist, Winnicott later converted to Anglicanism. His second
wife, Claire, a social worker whom he met and married, and with whom
he enjoyed a long collaboration, during war-time evacuation work with
children, describes Winnicott as deeply happy in his work, first as a pediatrician and later as an analyst. He died following a series of heart at-
tacks. Most of Winnicott's direct references to religion were in the context
of discussing transitional space and phenomenon (1953, 1965, 1971, 1975),
although he did make other incidental comments about religion
throughout his works. These biographical details were taken from Phillips
(1989) and Hughes (1990).

Harry Guntrip (1901–1975) was the son of a Methodist minister and
himself a Congregational minister for eighteen years. Not until 1946 did
he finally decide to be a psychotherapist. He was analyzed by both Fairbairn (completing over one thousand hours) and Winnicott; Fairbairn's
illness forced an early termination of their work. Guntrip's mother came
to live with Guntrip and his wife nine years prior to his mother's death,
and during that time she declared to him that she ought never to have
married and had children, but was better suited for business. Guntrip's
younger brother died when Guntrip was three and a half, a memory he
repressed for many years and an experience from which his mother never
fully recovered. These tragic details are examples of the impoverished,

painful and cold early world from which Guntrip withdrew. The intrapsychic and interpersonal tension between withdrawal and relating
would dominate Guntrip's life. He began religious life in the Salvation
Army before becoming a Congregational minister. Guntrip left full-time
ministry to become a psychotherapist in the department of psychiatry at
Leeds University (prior to his analysis with Fairbairn and Winnicott). In
addition to synthesizing and extending the work of others (Guntrip, 1971),
Guntrip focused some of his original work on religion (1949, 1969a).
These biographical details were taken from Dobbs (2009).

THEORETICAL AND CLINICAL CONTRIBUTIONS
OF KEY THEORISTS

Motivation. All object relations theories describe the fundamental
human motivation as relationship. The basic drive is not biological
toward gratification but toward the other for connection. Hughes (1990)
notes that Fairbairn came to this realization when a patient exclaimed,
"What I really want is a father" (p. 95), in protest to Fairbairn's talk of the
desires to satisfy drives. Winnicott (1961, 1965, 1971, 1975) contributed to
the understanding of motivation from his unique perspective as a pediatrician. His oft-quoted axiom "there is no such thing as a baby . . . one
sees a nursing couple" (1975, p. 99) was likely inspired (at least in part)
from his reading and review (1942) of a book titled *The Nursing Couple*
(Middlemore, 1941). The focal point in Winnicott's theory was the
mother-infant bond and the crucial importance of a devoted mother for
healthy development. Having been analyzed by Fairbairn and Winnicott,
Guntrip (1969b, 1971) elaborated on the need and motivational drive for
relationship with both internal and external others.

Psychological structure. Within object relations theory, psychological
structure relates to the self. The shift is away from Freud's topographical
(unconscious, preconscious, conscious) and structural (id, ego, superego)
models of intrapsychic functioning to an elucidation of how relationships
with others are internalized in ways that lead to the structuring of a self.
Although the term *ego* is often used in the early writings of object relations

theorists, the concept being explicated is not the ego as Freud envisioned it, but a self that is in need of forming (structuring) through relationship with others and the internalization of these self-other relations.

Summers (1994) has noted that structure is formed through internalization of self-affect-other experiences and associations (what he calls "object relations units"). These are not once-and-for-all experiences, nor are they intact internalizations of actual experiences; they are more complex and nuanced internalizations of self-other-affect experiences accumulated over time along with the meaning ascribed to those experiences. Because the very self of the person is formed based on these internalizations, confrontation may be experienced as a threat to existence.

Fairbairn (1952) developed the clearest description and diagram of how the internal drama forms and unfolds. Repeated painful relational and environmental encounters in childhood result in aspects of self and other being split off and forming self-other constellations that are connected by affect. Bad or painful object relations are internalized and repressed, but the evidence of them may be inferred from present patterns of relating with self and others.

Guntrip (1969b, 1971) synthesized Fairbairn's model of psychic structure and expanded it primarily by adding the concept of the regressed ego: part of the self that longs for relationship (Fairbairn's libidinal ego) but may withdraw entirely from seeking connection internally or externally. He described this as *the schizoid problem*: when the other is experienced as neglectful or severely impinging, the ego's response is passive withdrawal from any seeking to connect.

In final versions of his work Winnicott (1975) localized his view of psychic structure around the true and false self. The true self, marked by spontaneity and creativity, emerges and becomes structured through relational experiences with a good-enough (not perfect) mother. Winnicott noted the importance of imperfect provision as necessary for healthy development. However, if the child experiences maternal failures or an intrusive or impinging maternal presence, a false self develops and the child becomes prematurely and compulsively attuned to the mother (and later to others). The child becomes the mother's image of her or him rather than developing an authentic self.

Development. Although each object relations theorist has a unique perspective on maturation, they all hold in common the view that development hinges on the capacity of early caretakers (primarily the mother) to provide a relational experience and environment attuned to the infant's needs. This *facilitating environment,* marked by an optimal balance of provision without perfection, allows a robust, authentic self to develop. Summers (1994) has noted that the paradigm of attachment motivated by relationship versus drive is soundly supported by three lines of research: infant attachment, naturalistic observation and experimental work with animals; naturalistic research of children showing that they attach to caretakers whether the caretakers are good (provide for needs) or bad (neglectful or abusive); and that these attachments endure. To these lines of research is added the crucial element of meaning making.

For Fairbairn (1952), development was described in terms of three broad phases: *infantile dependence,* when the infant is wholly and utterly dependent on the mother or early caretaker(s); followed by a *transitional phase,* during which the key developmental task is the capacity for separation from the caretaker (mother) while maintaining a meaningful bond that is not threatened by abandonment or engulfment;[1] then *mature dependence,* the capacity for healthy interdependence based on mutuality and reciprocity. Guntrip's (1969b) view of development followed Fairbairn's, with the added consideration of possible complete withdrawal from object seeking (regressed ego), in contrast to Fairbairn's view of continuous object seeking.

For Winnicott (1965, 1975), development was centered on an intricate dialectic between intimate contact with others and differentiation/individual existence (Greenberg & Mitchell, 1983). Development begins with a phase of *absolute dependence* when the infant is in blissful union with the mother. When the infant becomes aware of a distinction be-

---

[1]The navigation of this phase is quite similar to Mahler, Pine and Bergman's (1975) description of separation/individuation.

tween herself and mother, this ushers in a phase of *relative dependence.*
The infant realizes he or she and mother are not one, with a concomitant
loss of sensed omnipotent control; reality and ambivalence enter the
picture. During this often-tenuous phase, capacities to care for the self
are internalized through the experience of maternal provision. The capacity for whole object relations (to experience both positive and negative feelings toward the same person) occurs during this phase. The final
phase *toward independence* results in, among other developmental
achievements, the capacity to be alone. From this master pediatrician and
analyst the field of psychoanalysis received key developmental concepts
(with clinical correlates) such as primary maternal preoccupation; good-
enough mothering, which includes a holding environment, mirroring, a
nondemanding presence, bringing the world to the child, graduated
failure of adaptation, survival in the face of aggression, failure to retaliate,
the opportunity to contribute and offer reparation after times of aggression; and the notion of transitional phenomenon/objects (where he
referenced religious experience). For Winnicott, play (1971) and transitional space (1953) were essential for creativity and thriving.

Psychopathology. If early life relationships and environment are full
of problematic or traumatic omissions or commissions, the formation of
a self will be hindered or arrested and functioning crippled. Each object
relations theorist has a unique view of how and why pathology occurs;
however, in every variant of the paradigm, psychopathology is a product
of distorted or disrupted object relationships that interfere with the
structure and functioning of the self (Summers, 1994).

For Fairbairn (1952), psychopathology resulted from the fragmentation of the ego and the devotion of the various split-off parts of the ego
to their internal objects (at the expense of relations with real people).
Powerful affects link these internalized object relations, and repression
prevents movement toward healthier relating. Qualitative and quantitative differences among the types of pathology are based on the type and
degree of splitting off of the ego that occurs (Greenberg & Mitchell, 1983).

Winnicott (1965, 1975) considered integrity and spontaneity as signs of mental health, and constriction in the expression of the self reflects pathology. Impairment in functioning of the self is due to a lack of good-enough mothering (deprivation or impingement). When maternal provision is missing, maturation is hindered and the resulting developmental needs dominate the relational landscape. If a patient regressed, it reflected a search for missing relational experiences. In earlier theorizing, Winnicott made three distinctions among mental disorders, but by 1954 he viewed them as resulting from dysfunction and disruption during the earliest year(s) of life. He used the true and false self as a single diagnostic principle; true neurosis was more a tribute to the fact that life is difficult (Greenberg & Mitchell, 1983).

Guntrip's (1969b) view was that pathology resulted from failure of strong ego formation in earliest infancy, the persistence of a fear-ridden and withdrawn (or regressed) infantile self in the depths of the unconscious that included unrealized potentialities of personality that have never been evoked. "*The rebirth and re-growth of the lost living heart of the personality is the ultimate problem psychotherapy now seeks to solve*" (pp. 11-12, italics original). Guntrip suggested that all forms of psychopathology were defenses against the schizoid problem: attempts by the patient to protect this vital core of the self, which together analyst and patient would try to reach. Guntrip described various schizoid characteristics (evidence of withdrawal from seeking objects): withdrawnness, narcissism, self-sufficiency, a sense of superiority, loss of affect in external situations, loneliness, depersonalization and regression.

Treatment. Within object relations theory, treatment is focused on facilitating internal structural change such that the (true) self may emerge, mature and function more effectively and adaptively. Although each theorist articulates the process uniquely, the two primary therapeutic interventions in this modality are interpretation and the provision of a new relationship (Summers, 1994).

For Fairbairn (1952) the analytic process was understood not as consisting of a resolution of unconscious conflict over pleasure-seeking impulses, but as a process through which the capacity for making direct and full contact with real other human beings is restored. From this perspective the task of psychotherapy is to release bad objects (understood as relational units by Summers, 1994) from the unconscious, for they are the origin of mental disorders. For Fairbairn the therapeutic aim in analysis was to help the patient change from a closed system of intrapsychic life to an open system, where the patient was free to interpersonally relate with real others.

Winnicott (1965, 1975) articulated the curative factor in psychoanalysis not as a result of accurate interpretations of psychological dynamics but rather from provision of missing maternal ministrations and meeting of early developmental needs. The analyst was called on to compensate for various early maternal failures by providing a holding environment that included reliability, attentiveness, responsiveness, memory and durability. Winnicott also noted the value of play (including creativity, illusion and humor). Ideally, treatment provided a holding, facilitating relational environment that allowed the true self to emerge and mature. Winnicott understood and used regression as a means to locate the point of arrested development; provision that compensated for early life deficits facilitated maturation.

For Guntrip (1969b) the initial goal of treatment was to encourage relinquishment of defensive attachments; this allowed the weak infantile ego to emerge. Then through *replacement therapy*, relationship with the analyst allowed the ego to reintegrate and enter the world on a positive basis. Guntrip emphasized that pathology resulted primarily from inadequate early caretaking and that analysts were called upon to provide an experience of adequate caretaking that encouraged the person to attach in healthier, more hopeful ways. Being accepted and understood when in a withdrawn (schizoid) place enabled the patient to feel hopeful and to be "born again" (Guntrip, 1949/1971, p. vi). For Guntrip, treatment unfolded in three phases or stages: (1) dealing with Oedipal defenses and conflict concerning ambivalent object relations of love and hate, primarily with parents and siblings that transferred into wider areas of living, (2) dealing with the schizoid compromise (feeling half in and half out of relationships and life), and (3) regression and regrowth (the most in-depth type of work when the analyst "begins to gain contact with the terrified infant in retreat from life and hiding in his inner citadel") (Guntrip, 1969b, p. 282).

PARTICULARITY OR PECULIARITY: TRADITIONING AS A FOUNDATION FOR INTEGRATION

While my husband and I were living in Oxford, England, a few years ago, we participated in a yearlong lecture and discussion series called "Developing a Christian Mind," which was hosted by Oxford University academics who were interested in theologically related academic dialogue. Theologian and scientist Alister McGrath was a frequent and popular speaker who spoke eloquently (and what seemed like effortlessly) at a rich, thick and deep level on the ways Christian theology and faith shape our work as academics and practitioners. He often began his talks with this quote from C. S. Lewis (1980): "I believe in Christianity as I believe that the sun has risen; not only because I see it, but because by it I see everything else" (p. 140).

Christianity provides the basis and foundation for my understanding of reality, so it is both my starting point and my anchor for integration. I appreciate the opportunity to speak openly about my Christian identity and how it shapes my understanding and critique of psychoanalysis. I appreciate Brad and Earl inviting us to extend hospitality and respect to one another as we detail our particularity; I am certainly aware that to what one person is *particularity* may seem to another to be *peculiarity*.

THEOLOGICAL AND SPIRITUAL NARRATIVE

I was raised Roman Catholic; both my parents were very devout. However, not all the branches on my family tree are Catholic; my ancestry includes a Methodist bishop, an itinerant Baptist preacher and a number of Anglicans. I attended Catholic school until eighth grade, went to catechism classes, and received the sacraments of baptism, penance (or reconciliation), Holy Communion, confirmation and the sacrament of the sick.

Growing up, my family often said the rosary together in the evening, and we attended mass weekly and observed all the seasons of the church year.

During high school I participated in Young Life and had a powerful encounter with God one starry night on a hilltop. That was the beginning of my introduction into non-Catholic expressions of Christianity. Across my life I have been part of many Christian communities (Southern Baptist, Vineyard, Episcopal, Presbyterian, to name a few). I was never comfortable with the sometimes "us-them" tone of these various communities (especially about Catholics and other Christians who did not maintain a similar theological or sociopolitical view). I was drawn to various traditions and churches at different times, depending on what God seemed to be teaching me during that season of life. I loved Southern Baptists for their emphasis on prayer, Bible study and faithful living. I loved charismatics for the abandon they showed toward God, the unswerving belief in the imminent presence of God, the deep encounter with God during worship and the faith to believe that when God showed up things happened.

This variegated Christian experience often left me feeling like something of an outsider, never quite belonging in any one tradition or denomination. These explorations also created a lot of dissonance for me regarding my Catholic tradition and identity, and I entered a prolonged state of liminality with respect to my Catholicism. God's redemptive and transformative movements in and through my life (which I don't have space to explain here) have brought about a rapprochement with my Catholic roots, which now provide a rich foundation for my Christian identity. I have what I would call a liturgical soul. Following the liturgical calendar and seasons of the church year provide a depth, meaning and resource that is spiritually enriching, intellectually stimulating and emotionally satisfying.

My participation within many different Christian traditions has led me to adopt what I refer to as an ecumenical identity. I almost want to whisper this for fear it will conjure up the oft-expressed disdain related to a word or notion from our clinical lexicon: *eclectic*. Rest assured I have no notion of ecumenism as a diluted form of Christianity. I embrace ecumenism out of a desire for connection across Christian traditions around the shared vision of being members of the body of Christ, through whom the Holy Spirit is actively at work bringing about transformation and redemption, which is taking place systemically (that is individually, interpersonally, culturally and globally), and out of a desire to promote a sense of community where there is recognition and value of the particularity of the many historical and contemporary traditions that represent the body of Christ. I am drawn to this expression of ecumenism because I need a larger framework to conceptualize and contain Christianity due to my diverse theological and spiritual background. I am inspired by *Streams of Living Water* (Foster, 1998) because of the thorough and balanced presentation of Christian traditions as well as the gracious and hospitable tone.

ESSENTIAL THEOLOGICAL AND SPIRITUAL BELIEFS

My understanding of Christian spirituality is bounded by orthodox theological beliefs drawn mainly from the creeds (the Apostles' Creed and the Nicene Creed), because they articulate the essentials of Christianity, what Lewis (1952) wrote about in *Mere Christianity* (*mere* being "essential" rather than "diluted"). In addition to the creeds, I draw from historical, orthodox Christian theology, and for the past decade or so I have found Alister McGrath's (2001a, 2001b, 2011) work quite helpful because of his thorough, careful research and accessible writing style. My beliefs are formulated based on church history (tradition), reason and experience with a foundation in God's incarnate and revealed word.

I believe we have both a longing for God and a propensity for sin. In the state of original sin (created by the fall) our awareness of God is dulled. I understand the context of original sin as a loss of trust and an unwillingness to acknowledge the need for and dependence on God. We are affected by both our own sin and being sinned against. Healing is possible through God's grace via a restored connection with God, self and others. Before we have had an awakening to God at a conscious level, our longing for God is more outside awareness, and the propensity for sin (living independently from God) is heightened. As God's overtures come more into conscious awareness, we reach crossroads where our intentionality in response to God is operative; we have the choice to respond to God's grace and yield to transformation or not.

Second-century church father Irenaeus said, "The glory of God is man fully alive." I believe the capacity to be fully alive is possible only in relationship to and with God. The behavioral sciences provide compelling evidence that humans are hardwired to connect, and will experience existence and find identity in relationship with others. As is explicated in object relations theory, this process may unfold for well or for ill based on the nature and quality of early life relationships. Existence and identity will be found in relations with others; what is crucial is who those others (or Other) may be. The familiar words of the Westminster Catechism come to mind in response to the question: "What is the chief end of man?" The answer is: "To glorify God and to enjoy Him forever." This succinct and beautiful phrase captures both purpose and relationship, or better said, purpose *in* relationship. The teachings from my Catholic roots about living a sacramental life invite and encourage me to live all of my life as worship to God. Living with a contemplative, mindful awareness of God's presence helps me to be a better wife, therapist, teacher, family member and friend.

I appreciate the work of Dallas Willard (2002) in returning our sensibilities to a holistic understanding of persons (philosophically and theologically). In his book *Renovation of the Heart* he articulates an aspective rather than partative view of human persons. He relates this holistic view theologically and philosophically to Jesus' response to the question, "What is the greatest commandment?" which is, love the Lord your God with all your heart, soul, mind and strength, and to love neighbor as self. Biblical scholars note how this profound and elegant phrase at once expresses God's intentions that we be integrated persons who are connecting with God in all aspects of our life and that this connection is motivated by love. It is curious and significant, because Jesus could have said serve, obey, follow, but he chose love. This integrated, aspective view of human

→ our love for God is always a response

persons is supported by discoveries in psychology, medicine and neuroscience (Koenig, King & Carson, 2012; Miller, 2012). We now have the
capacity philosophically, theologically, spiritually and psychologically to
understand human persons holistically; this is a significant shift from
dualism or other partative models or formulations of human experience
(Brown & Strawn, 2012; Thompson, 2010; Willard, 2002).

Based on my study of Christian theology and spirituality (Foster, 1998;
McGrath, 2011; Shelley, 1995), I understand God's activity in the world in
terms of reconciliation and redemption. From the time of the fall to the
present, God is ever at work making overtures to humankind to return to
the relationship we were created for. I believe that sin and psychopathology
(along with sickness) are in the world as a result of the fall. We are affected
by sins of omission and commission by others as well as by our own. We
will contend with sin, sickness and psychopathology as long as we are in
this age. When we encounter God in transforming ways that enliven our
eternal spirit to God, we have the potential to experience a measure of
transformation and redemption with respect to our own sinful patterns
and brokenness. Without connection to God, we will live a shadow of the
life we were born to have. We may experience encounter with God directly;
most often we experience it through community with others.

RESONANCE AND DISSONANCE IN THE MIDST
OF MUTUAL INFLUENCE

My theological beliefs and spiritual practices inspire me and give me
hope in my psychoanalytic work. Because I understand God is actively
at work to redeem humankind and creation, I see my work as sacramental and liturgical, participating in God's redemptive purposes in the
world and in the lives of my patients. Not that I have a priori understanding of *what* that redemptive work is for each of my patients; however,
I am persuaded *that* it is taking place. I believe in God's common grace;
therefore, I believe that God is at work in my patient's life even before she
or he has a conscious awareness of it or even welcomes it. Appropriate to
my therapeutic role, I am accompanying my patients on their journey as

it unfolds, including attending to whatever ways spirituality may be expressed during our work together. Believing in a trinitarian God who created humankind in God's image leads me to the fundamental premise that humans were created for relationship; connecting with God, self and others is essential to what it means to be human and alive.

I believe it is the most interesting and compelling aspect of this book that we are each considering how our particular theological and spiritual perspectives, practices and traditions inform how we think and work analytically and how our analytic practice enriches our theology and spirituality. I am drawing from my Catholic heritage because it was most influential in my formative years and continues as an anchor in my life. I am including reflections on the liturgical year because it orients me to time, the Eucharist because it compels me to remember and believe that Jesus is present, and the communion of saints because it provides an enlarged understanding of Christian community in the body of Christ.

The church year. For the whole of my life I have observed time in the context of the liturgical year. The word *liturgy* means "work." In Catholic teaching the liturgical or church year is oriented to the life and work of Jesus, and through intentional observance of each season, one is invited to participate in God's work in the world. Each season has a unique focus that mingles past, present and future; there is a dialectic between there-and-then and here-and-now.

The church year begins with Advent (Latin for "coming"). This is a season of waiting: remembering others waiting for Jesus' birth there and then as well as our waiting here and now in joyful hope for his second coming. Christmastide includes the traditional twelve days of Christmas that concludes with the Feast of Epiphany. Epiphany (Latin for "showing"), commemorates the manifestation of Jesus to the magi, who represent all the nations of the world. In the Church of England the Epiphany season continues until the Feast of the Presentation of Jesus in the Temple (on or around February 2). A season of what is called ordinary time (from the word *ordinal* or "counted") follows for a period of weeks. Lent begins with Ash Wednesday, when with the imposition of ashes we hear the words "remember you are dust and unto dust you shall return." Forty days of repentance through prayer, fasting and almsgiving provide focus on the reality of sinfulness and the need of a Savior. Palm Sunday commemorates Jesus' triumphal entry into Jerusalem. Holy Week begins the next day, and lectionary readings for each day of the week detail the events leading up to Jesus' death. The Paschal Triduum (Latin for "three days") begins the evening of Holy Thursday and concludes the evening of Easter Sunday. The days between Palm Sunday and Easter are a movement from triumph to tragedy to triumph again. The rhythms of Jesus' life are the rhythms of our life, individually and collectively. We all have seasons or days in our life that are like Good Friday, full of death (psychic or actual) and loss and betrayal and purgation; we have seasons that are like Holy Saturday, that feel dead and empty, all hope is gone and we are hollow; and we have seasons that are like Easter, where there is new life and resurrection and restored joy. The forty days following Easter commemorate the forty days Jesus appeared before his ascension into heaven. Pentecost comes at the conclusion of Eastertide; this day commemorates the coming of the Spirit and the reality of the eternal presence of Jesus with us now until he comes again. This feast is followed by a season of ordinary time until the year begins again at Advent.

For me, the liturgical church year provides a deep and rich grounding to life, a compass that is always pointing me toward true north, who is Jesus. The seasons are invitations for reflection, contemplation, repentance and rejoicing. Revisiting these seasons year after year allows me to find myself, God and others in fresh, new ways. In each season of the church year I find inspiration for my work with patients through the comfort of knowing and remembering Jesus, who descended to the depths of human experience, experienced triumph over human suffering, remains with us and in us through the Holy Spirit, continues to work through his living body to accomplish God's redemptive purposes for humanity and creation, and will come again in glory.

Celebrating the Eucharist. Eucharist means "thanksgiving." It is a celebration of our redemption through the life, death and resurrection of Jesus.

It is a sacrament in most Christian traditions. The God who is proclaimed and affirmed in the creeds and obeyed through the commandments is encountered in the sacraments (Kreeft, 2001). At one point in the mass, when the priest prays the words Jesus spoke at the Last Supper, the bread and wine (although they continue to appear as such) are transformed into the body and blood of Christ. Catholics refer to this as *transubstantiation*; Christ is really, truly and substantially present—body and blood, soul and divinity (*Catechism of the Catholic Church*, 1995; Kreeft, 2001; Smith, 1955). This is not magic, but it is surely a mystery and a miracle. Receiving the transformed bread and wine is called Holy Communion; it is a time of receiving and communing with the living God.

In object relations theory the relational experience of others is internalized.[2] Although theorists have attempted to describe it, I think there is also mystery around how this process happens. Each person, given her or his unique temperament, perceptions, sensations and emotions, internalizes real or perceived encounters with others in a way that forms the structure of the self (who she or he becomes). Relational experiences that occur over and over lead to the formation of self and personality. Through therapy, especially psychoanalytic psychotherapy or analysis, what we hope happens is change through relational experience; this is the taking in of a new other that leads to a re-formation of the self. Taking in Christ through the Eucharist contributes to Transformation (capital *T* for emphasis). Taking in the other through therapeutic encounters leads to transformation (small *t* for emphasis). Therapy as vocation, done through Spirit-led empowerment, has the potential to help lead the way from transformation to Transformation.

The communion of saints. In the final lines of the Apostles' Creed there is an affirmation of belief in the communion of saints, which I first learned about through my Catholic education. The communion of saints is made up of those who have died in Christ and who now are part of the great cloud of witnesses as living members of the body of Christ. In some

---

[2]A word used to refer to taking others in is curiously termed *incorporation*, taken from the Latin *incorporare* meaning "to form into a body."

Christian traditions (Catholic, Orthodox, Anglican) there are particular people whose lives of faith are so exemplary they are given a special title of Blessed or Saint. These include many of the early church fathers such as Augustine and Aquinas; founders of rules or religious orders such as Francis of Assisi, Benedict of Nursia or Ignatius of Loyola; mystics such as John of the Cross, Teresa of Ávila and Therese of Lisieux (for whom I am named); and contemporary figures such as Teresa of Calcutta, Pope John Paul II and Padre Pio. I am inspired in my faith as I learn about the lives of these women and men who have faithfully followed Christ and lived very holy and human lives. They may be asked for intercession as we would ask a friend or family member for prayer (Kreeft, 2001). Because of a unique ministry they had on earth they may have particular significance for those with a similar vocation.

In my spiritual life I draw inspiration and comfort from the communion of saints. The certainty and witness of those who have gone before me, who have suffered and persevered, draws me to Christ. In my practice I am inspired by the reality of the perseverance through suffering that is the life story of so many saints who faithfully followed Jesus. The reality of a communion of saints that is present though not visible may provide hope particularly for those for whom earthly relationships are or have been too terrifying or difficult to attain or sustain. In the communion of saints, meaningful connection with real others is possible. The witness and life of the saints who persevered through suffering can be taken in, internalized. While I do not initiate conversation with my patients about the communion of saints, I have encountered patients who feel connected to significant others who have died, drawing inspiration and comfort from the reality of their loved ones' continued existence and presence with them even after death.

So far I have mostly reflected on resonance and mutual influence between my faith and practice. There are dissonant chords as well. Most obvious to me are the ontological and teleological contrasts between Christianity and psychoanalysis. While there is reason to believe that the theological beliefs and spiritual lives of Fairbairn, Winnicott and Guntrip informed and shaped their unique articulations of motivation, development, pathology and treatment, the fundamental presuppositions of psychoanalysis as created by Freud remain unchanged in the negative tone toward religion. And the ways religion is discussed in the published works of these influential men are curious and at times seem somewhat contradictory. For example, Fairbairn's diaries are full of references to his personal faith (Hoffman, 2004), and, as noted earlier, he repeatedly uses theological language to describe psychological reality. However, his articulation of humans as born with a pristine ego seems to eschew his Calvinist upbringing, which would certainly have included some notion of original sin (which ironically seems reflected in the work of Freud and Klein, who posit the reality of innate aggression). Winnicott mentions religion in his highly original and compelling notion of transitional space and phenomena, and makes some connections between religion and other aspects of his theory in the large corpus of his work, but these ideas are not thoroughly explicated. Of the three, Guntrip comes closest to actively grappling with religion and psychoanalysis. Perhaps his life as both a minister and a psychoanalyst, as well as his analysis with both Fairbairn and Winnicott, uniquely prepared him for the formidable challenge of more focused discourse relating these two seemingly distant and dichotomous considerations of human experience. The lack of ontological and teleological fidelity to Christian theology has for decades caused a deep fissure between psychoanalysis and religion that needs healing. It is unlikely, if not impossible, for the dissonance to be fully resolved. There is sharp and profound dissonance and discord *within* Christianity and psychoanalysis; therefore, the relationship *between* them becomes even more complex. While attempts at full resolution may not be possible, what may be fruitful is the relocation of the conversation between Christianity and psychoanalysis from silos marked by mutual suspicion into transitional space (of the sort Winnicott described). In this transitional space the resonance (me) and dissonance (not me) within and between both Christianity and psychoanalysis may be acknowledged and respected with an attitude of humility and hospitality, and a desire for genuine dialogue and authentic engagement; the conversation would also benefit from inclusion of humor and play to facilitate the creative potential of this exchange.

CASE STUDY: TONY

Theoretical formulation. Tony is a young man struggling to connect with God, himself and others. He is experiencing "troubling lethargy regarding vocational aspirations," suggesting conflicts with identity and difficulty finding his purpose and place in the world. Descriptions of his early life suggest a home environment that was not entirely lacking in warmth, but mostly remembered by Tony as a place of fear, shame, intrusion and conflict. Tony describes his relationship with his mother as "warm but somewhat ambivalent"; the ambivalence resulted from his experience of her as intrusive. Winnicott's notion of the false self comes to mind here, as does Guntrip's idea of schizoid withdrawal as a response to inadequate provision and impingement.

Tony also feels conflicted about his father. Growing up, he wanted to be close and identify with him, but instead was met with ridicule and rejection, which led to feelings of shame and anger. I wonder whether the critical, demanding tone of the father-son relationship included specific references to God or religion. Whether or not these connections were overt, theoretical and empirical research suggests that Tony's understanding and experience of God was likely profoundly affected by this conflicted relational family scene.

I am also curious about the nature of the relationship between Tony's parents. Was his father as critical and demanding of Tony's mother? Was Tony's mother warm but intrusive toward her husband? Tony sought refuge from his father with his mother, but did she also seek refuge from her husband with Tony? These dynamics might be less consciously available to Tony but could be contributing to Tony's conflicts with women. I also wonder about Tony's relationship with his younger sister, specifically their age difference, the tone of the family at the time of her birth, and the family dynamic between various dyads and triads during his boyhood and young adulthood. Elaboration on these other family dynamics may be relevant to contextualizing and understanding Tony's struggles and conflicts with identity and purpose.

At the present time, what Tony is aware of is his painful sense of disconnection from others. He is not able to meaningfully engage with women in a consistent manner; initial interest turns to boredom and withdrawal. His relationships with men are overshadowed by competition and conflict. His current life is marked by both longing and fear. He longs to connect in satisfying and sustaining ways with women and men, and yet finds himself becoming avoidant with women and competitive with men. There is a hint of paranoia or persecutory feelings vis-à-vis his relationships with others as he wonders if "maybe he was being taken advantage of." He vacillates between anxiety and depression as these painful and unsatisfying scenarios unfold. Although not specifically articulated by Tony, the narrative suggests, if not reveals, that Tony is also disconnected from himself and from God. He compulsively masturbates in order to experience some self-soothing (his word) and aliveness (my word). While he does acknowledge some level of theological belief, he does not seem to experience any sort of personal or relational connection with God.

Tony has internalized his relational experiences of others in myriad complex ways that manifest in different relational expressions at different times depending on the situation (shifting states of self-other relation). For example, the narrative includes descriptions of Tony in relation to his father: "one moment desperately wanting his approval and the next minute belittling him as being uneducated and old-fashioned." There is also evidence in the narrative of varied internalizations of his mother: at times as a source of refuge, which likely brought about feelings of comfort, while at other times experiencing her as intrusive, which led to feelings of resentment. These variations are not by definition a problem. As Summers (1994) has noted, what becomes problematic is when these internalized constellations become fixed and rigid, leading to decreased options and diminished experiences in relationships with others in the present. This is evident in Tony's narrative. While Tony may have some conscious awareness of this link, he is likely less aware of how his very sense of existence is predicated on maintaining these relational patterns. This annihilation anxiety is too much to face alone. Ideally and hopefully, his relationship with his therapist will become a place for him to face himself and his fears.

Clinical application. The narrative suggests that Tony is eager to connect with his therapist, a man with whom he can bond and discover himself. There is a hint of some schizoid withdrawal or perhaps some hypervigilance around the responses of his therapist (real or perceived) as Tony expresses a preference for using the couch. Tony's ability to free associate rather readily is a good sign that initially he is able to express his thoughts and feelings. A positive transference may evolve fairly quickly, which would facilitate the healing process. He would likely come out of hiding and become more fully alive in response to empathy, feeling heard and understood, mirrored, accepted and emotionally held—what Winnicott called the facilitating environment.

Given the case narrative, there are a few additional clinical assessments that might be useful. One is the degree of Tony's depression and anxiety; is he or has he been suicidal? Depending on the severity of Tony's symptoms, a referral for medication evaluation might be in order. Also of interest is his general medical health; a recent thorough exam would help rule out organicity. These biological considerations notwithstanding, Tony's narrative strongly suggests that he needs a stable and trusted other to provide what he did not receive in early life: a steady diet of provision through experience (Stark, 1999) will lead to filling in deficits in development and to filling out and consolidating Tony's self.

However, provision alone will not likely be enough for Tony; he also needs insight. He is stuck in repetitive patterns in his relationships with his parents and others (particularly women) and he compulsively masturbates. Although he reports the locations as private, they seem in actuality to be quite public (public bathrooms, his car, etc.). If Tony is hiding, he is hiding in plain sight. Consciously, he has connected these episodes to stress and boredom. Horner (1991) has suggested that patients with obsessive tendencies may be suffering from approach-avoidance conflicts related to earlier phases of development where movement away from others may trigger fears of loss of love, and movement toward others may be fraught with fears of disappointment because of impending rejection and criticism. These are plausible hypotheses with respect to Tony's early life. Tony's therapist will need to formulate and offer interpretations that may elucidate the nature and extent of some of Tony's unconscious conflicts that are contributing to his compulsive behavior, feelings of anxiety and depression, as well as to his struggles in relationships and with vocational identity. These interpretations will connect his past relationships, his current struggles and the ways in which these dynamics will likely manifest in his relationship with his therapist.

In addition to interpretations (for gaining insight) and corrective emotional provision (for healing deficits), Tony also needs engagement and experience in relationship with the authentic self (subjectivity) of his therapist to facilitate resolution of his relational difficulties. Through mutual engagement, where the subjectivity of both patient and therapist is embraced, Tony will be able to work with his therapist to confront his interpersonal conflicts and relational patterns, and begin to experientially learn new ways of being himself as a person in relation to others. As Tony and his therapist enter into these exchanges together, new experiences in relationship are cocreated. Due to Tony's motivation, capacity for insight and capacity for a positive connection with his therapist, it is likely that therapy will be of great benefit to him. Through insight, provision and experience Tony will be able to move closer to having meaningful connection with himself, others and God.

As Tony gains insight, a stronger, more stable sense of self, and increased capacity for authentic and meaningful connection with others, he will likely be able to make clearer decisions about satisfying work. I cannot help but wonder whether Tony identifies in some ways (perhaps unconsciously) with the developmentally disabled man for whom he is caregiver. Perhaps in caring for him Tony is caring for some part of himself that he has projected onto this man. As Tony becomes more whole he may be able to see more clearly a vocational path and so attain the marks of health that Freud noted: love and work. McWilliams (1999) has noted that Chessick (1983) has added "play" to Freud's oft-quoted phrase about love and work. For Chessick, play is a restoration of the capacity for pleasure through creativity and recreation. McWilliams notes this capacity for play may be a fruit of successful therapy. Tony's life at present seems void of any genuine pleasure or creative expression.

As his therapy progresses the potential for Tony to experience himself coming alive and able to thrive in love, work and play will increase. Irenaeus's poignant words "The glory of god is man fully alive" will hopefully and prayerfully become a reality for him. Tony is in need of deep, sustaining, life-giving connection with God, through whom Tony may discover himself and his unique purpose in life. Tony's therapist has the opportunity to serve as a faithful companion on Tony's journey of becoming the person he was created to be, living a meaningful and purposeful life in community with others and at deeper peace with himself and God.

5

Self Psychology and Christian Experience

Earl D. Bland

U nfortunately, in many ways the history of psychoanalysis contradicts a progressive and normative intellectual development. After Freud's death, in their effort to systematize and monitor correct practice, psychoanalysts created a virtual theocracy that significantly hampered creative exploration and innovation. In particular, the coopting of medical psychiatry as the psychoanalytic gatekeeper not only went against Freud's (1926) original vision but by the 1970s resulted in the increasing marginalization of psychoanalysis as a preferred psychological treatment for most disorders (Stepansky, 2009). Elite isolationism and resistance to scientific advances in the field of mental health and neuroscience moved psychoanalytic thinking away from progressions in academia and the contemporary intellectual zeitgeist. Internally, competing theoretical models battled a stagnating classical view, and myopic training institutes were fast becoming insular fiefdoms (Bornstein, 2001; Kirsner, 2001,

2004; Goldberg, 1990; Ornstein, Ornstein, Zaleznik & Schwaber, 1977; Rubin, 1998; Rangell, 2004; Stepansky, 2009).

It is surprising perhaps that in the midst of this growing psychoanalytic malaise, self psychology emerged from the foment of object relations theory and ego psychology to become a principal contributor to the relational renaissance that has captured psychoanalytic theory in the last thirty years (Mitchell, 1988, 1991; Lee & Martin, 1991; Wolf, 1988). Self psychology, a contemporary movement in psychoanalysis, owes its genesis primarily to the work of Heinz Kohut. A Viennese-trained physician who immigrated to the United States during World War II, Kohut received his psychoanalytic training at the Chicago Institute for Psychoanalysis, where he remained an instructor until 1972. He died in 1981. An avowed Freudian in his early career, Kohut's construction of self psychology was a slow progression stemming from his extensive clinical work with narcissistic disorders (Siegel, 1996). Beginning with technical changes to the analytic mode of inquiry (Kohut, 1959) and culminating in a substantial reformation of psychoanalysis (Kohut, 1984), self psychology anchored paradigmatic shifts in psychoanalytic perspectives on development, the causes of psychological disturbance, the nature of self and object relations, and our understanding of treatment and cure (Fosshage, 1998; Lee, Roundtree & McMahon, 2009; P. H. Ornstein, 2008; Siegel, 1996).

To introduce the ideas of self psychology I start with three interrelated leitmotifs: empathy as the definitive therapeutic position, narcissism as the orienting psychic disturbance, and self as the center of psychological life. These broad clinical themes activated theoretical shifts in Kohut's thinking, moving the focus of psychoanalytic inquiry away from the tripartite mind and intrapsychic conflict, toward the development and vicissitudes of the self and *selfobject* functioning. Motivation, development, psychopathology and therapeutic change are all understood in reference to self-processes. I end our discussion with a brief critique and reflection on how my faith tradition engages the theory of self psychology, and I will consider the case of Tony through the eyes of a self psychologist.

EMPATHY

Recall from our first chapter that by the mid-twentieth century significant change was afoot regarding the traditionally accepted verifiability of scientific objectivism. As Kohut's theory developed, it was becoming increasingly evident that the ideal picture of a detached, neutral scientific observer gathering objective truth was as mythical as the fictive, fact-obsessed Thomas Gradgrind in Charles Dickens's (2005) novel *Hard Times*. As Donna Orange (2011) points out, Kohut's most prominent shift was his early move to emphasize the empathic introspective position as a primary method for gaining knowledge relevant to the psychoanalytic enterprise. Revealing an incline toward the "philosophy of experience" (p. 175), Orange explains Kohut's argument that a scientific discipline (psychoanalysis) was defined by its methods of observation or data gathering. Empathy as the primary tool of inquiry creates an *experience-near* perspective wherein the therapist is able to understand clinical material from within the patient's point of reference. For Kohut this was the only type of data relevant to psychoanalytic treatment. As the therapist sustains a deep empathic stance toward the patient, he or she is able to understand the meaning of the patient's inner experience, including symptoms, transferences and developmental path.

Ironically, perhaps, and it is unclear how much Kohut (1959) was cognizant of its implications, his focus on empathy confronted the established psychoanalytic community about what it meant to know something in the process of treatment. The use of the sustained empathic mode of inquiry was actually a subversive stance within the hierarchical one-person psychology that dominated psychoanalysis in the middle of the twentieth century (Stozier, 2001). Persistent empathy fundamentally changes clinical material because detached therapeutic observation and interpretation from preexisting knowledge categories are no longer valid. The observing tool, empathy, is an idiographic method for obtaining data (Stolorow & Atwood, 1992). In turn, the meaning of data is determined through a hermeneutical co-construction as both patient and therapist contribute to eventual understandings. Kohut (1975) believed,

and many have subsequently observed, that an empathic position re-
moved much of the hierarchy in therapy, making the logical endpoint of
Kohut's stance a two-person therapeutic process wherein therapist and
patient were collaborative coparticipants in the formation of perception
and meaning (Fosshage, 1998; P. H. Ornstein, 2008; Stern, 1992; Stolorow,
Brandchaft & Atwood, 1987).

Although he was not the first to identify empathy as an important
mode of attending in psychoanalytic treatment, Kohut made empathy a
principal construct within self psychology (Lee & Martin, 1991; Levy,
1985). Memorably, in a heartfelt lecture given four days before his death
from lymphoma in 1981, Kohut chose to underscore the importance of
empathy not only as a tool to gain access to the subjective world of the
patient but as a broad, life-enhancing action. Echoing an earlier comment
about the healing effects of empathy as "a bridge between human beings"
(1975, p. 361), Kohut's mature perspective saw empathy as critical to the
formation and maintenance of healthy self-functioning. Empathy provides the information necessary for understanding, interpreting and explaining therapeutic material; empathy between humans wards off isolation, it has healing and self-reparative effects, and it is a necessary
component of a responsive developmental environment. Bacal and
Carlton (2010) clarified these different meanings of empathy in clinical
settings by suggesting that the therapeutic impact of empathy could be
described by distinguishing empathy as a therapeutic _tool_ whereby the
therapist understood the subjective experience of the patient. Second,
empathy is a therapeutic _response_ of understanding and attunement,
which may have ameliorative effects apart from any interpretive process.

The self psychological focus on empathy, however, has lead to criticisms about the complexity of therapeutic action beyond empathy. Relational theorists argue that empathy is indeed critical for grasping the
subjective experience of the patient, but in itself empathy is not sufficient
for understanding psychoanalytic process because it does not clearly address the inherent two-person nature of treatment (Mitchell, 1993;
Wachtel, 2008). In essence, self psychology's emphasis on empathic at-

tunement says nothing about the character or subjectivity of the therapist outside of identifying a skill level necessary for effective listening (Aron, 1991). Emphasizing the relational bond originally acknowledged by Kohut, Aron (1996) writes, "Empathy, or analytic love, must be mutually given and mutually accepted" (p. 136).

These criticisms help bring clarity to the self psychology position, which has never argued for psychoanalytic treatment based solely on the empathic stance. Precluding the singularity of empathy, there are always theoretical assumptions therapists use to understand a patient (Goldberg, 1988). Moreover, external material in the form of infant research, treatment outcome data, neuroscience and expanded theoretical developments are important contributions to effective treatment (Basch, 1990; Lichtenberg, 1989). Teicholz (2006), taking a cue from research regarding the mutual regulating nature of the parent-infant attunement, states, "any joint endeavor between patient and analyst—if it is to be therapeutically successful—will involve an implicit striving toward mutual empathy, regardless of what other qualities of engagement are called forth" (p. 55). Distinguishing between modes of listening, Fosshage (1997a) identifies an experience-near mode of listening—one that empathically connects to the patient's experience—and an "other centered listening perspective" (p. 38), which honors an external view of the patient. Geist (2007) directly disputes the relational critique by suggesting that the deep, powerful bond established within a sustained empathic relationship facilitates the experience of being deeply understood. For Geist, sustained empathy does not diminish the therapist's subjectivity but increases his or her ability to respond effectively out of the subjective position:

> Prolonged empathic immersion is not a technical maneuver; it is better defined as an analytic sensibility that helps to inform the analyst how to respond to the patient. These responses include the analyst's inevitable expression of his or her subjectivity and authenticity. (p. 16, italics original)

More recently Geist (2013) spoke to a contemporary self-psychological view of the empathic connection as mutual or bidirectional wherein we "convey our understanding of what we experience to the patient in a way that invites the patient to emend, clarify, or correct our understanding in the context of our own subjectivity" (p. 267).

In these post-Kohutian discussions the topic of empathy is less about the definition and characteristics of empathy and more about the sufficiency of empathy as a therapeutic instrument or its relational function between therapist and patient. Suffice it to say that all psychoanalytic theories recognize the importance of empathy as both a mode of inquiry and a facilitator of therapeutic effectiveness. Perhaps the most salient feature of a contemporary self psychology view on empathy would be the continued prominence of sustained empathic immersion as the preferred psychotherapeutic stance. As Goldberg (2011) points out, momentary empathy is different from a sustained empathic stance that views the patient over a long period of time. Psychological, behavioral and relational dynamics are apprehended at deeper levels when the therapist has been connected to the patient in a sustained empathic relationship.

NARCISSISM

Kohut's favoring of empathy as the preferred therapeutic stance emerged primarily because he was working with a type of patient who needed significant levels of empathic mirroring. Increasingly he found some patients were exquisitely sensitive to variations in therapeutic understanding and had difficulty regulating their self-esteem. Instead of developing a classic transference neurosis, these patients experienced excessive disruptions in their sense of self and looked to him to acknowledge and affirm the validity of their narcissistic needs. These clinical experiences led Kohut (1966, 1968) to explicitly challenge the classical view of narcissism by suggesting that health did not mean the eradication of narcissism but its transformation into virtuous expressions of one's vitality and engagement with the world.

Originally Freud (1914) viewed healthy development as libidinal or psychic energy moving from a primary investment in the ego to a mature object-focused libido. Essentially the move is from self-love to object relations. In contrast, Kohut opened the possibility that narcissism followed its own developmental trajectory separate from ego development. Rather than the suppression and eradication of self-love, Kohut argued that altruistic Western values diminished the validity of self-needs such as affirmation, ambition, idealization, relational connection and growth (Kohut, 1977). He saw development and interest in the self as legitimate psychological processes that could be the focus of psychoanalytic treatment (Lachman, 2008). As Kohut shifted his attention from interpreting the transference as psychic conflict based in the patient's repetitive patterns from childhood to an empathic understanding of the patient's vulnerable self-esteem and emotional fragmentation, deeper levels of healing and symptom amelioration ensued. In essence he found that the patient was using the therapist to support and cohere a sense of self. The transference dynamics displayed were of a narcissistic origin and included the need for mirroring and an affirmation of grandiosity, the need to idealize the therapist, or the need to evoke experiences of sameness and similarity (twinship) to the therapist.

What precipitated the eventual departure of self psychology from the Freudian perspective on healing in psychoanalytic therapies was not so much an eschewing of the classical perspective but the realization of its limits in the face of "era-specific" cultural currents (Kohut, 1984, p. 57). Kohut (1971, 1977) argued that Freudian analysis was bound to a particular understanding of the psychic world deeply embedded in the evolutionary cultural metaphor of conflict in the mind. The mind was a battlefield with undesirable primitive wishes pitted against humanity's attempt to civilize through the abolition of libidinal and aggressive drives. In essence the Freudian description of psychological life privileges guilt as the endemic emotional process in all expressions of neuroses. Kohut (1977, 1984) contrasted this *guilty man* with the fundamentally different dilemma facing contemporary humans: the striving for self-fulfillment, meaning and the realization of the self's potential, or what he called the "nuclear program of [the] self" (1984, p. 148). Tragically, contemporary life is filled with obstacles, barriers and missed opportunities that hamstring our ability to achieve or realize the full potential and purpose of

the self. Kohut referred to this modern psychological disquiet as belonging to *tragic man*. As the expansion of ego control over the drives
was the goal of Freud's *guilty man*, the fully integrated expression of the
self is at the heart of Kohut's *tragic man*.

SELF

The construct self has a complex history (Taylor, 1989), and Kohut was
not the first or the only one talking about the self within psychoanalytic
circles.[1] While Kohut (1971) initially conceived of self as a structure in
the mind, not unlike how Freud conceived of the id, ego and superego, as
his theoretical insights matured Kohut (1984) deemed self the preferred
psychic configuration for understanding all human psychology. By the
mid-1970s he was keen to expand the territory and function of what he
called the nuclear self. His elaboration in relation to development, motivation and its centrality to psychoanalytic cure demonstrated the usefulness of self as a construct for understanding complex clinical disorders.

> This structure [self] is the basis of our sense of being an independent
> center of initiative and perception, integrated with our most central ambi-
> tions and ideals and with our experience that our body and mind form a
> unit in space and a continuum in time. (1977, p. 177)

Present at birth and emerging within a relational context for Kohut
(1984), the self became a superordinate psychological structure that captured the core of personality and served to organize psychological experience. He was loath to get too philosophical about the self and preferred
to keep his musings close to the clinical exchange where self-experience
could be apprehended via the empathic mode of listening. "It [self] is that
. . . which we experience as the 'I' of our perceptions, thoughts and actions"
(1970, p. 9). Moreover, while Kohut did refer to the self as a mental
structure implying some degree of constancy, he also wanted to preserve
the experiential nature and origins of self (Teicholz, 2000), keeping open

---

[1]Kohut (1971) recognizes that Heinz Hartmann was one of the first to conceptualize the self
as independent of the ego. It is worth noting, however, that D. W. Winnicott (1965) had been
writing about the self in the 1950s, and Carl Jung addressed the self decades earlier.

the possibility "of different and even contradictory selves in the same person, of selves with various degrees of stability and of various degrees of importance" (Kohut, 1970, p. 10).

In a helpful summation of the Kohutian perspective on self, Ronald Lee and his colleagues (Lee et al., 2009) describe three different dimensions of self-experience present in Kohut's writings. First is the fragmentation-cohesion dimension, which addresses the deterioration or consolidation of self-functioning alternatively seen in pathological versus healthy states of being. Second, the idea of peripheral versus nuclear self uses a spatial metaphor to demonstrate how some aspects of self-experience are more surface, and others, such as a person's ambitions, skills and ideals, constitute the core or nuclear self. Finally, there is self-partitioning (vertical split) or unique sectors of the self that are relatively permanent and sustained (e.g., religious or professional identities, specialized skill sets, or aesthetic pursuits). As Lee and colleagues point out, Kohut's ability to identify different sectors of the self allows for an expansion of what it means to be psychologically healthy or unhealthy. The notion of a complete and total analysis that resolves all unconscious conflicts is contrasted with a more bounded and perhaps realistic understanding that robust health in at least some sectors of the self may be enough to sustain a deeply meaningful and engaged life.

In the wake of Kohut's rather loose and general description of the self, there has been significant support, debate and consternation within psychoanalysis about what is meant by *self*. In lieu of a prolonged discussion I will highlight two streams of thinking that have significantly challenged and expanded our understanding of self within the psychoanalytic frame. The first challenge highlights the confusing theoretical and philosophical nature of Kohut's use of the term *self*. Consider the common statement "I am not myself today." How is this possible? How can my self, experienced as the subjective "I," be different than what I describe as my self? In other words, how can one's self disengage from its own experience and comment on it from the position of an agent? As Riker (2010) asks, "How can the 'I' 'have a self' or 'be a self' if the 'I' is the same as the self?" (p. 73). Surely there is the subjective experience of "I" that must be different from the self which the "I" experiences as a self. Stolorow and Atwood (1992) pointed this out by highlighting the dual meaning of self in the Kohutian system. The term *self* in self psychology can mean (1) an organization of experience called the self—which can experience fragmentation, and (2) the agent that experiences something to restore the feeling of cohesion. Consequently, self cannot be understood as a reified construct or structure in the mind. The notion of a unitary constant self is challenged by assumptions that self experience is always developed and maintained within intersubjective or relational contexts, and, in fact, the notion of a mental structure called the self is a construction that only makes sense within an intersubjective field (for more about the intersubjective notion of self see chap. six).

The second challenge to the notion of a unitary or cohesive self-structure is highlighted in the recent work of the interpersonal psychoanalyst Philip Bromberg. Drawing on extensive work with traumatized patients and recent neuropsychiatric findings about the nature of self, it appears that the experience of self-constancy is really an illusion of fluidity between multiple self-states that are highly context dependent and formulate around affective experiences with particular memory configurations, thoughts, behavioral repertoires and relational expectancies (Siegel, 2012). It is quite evident at this point that various emotional functions or self-capacities are constructed and emerge from different interconnected regions or structures of the brain (Lindquist, Wager, Kober, Bliss-Moreau & Barrett, 2012). Although the left hemisphere appears to be the "seat of language" (Pinker, 1997, p. 271) and conscious verbal expression, our experience of emotion is much more distributed with no one region holding sway (Uttal, 2011). Moreover, implicit emotional or affective processes may be activated independent of the brain's conscious processing or behavioral responses.

In a series of books and articles Bromberg (1998, 2011) and others (Panksepp, 2009; Schore, 2011; Siegel, 2012) demonstrate that self is best understood as a nonlinear and nonstructural affective configuration of variable states of reflective consciousness that deal with different reality needs and relational demands within shifting contexts. In other words, we are not one singular unitary self, we are a configuration of self-states. Our sense of continuity between these states is reflective of our non-dissociative healthy processing that does not need to sequester or isolate (dissociate) particular ways of being our self from other states. Healthy self-functioning demonstrates a nonconscious fluidity between different self-states. Those who have suffered significant trauma are more likely to experience disjunctions between various self-states.

In light of these challenges contemporary self psychology has allowed its understanding of self to evolve. In the wake of Kohut's turn to the self as the locus of psychoanalytic inquiry, the meaning of *self* has proliferated and expanded. It appears the self is best construed as a relationally embedded, emergent, biopsychic, affective system that organizes emotional and perceptual input allowing one to experience a sense of continuity, agency and uniqueness as well as connectedness and communal affiliation within the limits of embodiment.

SELFOBJECTS

When Kohut (1971, 1977) recognized that transference patterns went beyond repetitions of past relationships to influence self-regulation, he realized he was serving psychological functions for his patients. In particular he noticed three specific self-needs within the analytic relationship: (1) the need to idealize the therapist, (2) the need for perfect attunement and understanding by the therapist and (3) a need to be similar or like the therapist. In order, Kohut described these as idealizing, mirror and twinship transference needs. Further, he discovered that when the therapeutic relationship met these needs for idealization, mirroring and twinship, the patient responded with a sense of self-coherence or vitality. Essentially, the therapeutic relationship contained self-enhancing properties, and he called this process a *selfobject* function (Kohut & Wolf, 1978). However, the selfobject experience is not just a clinical phenomenon. Fundamental to the existence and maintenance of the self is a responsive relational milieu in which the expression of self is, to varying degrees, acknowledged, supported and validated with a sufficient amount of empathic attunement. In other words there are objects (persons) within the psychological space of the self that help to maintain its sense of integrity and cohesion. One's self uses these selfobject experiences narcissistically to fulfill self-needs and sustain psychological life. Selfobjects are understood not in terms of interpersonal qualities or external attributes, but as part of self-experience, performing needed self-functions (Kohut, 1971, 1977, 1984).

Although there have been some attempts to clarify its meaning and applicability, the selfobject concept is an enduring Kohutian legacy. Recently the definition of the selfobject experience or function has become central to self psychology's place in the tension between one-person intrapsychic psychoanalytic theory and two-person relational psychoanalytic perspectives. Kohut initially saw the selfobject as a function of the individual psyche. Although the concept suggests relationality (one needs actual people to provide selfobject experiences), it appears he was ambivalent and spoke in terms of the individual self-function of the selfobject, linking his ideas to the intrapsychic model of Freud (Goldberg, 2002, 2011; Bacal & Newman, 1990; Stolorow, 1994a). In contrast, those who maintain Kohut's theory as relational highlight his extensive discussion of self-selfobject experiences and the obvious implications of the selfobject concept for a two-person psychology. If the self is born into a selfobject milieu and needs responsive selfobjects throughout its life, relationality is clearly inherent within the self psychological paradigm, even if it does not embrace the explicit relational epistemology found in the current relational and intersubjective psychoanalytic theories (see chaps. 6-7) (Geist, 2008; Lee et al., 2009; Summers, 1996; Tolpin, 1986). Intersubjective theorists Stolorow, Brandchaft and Atwood (1987) clarified the relational nature of selfobject ties by suggesting that selfobject functions were primarily about the integration of emotions "into the organization of self-experience . . . the need for selfobject ties pertains most centrally to the need for attuned responsiveness to affect states in all stages of the life cycle" (p. 66). Moreover, while Geist (2008) maintains the asymmetrical self-enhancing and vitalizing function of the selfobject tie, he describes these experiences as best accomplished within a form of selfobject relatedness he terms *connectedness* or "the consciously or non-consciously felt sense of sharing and participating in another's subjective emotional life while simultaneously experiencing another as participating in ones own subjective life" (p. 131).

To summarize, organizers of self-experience are the emotions and feeling states that operate throughout life and obtain meaning and validation within a relational matrix. Humans need responsive others to provide selfobject experiences to help differentiate, integrate and contain various affective impressions resulting in a cohesive sense of self. In other words, selfobject experiences are relational experiences that provide a psychologically sustaining function for the self within symmetrical and asymmetrical relational contexts. When selfobject ties are absent or inadequate, the self is prone to fragmentation because of the unruly, frightening, traumatic and contradictory nature of affect states.

MOTIVATION AND DEVELOPMENT IN SELF PSYCHOLOGY

Developmentally, Kohut conceived the self as emerging out of a primary narcissistic position along two lines or poles. He described a grandiose or exhibitionist expression of self that seeks affirmation and mirroring, along with an alternative idealizing self pole that seeks to maintain security, power and goodness by projecting these perfections onto an important attachment figure, typically the parent. In the absence of trauma these early, archaic forms of narcissism gradually transform to their mature arrangement of ambitions and ideals that motivate and guide the self to the realization of its potential within the constraints of inborn talents and acquired skills. P. H. Ornstein (1995) summarizes: "The fundamental human motive is the establishment and maintenance of a cohesive self. Once cohesion has been achieved, living out one's inner design in keeping with one's ambitions and ideals, while maintaining connection to others, are lifelong, basic motives" (p. 51).

Despite Kohut's recognition of the interrelationship between the desire to maintain and restore self-cohesion, and the importance of an environment that is empathic and responsive, self psychology did not provide detailed explanations of how this was achieved in actuality. For instance, similar to Winnicott's (1965, p. 145) broad notion of the "*good enough mother*," Kohut assumed perfect mirroring or attunement was neither possible nor preferred for healthy self-development. He proposed the term *optimal frustration* (later expanded by Howard Bacal [1985] to the notion of *optimal responsiveness*) as way of accounting for the inevitable failures and breaks in selfobject functioning that characterize the parent-child bond. If the selfobject ruptures are nontraumatic, bracketed by adequate resonance and efforts to repair the empathic breach, children incrementally establish a sense of self through the internalization of selfobject functions—a process Kohut termed *transmuting internalizations* (Kohut, 1971, 1977; Tolpin, 1971).

Sustained engagement in self-selfobject relations is key to the solidification and maintenance of the self. Recent advances in infant research, attachment theory and cognitive neuroscience validate self psychology's recognition that the principal human motive for self cohesion, vitality and growth requires a developmental frame immersed in empathic attunement and responsiveness (Beebe & Lachmann, 1998; Lyons-Ruth, 2006; Schore, 2003; Sroufe, 2002). More specifically, a driving force in development of self is the movement from simplicity to complexity. Development is not a stepwise process but an unfolding or emergence of greater levels of complexity in interactions between children and the environment (Siegel, 2012; Thelen & Smith, 1994). The goal of the self is to initiate, organize and integrate experience so that a sense of cohesion and continuity is established and maintained. As children experience their own narcissistic grandiosity and expansiveness within an optimally receptive and admiring connection to the parent, self-delineation and organization of feelings, perceptual impressions, expectancies, memory and agency begin to take shape (Fonagy, Gergely, Jurist & Target, 2002; Siegel, 2012; Stern, 1985; Stolorow & Atwood, 1992). Consistency and cohesiveness of one's self depends on an ever-expanding memory of previously affirming experiences and the reinforcements that occur in specific conditions and contexts. Certain expressions of self become more probable as they become more rooted within consistent patterns of interaction and engagement. In the brain, emotional responses and affect states elicited during ongoing life experience are of primary value because these ingrained patterns of neuronal firing influence the way the self-system is activated and responds (Siegel, 2012).

Further, infant research has consistently demonstrated the interactive nature of development (Beebe & Lachman, 1988, 1998; Lichtenberg, 1989; Stern, 1985; Thelen & Smith, 1994). Where we once saw the baby as a largely passive/receptive partaker of an adequately responsive selfobject climate, it is now clear that infants enter the world capable of active influence. Specific motivational systems have been identified to include physiological regulation, exploration and self-assertion, sensuality (sexuality), attachment, caregiving, affiliation and withdrawal/antagonism (Lichtenberg, 1989; Lichtenberg, Lachmann & Fosshage, 2011). Guided by this bounded set of motivational systems that self-organize and assemble hierarchically depending on inner needs and external demands, the infant is engaged in a mutually influencing dance with its caregiver (Lichtenberg et al., 2011). Self-organization requires the perception of an inner need (hunger, novel stimulation, tactile engagement, etc.) along with an empathic confirmation from the mother or caretaker. In these mutually influencing and nonlinear exchanges the infant's motivational states are recognized as valid expressions of self. The emotional experience of vitalization and coherence within and across given motivational states allows for the eventual emergence of an "I," whose associational memory and perceptual expectancies continually shape environmental interactions resulting in the consolidated experience of agency and engagement (Trevarthen, 2009). In other words, one feels like they are coparticipants in determining their experience: the part-me, part-other exchange needed for healthy functioning.

PSYCHOPATHOLOGY

The absence of a receptive and empathic developmental environment extinguishes the self's effective organization as an independent center of initiative with adequate motivation and goals. One's sense of agency and relational connection is hamstrung by unrequited narcissistic needs that, to varying degrees, interfere with a vital, cohesive and consistent sense of self. This failure of adequate selfobject responsiveness throughout the lifespan can have devastating effects but is especially problematic during early development because primary narcissistic needs for grandiosity and idealization are not relinquished within the loving and understanding gaze of parents or other caregivers. Instead these needs are traumatically repudiated through disavowal or dissociation, making them unavailable for future modifying influences. Instead of an energetic and cohesive self, motivated by ambitions and compelled by ideals, one's self-experience is enfeebled, depleted and prone to fragmentation.

Self-pathology develops primarily because of deficits in self-development and functioning caused by an interference with the child's ability to effectively experience or make use of empathy and care in early relational connections. Development is *arrested*, which necessitates the pursuit of alternative pathways to achieve organization and regulation of the self. Because its tendencies and motivations generally seek to maintain attachments, the self is often able to make up for omissions in the primary selfobject environment by cobbling together other self-selfobject experiences to meet needs for mirroring, idealization and twinship. These compensatory relationships or *structures*, as they were originally called (Kohut, 1977; Tolpin, 1997), shore up fragile self-states and provide new opportunities to complete thwarted developmental strivings. Accentuating the fundamental hopefulness in self psychology, Kohut (1984) asserted there was more than one kind of healthy self. Lost or fractured early relational connections can be counterweighed in subsequent relational contexts that are adequately responsive (Fosshage, 1997b).

Although self-pathology is expressed in myriad behaviors and relational tendencies, traditional self psychology has distinguished between narcissistic behavior disorders and the more severe narcissistic character or personality disorder. The former is more acute and involves addiction, criminal acts, distorted sexual behavior or other conduct designed to vitalize or distract an empty self and soothe feelings of disintegration and fragmentation. More pervasive disturbance, like that found in personality disorders, could involve the already-mentioned behaviors but on a deeper level reflects a profound hunger for affirmation, acceptance and confirmation that often distorts and encumbers interpersonal relationships with emotional storms, excessive dependence and stinging rejection. Key to understanding this pathology is the recognition that symptomatic behavior and demanding relational exchanges are for the purpose of protecting the self from fragmentation and dissolution. Because the disordered self is fragile, emotional dysregulation caused by internal or external triggers can be extremely threatening to the integrity of self-experience.

In situations of psychological disturbance, two simultaneous factors are always at play. First, remember self psychology champions the notion of a progressive and forward-moving self that seeks wholeness and completion. Deficient self-organization retains a potential for unity and health as people constantly seek confirming selfobject experiences. However, this seeking is often colored by anxiety and apprehension due to previous disappointment of implicit expectancies of perfection caused by failures in the complex interaction of given biogenetic potentialities and available environmental responses. An ongoing dread of repeating the pain associated with unanswered selfobject needs keeps a person's interaction guarded and defensive, especially if the relationship activates fantasies of ideal attunement (A. Ornstein, 1974). The validation people urgently seek is caught up in the early grandiose needs for mirroring, idealization and twinship. When responsiveness is not forthcoming in adequate measure, the person experiences a repetition of disaffirmation and rejection, which confirms the need for defensive responses. In the words of Marion Tolpin (2002, pp. 168-69) every symptom has a "*leading edge*" that contains the hoped-for actualization of thwarted self-needs and a defensive "*trailing edge*" meant to protect and bolster fragile self-states.

Second, altering psychoanalytic meaning to reflect clinical and real life experience, Kohut discovered that it was not an aggressive drive that propelled his patients toward expressions of anger and destruction, but the failure of selfobject experiences to provide adequate responsiveness and support. With deference to developmentally adaptive capabilities for aversion and withdrawal (Lichtenberg et al., 2011), much aggression and narcissistic rage emerge from experiences of being wounded and are byproducts of failed relational connections. Those with fragile self-assemblage struggle to manage the rigorous demands of everyday life without skirting the edges of deflation and emptiness. Due to inadequate developmental responsiveness they are more prone to experiences of untoward anger or aggression because rage acts to protect, shore up and cohere these vulnerable self-states. The lack of adequate internalization of selfobject functioning causes an overreliance on the external relational environment to provide confirming selfobject connections. When the environment fails, as it inevitably does, the person feels hurt and may experience rage. Unfortunately, because of these negative interpersonal effects, anger and rage typically result, perpetuating destructive relational sequences.

Therapeutic Change

As originally conceived, the therapeutic process in self psychology was not a radical departure from the more classical understanding of interpretation and insight. The differences have been primarily understood to involve the salience of empathic immersion in the subjective life of the patient as a way to understand the exact nature of the selfobject disturbance and the patient's unique organization of self-experience. Although Kohut originally championed the empathic introspective position (introspective in the sense that the therapist grasps the patient's subjective experience by accessing his or her own feelings of identification regarding the patient's situation to inform one's stance of empathy) he did not necessarily see empathy as the primary road to symptom resolution or healing. Emphasizing the primacy of interpretation as the vehicle of therapeutic action, Kohut struggled to acknowledge relational components as anything more than a facilitating ambiance for effective interpretation of transference material. This more traditional and verbally anchored process between the patient and therapist accentuates conscious reflection on the theoretical meaning of therapeutic exchanges. Specifically, therapy involves exploration of emotionally heightened moments, explicit episodic declarative memories and the developmental context for increasing the patient's understanding of unconscious processes, particularly those active in the transference.

Unique to Kohut was the discussion of narcissistic or selfobject transferences. Instead of the more classical transference neuroses—for which cure was insightful remembering rather than repeating—Kohut experienced his patients as forming narcissistic attachments that contained one or more expressions of the bipolar self. In each therapeutic relationship selfobject transferences involve the search for mirroring, idealization or twinship sameness. As patients remain in the extended empathic environment of therapy a deep mobilization of these narcissistic needs in the transference relationship allows for the empathic connectedness of the therapist to provide needed selfobject functions.

As important as verbal processes are in the scaffolding of therapeutic meaning and understanding, in the years since Kohut's death a second pathway of therapeutic change has emerged (Fosshage, 2011, 2012). Critical to therapeutic change is the new relational experience where patient and therapist engage in novel and healthy interactions that verify and validate the patient's emotional life. In other words, along with the explicit cognitive and verbal domain of functioning there is an implicit sphere that involves emotion cues, procedural memory, hidden expectancies and meaning attributions, embodied communication, and self-regulation procedures (Fosshage, 2005; Schore, 2011). Unconscious communication exchanges between the therapist and patient, called *implicit relational knowing* (Stern et al., 1998) or the relational unconscious (Schore, 2009), are an ever-present reality. Self psychological treatment

provides the patient explicit and implicit support for self-enhancing processes such as emotion regulation, affirmation and connection, encouragement of ambitions, and the realization of life goals. In more severe
cases therapists allow for the mobilization of nascent and fledgling developmental strivings, which have heretofore remained split off, unrecog-
nized or only vaguely acknowledged despite their causal link to ongoing
interference in the patient's relational life and functional pursuits. What
constitutes therapeutic change is the reengagement of a gradual developmental process that allows for a deeper understanding of self-needs,
made possible by the sustained empathic immersion, making it possible
for the patient to safely address deficits in the self. As the patient experiences the empathic presence of the therapist, the patient is able to slowly
unravel his or her story and reexamine the deficiency and suffering that
are typically encased within a mixture of shame, guilt, fear and rage. Embedded memories and relational expectancies tied to the original negative and traumatic experiences are examined. Experiencing deep shame,
rage and fear in the empathic presence of the therapist who does not balk
but responds with understanding and compassion allows for new self-
experience in the form of emotional reorganization and the reconfigu-
ration of distorted perceptions, expectancies and procedural memories.
Essentially this therapeutic selfobject function amplifies a psychic space
or differentiation, making the previous compulsive, anxious or problematic behavior associated with troublesome self-states available for
conscious reflection and integration into a more cohesive and stable
sense of self.

In the midst of this process, and deeply necessary for its effective realization, is the therapist's ability to tolerate powerful narcissistic transferences and the capability of deftly negotiating disruptions in the therapeutic relationship that allow for effective repair and reengagement.
Specifically, when the therapist inescapably blunders, the disruption of
empathic resonance may echo the traumatic loss of selfobject responsiveness and activate a traumatic organizing pattern (Fosshage, 2012).
The patient's emotional response of shame, fear, rage, withdrawal or de-

flation must be recognized and processed in dialogue with the therapist, who is able to empathically recognize the error. Despite the intersubjective context in which the selfobject rupture occurs, which may involve the patient's provocation of the disruption, self psychology privileges the empathic position where selfobject failure is recognized as traumatic in the current relationship, and as a reverberation of the patient's previous trauma. As the therapist allows and accepts the patient's experience, there is the room to examine the disruption within the broader context of the patient's life. Moreover, the therapeutic relationship, including the patient's unconscious expectancies and selective attention, is explored to expand the patient's awareness of who and what contributed to the selfobject breach. Self needs and self-destructive processes are thoroughly examined within a mutually empathic milieu.

Regardless of the origins of the disruption, when repair is effectively negotiated the patient's sense of self is strengthened and enlivened through what Kohut called "transmuting internalizations." Essentially the developmentally appropriate internalization of selfobject functions is re-engaged. The self psychology–informed therapist leans toward the empathic position by examining his or her own failings and champions a safe interpretive frame that encompasses the hermeneutic of trust. Patient failure, even egregious action, is understood in light of the patient's unique organizational dynamics. As Geist (2011) clearly articulates in his discussion of empathic connection,

> Self psychological analysis is the reactivation of healthy development in the context of connectedness. More than interpretation of motivation or transference, more than technique, what distinguishes the forward edge of self psychological treatment is the subjective journey of two individuals seeking to rekindle healthy developmental strivings as they increasingly experience a felt sense of sharing and participating in each other's subjective emotional life. (pp. 235-36)

In other words, the therapeutic process is relational and asymmetrical, but it is not a process where the therapist eschews authenticity, wholeness or distinction. Rather as Donna Orange (2011, 2012) articulates, self psychological sensibilities embody the character of Levinas—the emphasis is on the other.

A TRADITIONED CHRISTIAN CRITIQUE

In situating myself theologically I hope to demonstrate the paradoxical experience of how we *choose* and are *chosen by* our psychological theories. If our sense of self is indeed reflective of multiple self-states woven together in the illusory experience of sameness, I agree with Pamela Cooper-White's (2011) suggestion that spirituality comprises a necessary developmental kedge or integrating braid in our humanness. To demonstrate the complexity of this braid I briefly engage in three areas of dialogue between my Christian heritage and self psychology. I begin by outlining my Wesleyan Pentecostal tradition's resonance with the virtues of self psychology through its preoccupation with lived experience as a means of understanding the self in relation to God. Next, I review the most popular way to think about religion from a self psychological perspective: the selfobject experience. Finally, I discuss empathic connectedness and the love of God.

My Christian roots sink deeply into the experiential world of mid-late twentieth-century Pentecostalism, specifically the Pentecostal Assemblies of Canada. Largely congruent with the Wesleyan-Holiness tradition but emerging from an amalgam of denominational traditions in the late nineteenth century, no tradition more fully embraces the pursuit of spiritual experience than the Pentecostals, whose distinctive preoccupation is postconversion, encounter-oriented spirituality. Anchoring its exceptionality in the baptism of the Holy Spirit, glossolalia, miraculous healing and other signs of spiritual renewal, Pentecostals embrace the narrative text of Luke-Acts over against the more didactic literature of Paul (Dayton, 1987; Wacker, 1999). Scripture is approached with a subjective, emotion-ready hermeneutic that echoes the anticipation of the first Christians waiting in the Upper Room through the day of Pentecost discussed in Acts 2. Speaking in tongues became the crucial identifier, but the non-academic, practical, communal piety surrounding emotionally oriented spiritual practices of ecstatic prayer, dance, singing in the Spirit, altar calls, healing services and prophecy emphasized a Holiness determination for right living. Absent a well-formulated systematic theology, the logic of Pentecostalism does not match that of the Reformed propositional and philosophically oriented dogmata. Rather, as Jacobsen (2003) observed, at least initially Pentecostal theology often followed Pentecostal experience. Spittler (1999) suggests these emotive dynamics can be very appealing and wonders whether Pentecostalism is better at bringing converts to Christianity than assisting them in mature spiritual formation. He describes Pentecostalism as a Corinthian spirituality, "a principled exaggeration of the worth of spirit over body" (p. 4). In contrast, while certainly vulnerable to unreflective experiential reasoning, the theological sophistication and depth of commitment to the Christian way of life is amply evident in Pentecostal writings even though much of the writing and theological discourse is narrative, anecdotal and specific to felt needs (Dayton, 1987; Jacobsen, 2003; Warrington, 2008). Soft on systematic theology (like its Wesleyan roots), Pentecostalism shifts the modes of understanding to more nonlinear, experiential and context-dependent categories.

Pentecostals also largely embrace the evangelical preoccupation with cultural distinction and separateness. Despite the encouragement of experience and spontaneity during worship, freedom and exploration are often bounded by cultural and communal language that promotes a *Spirit-filled* elitism. In my experience this communal religious frame was rather rigid, legalistic and somewhat prejudicial against non-Pentecostals. The experience of God derived its meaning within a grand eschatological vision of the Spirit *poured out* in the last days. Harvey Cox (1995) suggests this primal and affect-oriented nature of Pentecostalism eliminates any hierarchical distinction between cognition and emotion in spiritual functioning. Pentecostalism echoes the religious fervor of the early church seeking to bring believers into the potent and transformative presence of God. Early representations of God develop in a frame of deep emotive expression where feeling states measure attachment to God. When paired with a rigid interpretation of acceptable behavior and a pervasive suspicion of the secular world, self-organization is often split: the flesh, which seeks to destroy, and the Spirit, who brings life. In tragic situations this admixture of emotive spirituality and stultifying cultural rigidity mean one's spiritual life organizes around cyclical experiences of shame and guilt, confession and repentance, ecstatic belonging and backslidden disgrace.

At its best Pentecostalism resonates with Kohut's empathic, experience-near therapeutic stance by preferring and engaging the psyche's organization of affective self-experience. The threads to Jacobsen's (2003) description of Pentecostal theology as comprehended through vitalizing emotive encounters with the Holy Spirit are hard to ignore. This experience-oriented faith serves powerful organizing or selfobject functions as the cohesive and energizing potency of the Holy Spirit clarifies meaning and understanding of life and one's purpose in the world. Even though I no longer consider myself part of the Pentecostal community, I still find my spiritual rudder has a Wesleyan experiential bent. I tend to abjure dogma, instead seeking spiritually emotive communities within a broad creedal expression of Christianity.

While any religious experience can have selfobject properties (Kohut, 1985), mature Pentecostal faith seeks something closer to Geist's (2008, 2011) notion of connectedness. Christian experience is understood to be the ongoing practice of being inhabited by the Spirit and of living in the Spirit. This language of *indwelling* may evoke images of merger and the primitive vision of the powerful, idealized parent, but this is only one possible expression. Religious self-experience is complex, and meanings depend on context and available self-state organizations. In her discussion of religious selfobject experiences, Holliman (2002) identifies both compensatory or self-cohering functions that shore up fragmented and enfeebled self states, along with those that enhance development and transform our narcissism into deeper self-reflection and a connection to transcendent values and purpose that allows for self-differentiation mature relatedness. For Jones (2007) this dual manner in which faith serves a selfobject function moves us beyond surface understandings of religion in psychic life. Religion can sustain an object-hungry person without generating further development and transformation, or it can promote expansion and development of the self. For the latter to occur religious faith must be vitalizing, allow for spontaneity and creativity, and promote a differentiated expression of one's experience. For patients, identifying the leading-edge meaning of spiritual experiences may prove useful. For one, religion contains vital self-cohesive properties that sustain through trauma and tragedy while, for another, it is a self-enhancing and freeing link with a grander cosmic notion of love and acceptance of God and his creation.

In Pentecostalism, truth is understood within a reasoned understanding of the experiential world of our relationship with Christ. Because grace and love are most powerful in an experiential form of deep emotional connection with the transcendent God, we can evaluate the therapeutic relationship in light of its ability to communicate this love and grace. I believe the deep empathic understanding present in self psychological treatment embodies the transformative power of love so essential to the Christian message. Deeply connected relationships that happen within faith communities or within psychoanalytic consultation exemplify what David Benner (1983) articulated as the incarnational experience of psychotherapy.

For Lothane (1998) self psychology reimagines Freud's original statements (articulated most clearly by Ferenczi and later Ian Suttie) about the transformative power of love, cloaked in the language of empathic understanding. Unlike the classic psychoanalytic notion that loving others depletes self-love, Kohut's take on Matthew 22:39 would be that self-love is a necessary prerequisite to loving others effectively.[2] For Browning and Cooper (2004) and Riker (2010) Kohut's self psychology holds implicit and explicit ethical language that grounds the virtues of care, generative and empathic mutuality, trust, integrity, and courage in the embodied psychological realities of development and relational existence. The developmental process of the self within empathic and responsive selfobject

---

[2]"And the second commandment is like it: 'Love your neighbor as yourself'" (NIV).

relationships provides the essential emotional and relational contexts out of which emerges the self-organization necessary to act ethically in the world. Love, honesty, reciprocity, loving neighbor as self—all of these ethical ideas predate self psychology. Kohut established the parameters of a developmental environment that would most likely succeed in generating people of virtue. By responding to human narcissism with empathy and understanding, Kohut exposed the futility of culturally enforced self-denial and supplanted it with a call for the validation and affirmation of the created self. For Freud the goal was to weaken narcissistic desires in favor of love for others. For Kohut the transformation of our selfishness through deep and validating connection with empathic and loving others makes it possible for true transcendence and surrender of our selves. Loving and caring relationships foster trust, integrity of self-motives, reciprocity and other virtues that make the perpetuation of these same virtues in subsequent relationships more likely.

Geist (2008) captures the intimacy of this sentiment in his description of the relational priorities within self-psychologically oriented therapy: "connectedness is . . . a consciously or non-consciously felt sense of sharing and participating in another's subjective emotional life while simultaneously experiencing another as participating in one's own subjective life" (p. 131). With this sensibility Geist (2011) elaborates, saying therapists can "experience the patient's selfobject needs as a felt presence in [their] own [lives]" (p. 244). Inasmuch as this empathic connectedness within the therapeutic relationship reflects the *agape* presence of God, suffering is transmuted. This process is not simply the internalization of selfobject experiences that lead to the emotional reorganization of self, but encompasses the active work of the Spirit, who transcends and indwells the connected therapeutic relationship. Suffering is neither vaunted nor pacified; we do not ignore or pursue its disclosure. Yet still, in the safety of deep connectedness as both therapist and patient explore the limits of mutual empathy, suffering is laid bare. In these moments we, as therapists, become most like our suffering Savior and our patients most clearly experience the Holy Spirit. As an extension of the very presence of Christ, therapists embody the penetrating and irresistible knowing of the patient that comes from the surrender of one's own self. In this empathic immersion one finds the truth about one's self—a free expression of self—and what is the necessity for freedom? Truth—it will set you free, and "if the Son sets you free, you will be free indeed" (Jn 8:36).

CASE STUDY: TONY

The clinical application of self psychology assumes an experience-near stance that aids our therapeutic understandings by serving the dual purposes of description and explanation (Carlton, 2009; Colburn, 2011). In other words, self theory can be understood in a descriptive or phenomenological sense in which we attempt to grasp the *what* of Tony's life. What is it like to be Tony? What does he think or feel? What does he fantasize about when he is dating, masturbating, with his family or sitting in the consulting room? Alternatively, self can be understood in an explanatory way where we attempt to understand the context or conditions that have lead to Tony's current self-organization and expression. In this latter sense we are looking at the various pressures and contexts that evoke or provoke Tony's self-experience. In essence we are looking at the *why* of Tony. Both of these methods are instructive and provide different insights into how we might understand and respond to Tony in the therapeutic encounter.

In many ways Tony's story exposes the heart a *tragic self* (Kohut, 1971). His anxious depressive states betray a plebeian existence, striving for zest, cohesion and affirmation, but unable to conjure sustained meaning or passion from his pursuits. Tony's stagnant and lusterless self-organization alternates fervent quests for connection and vitality with deflating states of inadequacy or painful feelings of failure. Four main self-states capture, in a broad stroke, the *what* of Tony's life: (1) the hopeful pursuit of relational engagement, recognition and reciprocity; (2) a depleted and deflation-prone sense of self lacking vim and vigor; (3) relational ambivalence as demonstrated by concomitant feelings of love and hate, anger and longing, desire and fear; and (4) stultified and insipid ambitions that leave him enfeebled and isolated. Tony's developmental lagging seems palpable. His need for therapeutic permission to focus on just himself demonstrates a mirror-hungry young man who is tired of competing for love and acceptance.

Using a self psychology explanatory framework, it is not hard to see the troubling developmental pathway that has led to Tony's current malaise. By the second month of life infants have developed rudimentary self-other differentiation and awareness (Rochat, 2003). As the responsive and attuned selfobject environment honors and promotes the unique qualities of the child and reflects this self-other dialectic, narcissistic needs for connection, confirmation and affirmation are validated and allowed to moderate through the normal channels of disruption and repair. The varied success of this process is what makes for unique self-systems (Bromberg, 2004; Siegel, 2012). For Tony, adequate selfobject responsiveness has allowed him to differentiate much of his experience from his parents, but it does not follow that his sense of self is sufficiently stable to effectively pursue satisfying life goals and operate within mutually rewarding and sustainable relationships. Three explanatory domains converge as we look at the *why* of Tony's life: selfobject experience, motivational systems and self-organization.

To begin, the inadequacy of Tony's developmental pathway is not related to gross trauma or neglect, but less dramatic and abstruse selfobject failures inescapably present in early life. Bookended by the threat of intrusive control and a relentless demanding-rejecting double bind, Tony was caught in a rigid relational system with very little room to breathe. Preoccupied by selfish needs and perceptions of who Tony should be, mother and father found it difficult to reflect, with any conviction, Tony's uniqueness or his possible difference from their own religious and relational demands. As Wolf (1988) describes, "a person's sense of self is enhanced by the knowledge that another person understands his inner experience" (p. 36). The catastrophe of this relational patterning for Tony is the crippling of multiple motivational systems, making it difficult for him to explore and assert his uniqueness with confidence. Needs for attachment, including friendship and mature sensual/sexual engagement, are unaffirmed. It is very likely that, in place of desired admiration and pride, many of Tony's narcissistic longings were disgraced and derided as inappropriate or pathetic. The resulting sting of shame is difficult to shake, and in light of its persistent presence becomes repressed and part of implicit affective relational expectancies. Hidden from conscious examination, which might help ameliorate its potency, these expectancies, procedural memories and implicit self-assessments emerge whenever he experiences the desire for assertion and intimacy. The hope of a new vitalizing relational experience or the fulfillment of a cherished ambition/ideal exists simultaneously with a dreadful emotional flood of shame and inadequacy.

The understimulation of self-strivings, matched with the over-burdening expectations of others, impedes effective self-organization, leaving Tony enfeebled and prone to depression and despair. Emotional regulation is achieved with passive withdrawal and soothing mastur-batory fantasies. The concomitant fear of being engulfed within intimate connections and distress about his acceptability and adequacy severely constrict exploration of his own needs and desires both vocationally and within an intimate relational exchange. A clear example is his emotionally disengaged experience of God. Relational interest is retained, but wary detachment prevents the pursuit of a connection that could serve as a reparative home.

Although description and explanation may seem like distinct functions in our discourse about Tony, Carlton (2009) points out that each method of theorizing influences the other. When we talk about what Tony is experiencing, we invariably tread into concepts and categories that explain why Tony is experiencing a particular self-state. Conversely, it is very difficult to explain why something happened or exists without exerting a powerful influence on the description of what we are talking about. Description and explanation interconnect, depending on the vantage point one takes. The language Tony chooses when he describes himself or his experience (*what*) helps to form how we understand the cause (*why*) of his self-experience. Self psychology prizes both; the empathically informed connection so important to understanding Tony leads to, and coconstructs, our categories of explanation. In treatment, an asymmetrical *being with* and *being for* Tony embodies the sacrificial and kenotic love so central to our Christian story.

6

Intersubjective Systems Theory

Mitchell W. Hicks

Beginning with the publication of *Faces in a Cloud* (Stolorow & Atwood, 1979), intersubjective systems theory has evolved as a theoretical framework that has made a unique contribution to psychoanalytic thinking. Through the ongoing collaboration of Drs. Robert Stolorow, Donna Orange, George Atwood and Bernard Brandchaft, a number of major constructs from psychoanalysis in general and Kohut's (1977, 1984) self psychology in particular have been reconsidered in light of shifting philosophical assumptions to be detailed in the next section. What follows is an attempt to articulate these assumptions, their theoretical corollaries and their application to the case of Tony.

INTRODUCTION TO INTERSUBJECTIVE SYSTEMS THEORY

In many ways, intersubjective systems theory is best described as a field theory. An early formulation of this approach noted that "psychoanalysis seeks to illuminate phenomena that emerge within a specific psychological field constituted by the intersection of two subjectivities—that of the patient and that of the analyst" (Stolorow & Atwood, 1984, p. 64). Orange, Atwood and Stolorow (1997) further describe intersubjectivity theory as a metatheory: "It examines the field—two subjectivities in the system they create and from which they emerge—in any form of psycho-analytic treatment" (p. 3). While each of these quotations refers to the specific interaction between the patient and the psychotherapist, it is recognized that all of an individual's experiences of self, affect and interpretation are always embedded within a matrix of intersubjective contexts. These contexts can be populated by any combination of persons as well as one's historical and cultural context (Orange, Atwood & Stolorow, 1997).

It is important to distinguish intersubjective systems theory from other uses of the terms *intersubjective* and *intersubjectivity* that are used within psychoanalytic discourse. In contrast to the contributions of authors such as Benjamin (1990, 1999) and Aron (1996), these theorists do not consider intersubjectivity a developmental achievement. Though Orange and her colleagues (1997) suggest that mutual recognition may be a late developmental achievement, intersubjective systems theory is more focused on the relational context and process existing between two subjects.[1]

The major contributors to the intersubjective sensibility have gone to great lengths to articulate foundational assumptions of the approach while also interrogating what they believe to be philosophical and empirical problems in other psychoanalytic theories. The following is an introduction to these critiques.

PHENOMENOLOGICAL

Orange, Atwood and Stolorow (1997) state that the intersubjective approach is firmly rooted within phenomenology, with the focus being on the irreducible subjective experience of the individual in context. Orange (2009) offers at least three implications for a psychoanalysis imbued with a phenomenological sensibility.

---

[1]For a critique of the concept of mutual recognition, the interested reader is directed to Orange (2010a).

First, the phenomenologist will hold presuppositions, theories, scientific "facts" and cultural lenses as tentatively as possible while focusing on understanding the patient's lived experience and suffering. Leading intersubjective theorists have observed that preconceived notions derived from theories and other sources may in fact limit the psychotherapist's understanding of the individual, which can have the deleterious effect of not providing a space for the articulation of heretofore dissociated affective experiences (Atwood & Stolorow, 1993; Orange, 2009, 2011; Orange, Atwood and Stolorow, 1997).

Second, Orange (2009) observes that a phenomenological approach to treatment means accepting the premise that relatedness is "our primary human situation. This means that we are born into relatedness and that our coping capacities and our tangles develop, maintain, and transform relationally" (p. 120). Because an individual's subjectivity can only emerge and be modified within an intersubjective context, this approach is irreducibly relational (Orange, Atwood & Stolorow, 1997). This particular implication is directly related to Stolorow and Atwood's (1992) interrogation of the Cartesian "isolated mind" to be discussed later.

Finally, a phenomenological spirit places a heavy ethical requirement of asymmetry on the psychotherapist (Orange, 2009). Rather than expecting reciprocity, "psychoanalytic phenomenologists seem drawn to theories and clinical attitudes that emphasize our responsibility to stretch empathically, to reach for contact, to understand, just as good enough parents do for many years, without expectation of any adequate recompense" (p. 120).[2]

ISOLATED MIND

Stolorow and Atwood (1992) observe that many of the philosophical and theoretical limitations of earlier one-person formulations of psychic life can be boiled down to what they refer to as the "myth of the isolated mind" (p. 7). This myth presents the person as separated or alienated

---

[2]Cf. Shabad (2001), who notes that the child and the patient have needs to make offerings in these asymmetrical relationships.

from the larger contexts in which that person exists. "Viewed as a symptom of cultural experience, the image of the isolated mind represents modern man's alienation from nature, from social life, and from subjectivity itself" (1992, p. 8). Perhaps one of the most problematic implications of the Cartesian isolated mind is that it disconnects the individual from his or her relational context. But contrary to critiques of the intersubjective systems model, those espousing this viewpoint do not disregard or fail to adequately consider the intrapsychic. Orange, Atwood and Stolorow (1997) instead observe the reciprocal influence of the intrapsychic on the intersubjective context. More specifically, one's subjective experience influences and is influenced by the relational context in which that person now finds him- or herself.

REFORMULATION OF THE UNCONSCIOUS

Based on these theoretical reconsiderations, the major intersubjective systems theorists have also reconceptualized the unconscious as a set of processes that cannot be understood outside the patient's intersubjective context. What follows is a delineation of four interrelated facets of the unconscious that draw from several sources (e.g., Stolorow, 2007; Stolorow & Atwood, 1992; Stolorow, Brandchaft & Atwood, 1987).

The *dynamic unconscious* is constituted by those affect-laden experiences that were not able to be fully articulated because the individual's caregivers were chronically misattuned to these experiences. Because these affects were experienced as threatening to a vital relational tie, they were repressed and may be the source of considerable psychic conflict. The *pre-reflective unconscious* comprises relational heuristics for making sense of patterns of experience. These heuristics, or core organizing principles, serve to thematize the individual's relational experiences at an affective level and generally operate outside one's awareness. For example, one may tend to feel that others do not understand how one is feeling for reasons inexplicable to the individual but that resonate throughout life whenever more emotional intimacy develops. The *unvalidated unconscious* includes those emotional experiences that, because of a lack of a validating or responsive relational environment, cannot be articulated. Finally, Stolorow (2007) has added the *ontological unconscious* "to denote a loss of one's sense of being" (p. 26). He is specifically referring to self-loss and deadening in response to trauma and the inability for these traumatic experiences to find a "relational home," or a set of interpersonal experiences where these emotions can be articulated and met with empathic attunement.

ESCHEWS REIFICATIONS

As can be seen thus far, much of what has influenced the developers of the intersubjective systems sensibility has been a philosophical interrogation of various constructs within psychoanalysis that suggest a "structure" or "thingness." In sharp contrast to the identification of reified structures, these theorists set out to articulate a metapsychology focused on the *process* of subjective and intersubjective experience rather than the identification of universally present contents (Orange, Atwood & Stolorow, 1997; Stolorow & Atwood, 1992; Trop, Burke & Trop, 2002). Further, they have approached theory development with the fundamental goal of formulating an approach to psychoanalysis where the "unfolding, illumination, and transformation of the patient's subjective world" is its primary project (Stolorow, Brandchaft & Atwood, 1987, p. 9). Consequently, the leading intersubjective contextualists have attempted "a 'minimally theoretical' psychoanalysis, working with experience-near concepts, and holding our judgments and diagnostic impulses as lightly as we can" (Orange, 2009, pp. 120-21). Thus, every psychotherapy consists of cocreating understandings of the patient's sufferings—understandings that can be drawn from any existing psychoanalytic theory or emerge in the particular therapeutic dyad. While this holds the appeal of not being forced to swear an allegiance to any one school of thought, it creates challenges to explicating central theories of motivation, development and psychopathology.

MOTIVATION

As noted earlier, the major contributors to the intersubjective contextualist approach have been very strongly influenced by the theoretical contributions of Heinz Kohut (1977), with one of his most important contributions being the articulation of the empathic-introspective stance and his emphasis on both conscious and unconscious self-experience (Stolorow, Brandchaft & Atwood, 1987). "A singularly important implication of this emphasis, which Kohut did not address directly, is that it leads inevitably to a theoretical shift from the motivational primacy of instinctual drive to the motivational primacy of *affect* and affective experience" (p. 16).

Stolorow (2002) observed that privileging the motivational influence of affect carries the implication of moving from an intrapsychic model to an intersubjective stance.

> Unlike drives, which originate deep within the interior of a Cartesian isolated mind, affect—that is subjective emotional experience—is something that from birth onward is regulated, or misregulated, within ongoing relational systems. Therefore, locating affect at its center automatically entails a radical contextualization of virtually all aspects of human psychological life. (Stolorow, 2007, p. 1)

Importantly, Stolorow's use of affect is far broader than is typical in the mental health disciplines. Drawing on the writings of Heidegger, who uses the term *Befindlichkeit* (translated "how-one-finds-oneself-ness"), Stolorow (2007) notes that affect for Heidegger implies not only how one feels but also the context within which this feeling is taking place. For Stolorow (2007), affect is "a felt sense of oneself in a situation" (p. 2).

Clinically, a major implication of this shift toward affect is the recognition that it is the principal way in which an individual organizes his or her experience. In one of the earlier works representing this perspective, Socarides and Stolorow (1984/1985) expanded the Kohutian concept of selfobject function to include the process of affect integration. Consistent with the findings of infant researchers (e.g., Beebe, Jaffe & Lachmann, 1992; Stern, 1985), intersubjective systems theory observes that the regulation or misregulation of affective experience in its relational context has significant implications for psychological development and subsequent organization of self-experience.

DEVELOPMENT

A hallmark of the intersubjective contextualist approach is that it attempts to understand the patient within his or her developmental context, and how that context is influencing the intersubjective space between analyst and patient as well as patient and the others that populate his or her world (Orange, Atwood & Stolorow, 1997). Stolorow and Atwood (1984) assert that psychological development must be considered within the specific relational contexts in which it occurs, and how those contexts either facilitate or impede the child's movement through various developmental tasks and phases. Drawing on the empirical work of Stern (1985), Stolorow, Brandchaft and Atwood (1987) note that from birth onward the central task of self-development and self-differentiation occurs through the child's mutual sharing of affectivity with the caregiver. While a number of contemporary theorists have attempted to integrate these findings, these authors return to their self-psychological roots to expand upon some of Kohut's (e.g., 1977) contributions.

One of the earliest contributions from the intersubjective contextualist school of thought was a reformulation and broadening of Kohut's (1977) concept of selfobject as a

> class of psychological *functions* pertaining to the maintenance, restoration, and transformation of self-experience. Thus, the term *selfobject*, when used in accord with its strictly psychoanalytic meaning, does not refer to an environmental entity or caregiving agent. Rather, it refers to an object *experienced subjectively* as serving selfobject functions. (Stolorow & Brandchaft, 1987, pp. 241-42; see also Orange, Atwood & Stolorow, 1997)

Rather than simply mirroring grandiosity or needs to align with a stronger, more potent force, selfobject functions pertain to those experiences of another person in the metabolizing of *any* affective experience (Socarides & Stolorow, 1984/1985).

The importance of selfobject functioning is difficult to overstate. With respect to the structuralizing of self-experience, Stolorow, Brandchaft and Atwood (1987) note that there are at least four important consequences.[3] First, in order for the child to increase his or her faculties in the articulation of self-experience, caregivers serving selfobject functions must be able to attune to shifting affective states that help the child to differentiate between them. Second, adequate selfobject functioning requires that the caregiver help the child to synthesize discrepant emotional states such that both positive and negative affects can be identified and integrated. For example, a child may have a *bittersweet* reaction to a visit from a relative. It may be quite enjoyable and enlivening to have a new partner in play and to receive attention not normally available. However, the visitor is likely to also require the attention and energy of the child's primary caregivers, which may be viewed as loss or point of competition.

Third, Stolorow and his colleagues (1987) suggest that the caregiver's responsiveness and ability to aid in the articulation and differentiation of emotional states helps the child develop the ability to tolerate and modulate overwhelming and unpleasant affect. The authors note that this function has been captured in various theoretical threads within psychoanalysis, such as with Winnicott's (1965) "holding environment" and Bion's (1977) container metaphor. Relatedly, this capacity for affect tolerance would also allow emerging emotions to be used as signaling changes in self-state rather than as impending psychological trauma. Finally, the development of an affective language allows for the desomatization of affect. This does not mean that affective states will not be experienced somatically. Rather, those physical sensations will have a corresponding linguistic structure that would allow for its articulation.

Ongoing maturational changes and increased self-organization bring with them the need for corresponding shifts in caregiver responsiveness. As the child displays varying degrees of autonomy, aggressiveness and sexuality, the caregiver needs to be able to modify how he or she responds

---

[3]It is important to note that intersubjective contextualists do not speak of structure per se. Rather, when speaking of structure they are referring to broad patterns of relational experience that organize ongoing relational experience in a prereflective manner. (See for example Stolorow, Brandchaft & Atwood, 1987.)

to and tolerates these changes. Failing to do so can have significant negative consequences for the child's psychological development (Stolorow & Brandchaft, 1987; Stolorow, Brandchaft & Atwood, 1987).

PSYCHOPATHOLOGY

As we have seen, the intersubjective field, its responsiveness to affect and the caregiver's ability to adequately provide selfobject functioning are keys to the healthy psychological development of the child. While disruptions in empathic attunement are normal, expected and perhaps even required for healthy psychological development, Stolorow (2007) observed that pervasive and substantial misattunement to a child's affective states results in the development of psychological conflict. "Such unintegrated affect states become the source of lifelong emotional conflict and vulnerability to traumatic states because they are experienced as threats to the person's established psychological organization and to the maintenance of vitally needed ties" (p. 3; see also Stolorow, Brandchaft & Atwood, 1987). Stolorow (2007) goes on to observe that developmental trauma involves the experience of unbearable affect that cannot be tolerated, articulated or integrated. This results in the disconnection of affect and cognition, disorganized states and possibly to the development of pathological accommodations (Brandchaft, 2007; see discussion of pathological accomodation below).

Stolorow (2007) observes that the experience of affective states that have historically been unvalidated, unintegrated and rejected by caregivers takes on persistent and devastating meanings. Previously unmet developmental longings and unacceptable affective experiences are disowned as they are seen as evidence of a repugnant defect of the self. Not surprisingly, such developmental trauma brings with it a significant restriction of affective experience. Moreover, a "defensive self-ideal" (2007, p. 4) is established in which these unacceptable feelings and yearnings are disowned and abandoned. The emergence of one of these offensive affective states is experienced as a violation of the self-ideal and often accompanied by feelings of shame and isolation that themselves must be defended against (Orange, Atwood & Stolorow, 1997; Stolorow, 2007).

Stolorow (2007) further notes three other important consequences of traumatic experiences that deserve consideration. First, trauma results in the shattering of what Stolorow calls absolutisms of everyday life. These include stable and predictable beliefs about the world that are not open to discussion or consideration, but that can serve defensive functions in pathological forms. An example given might be the assertion that "I will see you later." In everyday usage, life is lived as if routine partings are only temporary and that reunion will occur at a later time. Though such a statement is normative in American culture, it glosses over the reality that any parting may in fact be a final parting. However, it should be noted that such a statement could be considered pathological if it ignores the impending death of a loved one. Stolorow (2007) points out that the traumatized individual is disabused of these absolutisms; these normative illusions that nonetheless stave off death anxiety no longer function for the traumatized person.

Second, the loss of these absolutisms also brings with it a sense of aloneness, or a sense that no one can really understand what the traumatized person is experiencing. To illustrate this point, Stolorow (2007) described his own experience of being at a professional conference not long after the traumatic loss of his wife to cancer. He wrote,

> There was a dinner at that conference for all the panelists, many of whom were my old and good friends and close colleagues. Yet, as I looked around the ballroom, they all seemed like strange and alien beings to me. Or more accurately, *I* seemed like a strange and alien being—not of this world. The others seemed so vitalized, engaged with one another in a lively manner. I, in contrast, felt deadened and broken, a shell of the man I had once been. An unbridgeable gulf seemed to open up, separating me forever from my friends and colleagues. They could never even begin to fathom my experience, I thought to myself, because we now lived in altogether different worlds. (p. 14)

For Stolorow, trauma means in part that one is faced with the existential realities of loss, death and aloneness from which everyday absolutisms provide refuge.

Finally, trauma has the effect of destroying one's sense of being-in-time. Stolorow (2007) observes that the continuum of past, present and future collapses in the face of trauma. It is as if the traumatic experience is frozen in the present, a present from which the individual is unable to escape. While this could manifest itself as the reliving commonly associated with post-traumatic stress disorder, it often leads to one's continuing to view the world as though the trauma is ongoing and always present.

Brandchaft (2007) has further extended the intersubjective systems understanding of the consequences of persistent empathic failure. He notes that pathological accommodation occurs as a result of a child being forced to dissociate parts of the self in order to maintain needed object ties. Rather than being permitted the experience of a full range of emotion, interest and needs, the child must subjugate this self-experience in order to accommodate the needs of caregivers. Being overly attuned to the needs of caregivers, the child will internalize a list of imperatives or "shoulds" so as to avoid ongoing traumatic failures in the caregiver (Brandchaft, Doctors & Sorter, 2010). These imperatives then become a template that is carried forward into future relationships.

THERAPEUTIC CHANGE

Practicing from an intersubjective systems perspective does not lend itself well to technical recommendations as much as it does the assumption of a certain sensibility (Orange et al., 1997). "It is an attitude of continuing sensitivity to the inescapable interplay of observer and observed. It assumes that instead of entering and immersing ourselves in the experience of another, we join the other in the intersubjective space" (p. 9). Rather than dogmatically prescribing a neutral stance or therapeutic abstinence, Stolorow, Brandchaft and Atwood (1987) suggest that decisions about intervening or not intervening at any given moment should be guided by what is likely going to aid in the clarification, articulation and transformation of the individual patient's subjective experience. They go on to note that attention must be paid to what any given action by the psychotherapist may mean for the patient. Orange, Atwood and Stolorow (1997) further note that rather than focusing on technique, analytic discourse should focus on practice. "Unlike technique, practice is always oriented to the particular, . . . embodies an attitude of inquiry, deliberation and discovery . . . eschews rules and loves questions" (p. 27).

Indeed, drawing from different theoretical traditions within psychoanalysis (or any theory of psychotherapy, for that matter) can have profound implications for the therapeutic space. For example, an analyst whose formative training was heavily influenced by the work of Melanie Klein is likely to be tuned in to the experience of envy and aggression. Seeing the same patient, an analyst coming from the tradition of self psychology might empathically comment on narcissistic wounds. The purpose in making this observation is not to eschew theory altogether. Rather,

> the implication here is not that analysts should refrain from using guiding theoretical ideas to order clinical data, but that analysts must recognize the impact of their guiding frameworks in both delimiting their grasp of their patients' subjective worlds and in codetermining the course of the analytic process. (Orange et al., 1997, p. 21)

Orange and her colleagues further assert that holding an attitude of knowing in advance of what to expect from the patient is extremely harmful and is to be avoided.

Despite these comments, the philosophical and theoretical tenants of the intersubjective systems approach have implications for interpretation, self-disclosure and work within the transference-countertransference matrix.

INTERPRETATION

Through a stance of sustained empathic inquiry into the subjective experience of the patient, the psychotherapist collaboratively works with him or her to cocreate a therapeutic space where it is emotionally safe to "explore together those 'regions' of unconsciousness that make up the problematic aspects of subjectivity" (Orange et al., 1997, p. 8). Stolorow, Brandchaft and Atwood (1987) observe that both participants in the analytic endeavor are contributing to the relative safety or dangerousness of this therapeutic space through the ongoing mutual influence and the organizing activities of each. This has implications for interpretation, self-disclosure and the selection of interventions.

Stolorow, Brandchaft and Atwood (1987) note that interpretations do not come from within the analyst, nor are they uncovered through some archaeological dig into the unconscious, as Freud once suggested. Instead, the multiple meanings available to enrich the understanding of the patient's subjective experience are cocreated within the intersubjective space of the therapeutic relationship. Critical to understanding interpretation for an intersubjective systems sensibility is the critique of the practice of interpretation as an intellectual exercise separate from emotional understanding, a byproduct of the Cartesian dichotomy (Orange et al., 1997).

Indeed, Stolorow (2007) notes that the act of interpretation is an inseparable and crucial aspect of the emotional connection between the psychotherapist and the patient. He goes on to assert that a mutative interpretation not only communicates to the patient that his or her experience and feelings are being understood, but that such understanding carries with it specific transferential meanings "as the patient weaves that experience into the tapestry of developmental longings mobilized by the analytic engagement" (p. 5).

SELF-DISCLOSURE

Intersubjective systems theorists also note that the psychotherapist cannot avoid self-disclosure. In fact, it is impossible to *not* make self-disclosures because the therapist is an active agent in a system of mutual influence in the therapeutic space. In contrast to the typical attitude of psychoanalysts (e.g., Greenson, 1967), self-disclosure is viewed as a potentially vital contributor to the analytic process.[4] Through those things the therapist attends to, the ease or lack thereof with which the therapist approaches certain topics or emotions, and even the process of giving and

---

[4]It should be clear that therapeutically useful self-disclosures do not typically include information about the psychotherapist's history or circumstances. However, there may be times when such a disclosure could be very helpful in the context of any given therapeutic relationship.

withholding—all provide information to the patient (Orange, Atwood & Stolorow, 1997). This process of revealing and hiding has a significant impact on the therapeutic space, and it is incumbent on the psychotherapist to evidence an ongoing commitment to self-knowledge so that the impact of these disclosures can be appreciated, considered and utilized in the service of increasing the patient's self-articulation. Regardless of how these disclosures are addressed in treatment, what seems to always be required is an ability to decenter and reflect on one's influence on both the process and content of the treatment (Stolorow, Brandchaft & Atwood, 1987).

TRANSFERENCE AND COUNTERTRANSFERENCE

As with most approaches within the psychoanalytic tradition, the proponents of the intersubjective systems perspective place a particular emphasis on the transference-countertransference matrix. For Stolorow, Brandchaft and Atwood (1987), transference is viewed as a manifestation of the tendency of humans to organize experience (see *prereflective unconscious*) rather than as regression or distortion per se. As such, the goal of psychoanalytic exploration is not to relinquish it but rather the "acceptance and integration of the transference experience into the fabric of the patient's analytically expanded psychological organization" (p. 45). Drawing from the recommendations of Kohut (1984), this would be achieved through an empathic, introspective inquiry into the perceived disruptions, disjunctions and ruptures of the patient's selfobject experience of the psychotherapist (Orange, Atwood & Stolorow, 1997; Stolorow, Brandchaft & Atwood, 1987).

More archaic and rigid organizing principles are likely to emerge whenever the patient anticipates a retraumatizing experience with the therapist, and it often manifest in the form of resistance (Stolorow, 2007). This understanding requires significant consideration when working with what may be viewed as bad behavior or "acting out." Traditionally, such behaviors are viewed as resistance to the analytic process and constitute a threat to the individual's well-being. While the possibility that the behavior is ultimately self-destructive may be accurate, it fails to consider that it also is serving a salubrious end through the forestalling of retraumatization. To interpret these behaviors only or primarily as acting out is "likely to be experienced by the patient as part of the bond that shackles, because they superimpose alien and extrinsic organization of experience onto his own, thereby derailing the self-differentiating process and depriving it of a sustaining matrix" (Stolorow, Brandchaft & Atwood, 1987, p. 57).

Drawing on previous contributions by Brandchaft (1983, 1986), Stolorow, Brandchaft and Atwood (1987) are particularly concerned about how the analysis of transference can be misused to induce compliance in the patient. To guard against this, it is particularly important that the psychotherapist be willing to make room for the patient to explore affects or topics that for whatever reason may be experienced as threatening to him- or herself. Consider the following example. Dr. T. is a newly minted doctor of psychology, and as such she is very concerned about her adjustment to her new role and being an effective therapist. She has been working with Ms. M. for about six months in a treatment that started with about five months remaining in Dr. T.'s predoctoral internship. Ms. M. seems to talk quite a bit about how wonderful and helpful Dr. T. has been to her, though Dr. T. is unable to discern any major changes in Ms. M.'s emotional and relational concerns. It could be quite satisfying for Dr. T. to allow these accolades to permeate each hour, especially given that it would be threatening for her to actually talk openly about Ms. M.'s lack of progress. Opening up this threatening conversation has many possibilities for deepening Ms. M.'s self-understanding and has the potential to free her from a need to care for others to the detriment of herself. Regardless of the specifics elucidated in this exploration, failure to broach the threatening topic serves only to recreate the structure of pathological accommodation (Brandchaft, 2007; Brandchaft et al., 2010).

FAITH CRITIQUE

Traditioning. Though attempting to articulate the core components of the intersubjective systems perspective was a daunting task, it has proven to

be easier than attempting to clearly articulate my own theological tradition. It is hard to point to a core theological foundation in either of the
traditions that have shaped me as a follower of Christ. What follows is an
attempt to provide some sense of my subconscious influences.

I was raised in the Church of God (Anderson, Indiana), which began
during the Holiness revival that was occurring in the United States in the
1800s (Faculty of the Anderson University School of Theology, 2007).
Though committed to Scripture as the guide and standard for living, this
movement was also predicated on the principle that God's desire is for all
believers to live in peace and harmony even in the midst of differences.
As such, Christ is to be the common foundation. In addition to affirming
the dynamic nature of God's truth and revelation, there has been the
"conviction that the movement would be tied together not by a set of commonly held beliefs, but rather by a common experience in Jesus Christ"
(Faculty of the Anderson University School of Theology, 2007, p. 1). Honestly, I did not realize this foundational conviction until attempting to
align the Church of God with a particular theological tradition, yet I can
now see how it shaped my own desire to practice a faith that is widely
welcoming to all who profess faith in Jesus Christ despite very wide dis-
agreements on other matters.

For the past fifteen years I have been involved with the Messianic
Jewish Movement, which itself represents a wide diversity of beliefs and is
difficult to align with one theological tradition. According to Kinzer
(2000), the Messianic Jewish movement is composed of those Jews and
Gentiles who affirm Yeshua (Jesus) as the promised Messiah of the Hebrew
Scriptures (see also Schiffman, 1992). Further, we are committed to maintaining an identification with the larger Jewish community through participation in traditionally Jewish forms of worship, observance and cultural participation. This places the Messianic believer (whether Jewish or
Gentile) in an ambiguous place with respect to cultural identification and
religious practice (Yangarber-Hicks & Hicks, 2005).

Regardless of the specific theological influences on any Messianic
Jewish congregation or organization, most if not all would affirm the

centrality of the covenant relationship between God and Israel, and by extension between God and those grafted into the commonwealth through belief in Messiah Yeshua (Jesus Christ) (Kinzer & Juster, 2002; Yangarber-Hicks, 2005). In other words, Messianic Jewish believers place an emphasis on connection to the community. Further, the ethic of *Tikkun Olam*, or restoration of the world in preparation for the coming Messiah (or in the case of a Messianic believer, for Yeshua's return) through works of goodness, kindness and charity while taking a stand for the downtrodden and oppressed is a common refrain in Messianic Jewish thought.

Resonance and dissonance. So, how might practice from an intersubjective systems perspective fit with a theological tradition that places such a premium on connection and working toward the restoration of the world? First, one cannot escape Levinas's ethical mandate of recognition of the other, which is brought into sharp focus by the intersubjective perspective (e.g., Orange, 2011). No doubt deeply affected by the horrors of Nazi Germany, the concentration camp and the systematic murder by the Third Reich of the Jewish people (including his own family) and other persons deemed "undesirable," Levinas (1969, 1989) noted that the face of the other places a heavy ethical demand on the individual to see the other as other and not to commit violence through negation (Dueck & Parsons, 2007; Orange, 2011). While an exploration of the therapeutic implications of this has been more fully developed elsewhere (e.g., Dueck & Parsons, 2007; Goodman & Grover, 2008), a few important points are worth considering here. In response to the face of the other, it is an imperative not to objectify or otherwise taint or reduce a person's "otherness." This is a major reason why practice from an intersubjective sensibility seeks experience-near constructs and eschews approaching patients with a preconceived conceptualization of their concerns.

A serious consideration of the face of the other also highlights the divine connection between self and other. It reminds us that in each and every other is a glimpse of the *imago Dei* (Dueck & Parsons, 2007). As such,

the suffering widow, orphan, or stranger deserves my hospitality. . . . The
Other's need transcends me. . . . Just respond, and stop categorizing and
judging from your high horse, he would say. It is simple to respond. *Hineni.*
Take and eat. Take and drink. (Orange, 2011, p. 56)

What resonates is that it seems to be a violation of an ethical imperative
to *not* respond to the suffering of the other.[5] We may not just pass by
while the man beaten by thieves lays bleeding (Lk 10:25-37). We cannot
justify *not* responding to suffering.

Another theme resonating between these two traditions is the call to
offer comfort to those who suffer. In the words of the prophet Isaiah,

Comfort, comfort my people,
  says your God.
Speak tenderly to Jerusalem,
  and proclaim to her
that her hard service has been completed,
  that her sin has been paid for,
that she has received from the LORD's hand
  double for all her sins. (Is 40:1-2)

Isaiah goes on to proclaim the hope of God's redemption and triumph,
which would be easy to make the focus of offering comfort. But the full
meaning of the Hebrew word *nacham* (comfort) includes compassion,
being moved to pity and suffering grief (Goodrick & Kohlenberger, 2004),
suggesting a more inclusive response that makes room not only for hope
but for the experience of suffering in the present. Such a response to
trauma and suffering is similar to Stolorow's (2007) concept of the relational home where affective responses can be identified, articulated and

---

[5]Levinas is often understood to be saying that there is an asymmetry in the self-other relationship such that a complete or near-complete self-sacrifice is demanded. Despite what appears
to be at least a limited embracing of this perspective by Orange (2011), this actually seems
inconsistent with an intersubjective systems view that emphasizes the mutual participation
of two or more people in the creation of the intersubjective field. While psychotherapy practice certainly requires that the focus of treatment is on the patient's suffering, this cannot be
accomplished in an arena where mutuality and needs of the self are negated (M. Hoffman,
personal communication, August 2011). Fully embracing this position seems to create a
therapeutic space where the practitioner must make pathological accommodations.

understood rather than being disavowed or invalidated. Because such a response was missing in the patient's earlier life experiences, it is incumbent on the therapist to work to create such a safe place.

A final resonating theme is that of emancipation, which, as discussed earlier, is one of the seminal contributions of Brandchaft and colleagues (2010) to the intersubjective systems approach. His explorations have led to an increasing understanding of how parts of the self are dissociated in order to maintain object ties. In my experience many of my patients who truly desire to love and follow God are held back through systems of pathological accommodation in which religious language and behavioral standards were used in such a way that a full range of emotional expression was squelched. Such individuals have been pushed to submit rather than encouraged in a willful process of surrender. Benner (2011) suggests that such an empty and defensive religiosity robs the individual of a faith and connection to God that is life-giving and authentic (see also Ps 40:6; Hos 6:5-7; Mt 9). Perhaps this is another way in which psychoanalytic inquiry can lend itself to setting the prisoners free.

One area that could potentially be disconcerting to some believers is the intersubjective approach's reliance on a phenomenological approach as well as its apparent subjectivity. Indeed, Stolorow and colleagues (1987) assert that an individual's subjective reality is the only one that is accessible to psychoanalytic investigation. They go on to note that what is often believed to be "objective" reality is really a concretization of subjective truth, which is often used by psychotherapists and others to speak of concepts such as distortions. To not attempt to ascertain an objective, knowable truth is likely to give some Christian therapists pause. However, two cogent responses can be offered in defense of this subjective and relativist position.

First, the purpose of psychoanalytic inquiry is *not* to delineate what is objectively true and what is factually incorrect within the patient's experience. Further, it is not necessarily to explore ontological and moral truth so much as it is to aid in the exploration and articulation of the individual's experience. Take for example a twenty-three-year-old student currently enrolled in law school who consults the therapist to help her understand why it is that she feels unable to control her angry outbursts around her family. Any number of levels of inquiry could prove useful in understanding this unsetting emotional block. However, it is unclear why a discussion of the moral behavioral response or who or what is objectively "right" would be among them, beyond the patient determining what she aspires to accomplish in such conflictual situations with her family. But an exploration of her subjective experience of these encounters from an intersubjective frame may lead to the patient and psychotherapist being able to identify the ways that she has been organizing this experience and articulate the emotions being given voice through her angry outbursts. The goal of such an inquiry would not be to condone actions hurtful to herself or others, but to gain an understanding of their *meanings* so that the person is more free to explore alternative actions.

Second, when exploring a patient's personal history or experience of a relational situation, the psychotherapist almost never has direct access to what actually happened in any given situation. Even in the intersubjective context of the therapeutic situation the psychotherapist only can access his or her own *experience* of that situation. To revisit the law student discussed in the previous paragraph, it is quite likely that one way that insight will be gained into what occurs with the patient's family is through its enactment in the analytic situation. The patient may experience the therapist as emotionally distant and withholding, but when confronted with this the therapist may deny that this is occurring. Who is "right"? What is the "objective truth"? Though the therapist may be tempted to say that he was not being emotionally distant, it would be more accurate from an intersubjective systems perspective to state that he did not *experience* himself as distant. And therapeutically it is more important to understand what in the interaction between therapist and patient was experienced as distance.

Case Study: Tony

Given the phenomenological sensibilities of the intersubjective systems approach, responding to the case of Tony presents some interesting challenges. Specifically, interpretations and interventions emerge organically within the intersubjective space created between patient and therapist. However, it is possible to detail several themes that I might be considering after hearing this history during an initial session with Tony.

The first of these themes might be to wonder about the meanings of his reported inability to maintain more emotionally intimate connections with women. Tony indicates that he becomes "bored" and "passive," which leads me to wonder whether this is indicative of some type of self-protective measure similar to becoming "quiet and avoidant" as he does in response to his mother's intrusiveness. Thus, one may wonder whether this withdrawal serves to preserve his sense of self-differentiation.

Little is known about what goes wrong in his relationships with men, though after this initial contact I would be wondering whether this is part of a system of pathological accommodation that seems to have been required to maintain any type of relationship with his father. Tony tells us that this conflict-laden relationship was marked by competition, not feeling that he was measuring up and a felt sense that his father had to endorse his masculinity. Although he seems to have some awareness of feeling angry and ashamed in response to his experience of disappointing his father, one must also wonder whether he has also discovered that "winning" was going to destroy what relationship he did have with his father. The legacy of this dynamic may be playing out in what appears to be a lack of direction and initiative as well as apparent ambivalence regarding success. This hypothesis makes Tony's decision to lie on the couch to keep from monitoring his male therapist's reactions interesting, and could actually be an affirmative move toward emotional health and freedom. Moreover, it may reflect awareness that he must stop trying to live up to his father in order to find himself.

A third theme that I might be considering after this initial session centers around his reportedly compulsive masturbation, though it is questionable to what extent it is really a "private" matter insofar as he acknowledges being in fairly public places at times. Although such information might give me pause, it is important that the therapist take a stance in which this behavior can be understood in all its meanings rather than quickly moving to extinguish it. Given the potential for legal problems, this would be a real push for me. This is likely to affect the space between us, and it seems like it could be useful to disclose my tension between encouraging him to stop at least semipublic masturbation to avoid legal problems and wanting to make space for understanding and not intrude. With respect to initial hypotheses about what might be driving this behavior, my initial thoughts turn to questions regarding affective regulation, feeling intruded upon (boredom) and dissociated needs or affective states.

Finally, I might consider how Tony's reported impersonal and disconnected relationship with God in some ways brings together potential implications of these three other themes as well as some (admittedly assumed) elements of his faith education. He may be quiet and avoidant in response to an all-knowing (intrusive) God with impossible moral standards that he can never meet. This feeling seems to persist despite his departures from the traditional teaching on matters such as sexuality that he likely received. Further, one might consider spite or rebellion as additional motivators for compulsive masturbation.

CONCLUSION

It is hoped that the preceding discussion has illuminated some of the ways in which adopting an intersubjective systems framework with its phenomenological sensibilities can serve the psychoanalytically informed psychotherapist who also desires to find resonance with his or her Christian faith. As can be seen, practicing from this framework places significant relational and emotional demands on both psychotherapist and patient as they embark on a journey of what usually turns out to be mutual self-discovery.

7

Relational Psychoanalysis

Lowell W. Hoffman

R elational psychoanalysis may be thought of as an emerging tradition within psychoanalysis rather than an organized school of psychoanalysis. Greenberg and Mitchell (1983) first used the term *relational psychoanalysis* in the context of creating a more robust theory of interpersonal relations through forging an interpenetration of the interpersonalist psychoanalysis of H. S. Sullivan and British object relations. Stephen Mitchell was "committed to a dialogue among psychoanalysts and abhorred the authoritarianism that dictated adherence to a rigid set of beliefs or technical restrictions. He championed open discussion . . . and promoted new voices" (Aron & Harris, 2012a, p. ii). Relational psychoanalysis has since its inception progressively widened the girth of its tent to welcome the contributions of self psychology, empirical infancy research, attachment theory, contemporary Freudian and Kleinian theory, cognitive neuroscience, and neuropsychoanalysis. Relational psychoanalysts mostly write separately and value difference with one another to the extent that they do not have a unified voice. Individual relational psychoanalytic theorists often tilt toward a Sullivanian, Fairbairnian, Winnicottian, Kleinian, Kohutian or Freudian theoretical perspective.

Perhaps still relevant to the understanding of the heterogeneity of relational psychoanalysts is the research of Randall Lehman Sorenson (2004a). Utilizing multidimensional scaling, Sorenson empirically demonstrated that over a ten-year period published articles in *Melanie Klein and Object Relations* and *Progress in Self Psychology* tended to be homogeneous in their citations; authors of the Kleinian and self psychology articles resourced primarily theorists within their own respective orientations. By contrast, articles published in the relational psychoanalytic journal *Psychoanalytic Dialogues* frequently cited Kleinians and self psychologists, as well as Freudians, interpersonalists and so forth. According to Sorenson, "authors in *Progress in Self Psychology* and *Melanie Klein and Object Relations* were distributed in tightly associated conceptual space accounting for just 21% and 25% . . . respectively [of the psychoanalytic literature surveyed]" (2004a, p. 8). By contrast, Sorenson found that "Relationalists covered more than twice as much intellectual territory (54%)" (2004a, p. 8). More recently, Ringstrom (2010a, p. 197) and Reis (2010, p. 233) have offered anecdotal observations concerning these continuing tendencies that Sorenson empirically demonstrated.

The heterogeneity of relational psychoanalysis may also be understood because of a robust interdisciplinary interplay with feminist critiques advanced by relational psychoanalysts including Jessica Benjamin, Muriel Dimen, Virginia Goldner and Adrienne Harris—all are faculty in the relational track of the NYU Postdoctoral Program in Psychotherapy and Psychoanalysis (NYU Postdoc). A second major interdisciplinary influence in relational psychoanalysis is a variety of postmodern critiques; one shared sensibility that describes most relational psychoanalysts is that they rely on an epistemology of perspectival realism, or perspectival relationalism in Aron's usage (1996), or social constructivism in Hoffman's usage (1998).

The relational epistemology of perspectival realism has opened a berth in psychoanalysis for a previously excluded perspective: theistic spirituality and religion.

In fact, the very first article in volume 1 of the Relational Psychoanalysis series (Mitchell & Aron, 1999, p. 1) is Michael Eigen's article titled "The Area of Faith in Winnicott, Lacan, and Bion." The Relational Book Series, edited by Lewis Aron and Adrienne Harris, has published four volumes that are dedicated to spirituality and religion, including the work of Christian psychoanalysts Sorenson (2004a) and Hoffman (2011). Other relational psychoanalysts who have written on theistic religion include Aron (2004) and Starr (2008) from Jewish perspectives.

One further category is necessary to reveal the confluence of perspectives that contribute to relational theory. Many relational theorists are social activists whose social consciousnesses were birthed out of a philosophical shift that reacted to cultural trauma. For instance, Jessica Benjamin studied at the Frankfurt School, which was founded to study and influence cultural ideals such as how to avert another Holocaust. Perhaps most notable of the relational activism is Neil Altman's guileless but unrelenting protest against the American Psychological Association's participation with CIA interrogation practices, and his long-term influence upon applying a psychoanalytic lens to race, class and culture. There is the activism of Jessica Benjamin and Andrew Samuels in the conflicted Israeli-Palestinian relations, and the advocacy for human rights for women in Latin American terrorist states by Nancy Caro Hollander. Other relational activists include Ghislaine Boulanger, Stephen Hartman, Lynne Layton, Steven Reisner and Nina Thomas. These and many others both pursue justice for the objectified other and bring this lived experience to their psychoanalytic thinking.

Donna Orange (2012) has distinguished between "Relational psychoanalysis" and "relational psychoanalysis" in a manner that permits her to identify with the generic, phenomenological development of a "lower-case r" relational psychoanalysis without including herself within the branded explanatory category of the theoretical orientation of an "upper-case R" Relational psychoanalysis. It is likely that Orange makes this distinction to distance herself from what she might consider Cartesian trends in Relational psychoanalysis. Philip Ringstrom (2010a, 2010b), in dialogue with Clement (2010), Jacobs (2010) and Reis (2010), offers a most helpful discussion concerning alleged Cartesian trends in relational psychoanalysis. He writes, "*Relationalists* are unwilling to follow [Orange's and] the *Intersubjectivists* admonition that they must choose between the Cartesian world that Freud inherited and the post-Cartesian world of contextualism that the *Intersubjectivists* embrace" (2010b, p. 241). Ringstrom continues,

> Instead, the *Relationalists* value a dialectic position in which they take up these opposing world views. *Relationalists* typically embrace the intrapsychic complexities of a patient's issues (described by the Intersubjectivists as a remnant of Cartesian philosophy) while empathetically retaining a contextualist view of the analyst's participation in how those issues manifest. (2010b, p. 241)[1]

LEADING THEORISTS

Relational psychoanalysis has evolved as a tradition in psychoanalytic theory and practice in the wake of the seminal contribution of Stephen Mitchell and Jay Greenberg, who coauthored *Object Relations in Psychoanalytic Theory*. They wrote,

> The most significant tension in the history of psychoanalytic ideas has been the dialectic between the original Freudian mode, which takes as its starting point the instinctual drive, and an alternative comprehensive model initiated in the work of Fairbairn and Sullivan, which evolves structure solely from the individual's relations with other people. (Greenberg & Mitchell, 1983, p. 20)

Greenberg and Mitchell asserted that drive theory and the alternative model are incompatible and cannot be integrated because they derive from two different views of human nature.

---

[1]The complete text of this conversation is published in *Psychoanalytic Dialogues*, 20(2), 196-250.

Greenberg and Mitchell (1983) identified theorists of the alternative model, including Klein, Fairbairn, Winnicott, Balint, Sullivan, Fromm, Kohut and Loewald. This alternative model was given the name "relational" in 1988 by the five founding members of the relational track at New York University Postdoctoral Program in Psychotherapy and Psychoanalysis: Philip Bromberg, Bernard Friedland, James Fosshage, Emmanuel Ghent and Stephen Mitchell. To be sure, psychoanalysts elsewhere, including Merton Gill (1982) and Robert Stolorow, Bernard Brandchaft and George Atwood (1987), were contributing to the development of the alternative model. However, Aron (1996) asserts that "the track system at [NYU Postdoc] forced [relational psychoanalysis] to take shape with particularly sharp contours" (p. 4). Contemporary relational theorists include Altman (1995, 2010), Aron ([with Harris] 1993, 1996, [with Harris] 2005, [with Suchet and Harris] 2007, [with Harris] 2012a, 2012b), Atwood and Stolorow (1984, 1993), Beebe and Lachman (2002), Benjamin (1988, 1995, 1998), Bromberg (1998, 2006, 2011), Chodorow (1978, 1991, 2011), Davies and Frawley (1994), Ehrenberg (1992), Eigen (1981, 1998), Fosshage, Lachmann and Lichtenberg (1992, 1996), Ghent (1990), Harris (Aron & Harris, 1993, 2006, 2007, 2012a, 2012b), Hoffman (1998), Maroda (1999, 2004, 2009), Mitchell (1988, 1993, 1997, 2000), Ogden (1982, 1994), Orange (2010b, 2011), Pizer (1998), Renik (2006), Shabad (2001), Slochower (1996, 2006), Spezzano (1993), Stern (1997, 2010), Stolorow ([with Brandchaft and Atwood] 1987, [with Orange and Atwood] 2002, 2007), and Wachtel (1997, 2008).

There can be little doubt that until his untimely death in 2000 Stephen Mitchell was the most prolific and influential of the originators of the relational tradition, and his contributions are central to learning and understanding relational theory. Two other contemporary relational innovators who will be resourced for this chapter are Jessica Benjamin and Lewis Aron. Benjamin's work is resourced above all other relational theorists for her intersubjectivity theory, which informs so much of relational thinking. Aron is arguably to relational psychoanalysis what the apostle Paul was to Christianity. Not only has he extended the work and spirit of Stephen Mitchell, but he has expanded the relational paradigm shift through his commitment to resurrecting the legacy of Sandor Ferenczi (Aron & Harris, 1993).[2] Aron, along with Adrienne Harris and Jeremy Safran, was instrumental in founding the Ferenczi Center at the New School for Social Research.

A relational theorist who writes on the integration of relational psychoanalysis with Christian narratives is Marie Hoffman (2011). Of her work, Aron states, "One of the areas I'm really interested in is psychoanalysis and religion. . . . Marie Hoffman has been doing really interesting writing on the Christian influence on many analysts' work over the last hundred years" (Safran, 2009, p. 112). Aron has also recognized Hoffman's (2011) contributions to intersubjectivity theory, including her integrative linking of Benjamin's work in intersubjectivity theory, which "reverberates with Christian theology about the Trinity" (Aron & Harris, 2012b, p. 235).

PERSPECTIVES ON MOTIVATION

Stephen Mitchell's point of entry into a discussion of motivation is his assertion that all psychoanalytic theories understand persons as object-seeking (1998). For instance, Freud understood humans as seeking objects for discharge of sexual and aggressive drives. Sullivan believed that persons seek objects for the satisfaction of integrating tendencies. Both Harry Sullivan and Ronald Fairbairn sought a new paradigm for psychoanalysis in which the human person is in her or his very essence a social being. In contrast to Freud's human, who is existentially alone and drawn into human relating for a narcissistic purpose or need, Sullivan's and Fairbairn's human has an embedded desire to relate as a natural state of being; at birth, human beings are already "hard-wired" to seek relational matrices with others. According to Mitchell, "Fairbairn was suggesting that object seeking . . . is not the vehicle for the satisfaction of a specific need, but the expression of our very nature, the form through which we become

---

[2]Others who have contributed to Ferenczi's revival include Andre Haynal (2002); Judith Dupont (1988); Arnold Rachman (1997); Martin Stanton (1991); Peter Rudnytsky, Antal Bokay and Patrizia Gampieri-Deutsch (1996); Jay Frankel; and before and above all Michael Balint (1933, 1949, 1959, 1968) and Izette DeForest (1954).

specifically *human* beings" (1998, p. 117). Mitchell understood human motivation as mediated by "the very nature of that organism [which is] wired to be actualized only through exchanges with other minds" (1998, p. 121).

A relational approach to motivation insists upon a "dyadic, social, interactional, interpersonal" understanding of the human mind (Aron, 1996, p. x).[3] Mitchell's contributions to a relational conception of mind are foundational. Mitchell stresses a theory of mind that originates and is "structured through interaction" (1988, p. 4).

Mitchell asserts that the contents of a mind are an amalgam of "relational configurations" (1988, p. 3). He further asserts that the impulses of a relational mind are "experienced always *in the context of relatedness*" (1988, p. 3). Superordinate to Mitchell's relational mind is the understanding that the meaning assigned to one's experience derives from "relational patterns" (1988, p. 4). Extending Mitchell's model of a relational mind, Aron understands the context of mind as inextricably bound to "mutual and reciprocal two-way" encounters with real others (1996, p. x). Aron further asserts that a relational model of mind is "generated relationally and dialogically" in interpersonal relating to others (1996, p. xii). Mitchell understood relational configurations to be a source of motivation. Relational configurations are mental representations of oneself in relationship with another. These configurations can be further parsed as containing representations of the self, representations of the other and representations of the "specific interactions which transpire between self and other" (Mitchell, 1988, p. 33).

Extending Mitchell's understanding of motivation, Benjamin (1988, 1995) developed a model for describing a person's capacity for recognition, which she defines as a subject's ability to experience another subject as "a separate and equivalent center of subjectivity" (1995, p. 7). Benjamin understands a "good enough" childhood as one in which children receive recognition from caregivers and in turn learn how to

---

[3]Mind as a construct is utilized in this section, not in support of maintenance of a mind-body dualism, but as a signifier for the integrator of motivation and content of stored lived experience, both explicit and implicit.

provide recognition to others. This capacity to receive and give recognition enables the possibility of mutual recognition between subjects (1995, p. 30). Benjamin's intersubjectivity theory will be discussed more fully in the next section on development.

For the present consideration of a relational theory of motivation, it is important to emphasize about Benjamin's intersubjectivity theory that mutual recognition connotes the parallel processes of a subject recognizing other subjects as essentially different from oneself, essentially similar to or like oneself, and of equal value to oneself. When another subject can be recognized as being of equal value to oneself, this meaning concerning the other can motivate one to relate to the other for the other's benefit, rather than solely on the basis of one's interpretation of his or her own intrapsychic meaning with regard to the other. What may be derived from Benjamin's intersubjectivity theory is a model for relational motivation made possible by the subject's intention to be responsive to her own subjectivity while simultaneously being responsive to the other's subjectivity.[4]

PERSPECTIVES ON DEVELOPMENT

Vitz (Vitz & Felch, 2006) has asserted that object relations theory is unique in offering the only comprehensive psychoanalytic theory of development. It is likely that Mitchell would not have objected to Vitz's assertion since he relied upon Fairbairn (1952) for a starting place for understanding human development. Mitchell understood development as originating from primary internalizations of early object relations. However, rather than understanding the infant as differentiating an inside from an outside (a "me" and "not me"), Mitchell believed the baby begins life fully embedded in a relational matrix with his or her caregivers. He believed that a sense of oneself develops gradually out of an undifferentiated relational matrix. For Mitchell, "me" and "not me" does not come about through a defensive process of projections and introjections, or incorporations and expulsions, as Klein and Fairbairn believed.

---

[4] I am indebted to Drozek (2010) for his contribution to this section on motivation.

Rather, Mitchell understood the boundaries between self and others as diffuse, so that in the experience of intense emotional relational interactions, it is not possible to know who is who. In this conception Mitchell (2000) approvingly quotes Phillips (1995, p. 22), "When two people speak to each other, they soon become inextricable: words are contagious." However, Mitchell did not drift into a view of undifferentiated human selves. He believed it was possible to "combine Loewald's (1980) notion of primary *affective* unity with objects with Stern's (1985) notion of *perceptual* differentiation of objects" (1998, p. 124, emphasis added).

Greenberg and Mitchell (1983) proposed three historic core analytic theories of development: (1) drive-instinct models, (2) relationship models and (3) mixed models. The baby in the drive-instinct model is motivated to reduce internal tension and is only secondarily interested in differentiating him- or herself from other people. Freud's and Klein's developmental theories are examples of this model. By contrast, the baby in relational models is primarily motivated toward human relations. Interpersonal psychoanalysis, self psychology and attachment theory are encompassed within this relationship model. Mixed models are committed to incorporating specific integrations of the drive-instinct and relationship models. Winnicott (1960) and Anna Freud are exemplars of the mixed model.

Mitchell's seminal volumes (1988, 1993, 1997, 2000), which initiated the relational turn in psychoanalysis, asserted that a new paradigm in psychoanalysis was necessitated by many factors, including emergent feminism, neuroscientific and infant observation research, and the postmodern critique. Development must be understood as a *two-person* system in which the individual is cocreated in a relational matrix that is both the native motivator and organizer of psychic development. Hence, dynamic interaction between persons, rather than within an individual mind, is the essential crucible of human development. Moreover, "reality [is] on par with the intraspsychic, and past and present are in dynamic interplay rather than either being reducible to the other" (Seligman, 2003, p. 482). Stephen Seligman's description summarizes

Mitchell's commitment to hold the tensions between interpersonalist and object relationalist theories of development within the context of the emerging currents of an intersubjectivist-phenomenological philosophy and a hermeneutic-constructivist critique.

Seligman also enumerates the concepts from infant research that are directly parallel to a relational view of development. He writes that these parallels include

> a view of the infant-parent relationship as a mutual influence structure; the transactional systems perspective; the emphasis on affect and dyadic internal representations; the attention to interactions and nonverbal communication; the central role of reality in development; the assumption of continuity between earlier and later developmental stages; and the conceptualization of attachment and intersubjectivity as fundamental motivation systems. . . . The analytic interest in the development of subjectivity and intersubjectivity and the dynamics of recognition added a crucial [relational] dimension. (Seligman, 2003, p. 483)

Jessica Benjamin (1988) has significantly extended the developmental contributions of Mitchell with her intersubjectivity theory. Benjamin depicts the nascent dynamics of dominance and submission that occur in a two-person situation where the infant strives to establish his or her own subjectivity in the context of his or her dependence upon the caregiver. She posits an optimal developmental environment in which the child develops the capacity for mutual recognition between subjects (1995, p. 30).

Benjamin understands mutual recognition as the concurrent experiences of one perceiving another to be fundamentally distinct and fundamentally similar. Together these twin perceptions form "the two central elements of recognition" (1988, p. 170). Benjamin emphasizes that mutual recognition is more than the cognitive acceptance of another person's difference; mutual recognition includes the capacity for empathy for another person (1988, p. 76). This capacity for empathy is to be understood as akin to mutual respect, that ability "to respect the other subject as an equal" (1988, p. 8). Benjamin understands the achievement of mutual recognition as including affirmation (1988, pp. 15, 60), appreciation (1988, pp. 15, 28, 54, 177, 195) and love (1988, pp. 16, 106). For Benjamin, mutual recognition includes the simultaneous capacities to recognize the unique difference of another subject, recognize the shared similarity between another subject and oneself, and recognize the intrinsic value of the other subject as being equal to one's own value.

Benjamin constructed her intersubjectivity theory through utilizing the Hegelian conceptions of identification and surrender, and modulated the "absolutizing" tendencies in Hegel's system through resourcing Winnicott. The Christian foundation of Hegel's system and Benjamin's intersubjectivity theory are explicated by Hoffman (2011). Reis (2009), writing as a relationalist, has criticized Benjamin's reliance on Hegel:

> Hegel's paradigm of recognition as used by Benjamin, even while tempered by the addition of Winnicott's optimism, has a distinct world view associated with it. Hegel's world is one in which other people, referred to as objects, are seen as impediments, who struggle with each other in warring fashion to deny their mutual dependence. Intersubjective theories based in Hegel thus center around the *problem* of understanding how separated subjects can recognize each other as equivalent centers of experience. (Reis, 2009, p. 567)

Reis approvingly quotes Kelly Oliver in asking the question of Benjamin: "From the presumption that human relations are essentially warlike, how can we imagine them as peaceful?" (Oliver, 2001, p. 4). Reis (2009) then advocates for a worldview in which

> minds are transformed into embodied beings [who are born] already able to communicate their emotions and intentions to others with whom they are in immediate relations. Instead of a social context filled with tense antagonism and negation of others, this world assumes the joyful sharing of friendship and companionship and the motivation to share good company. (p. 560)

Reis (2009) concludes,

> Because our subjective life is our bodily life, all of our experiences and the meanings which animate our lives are based in our active corporeal, and

intercorporeal involvement in the world. Thus when we see others, we have no need to doubt their existence. Instead, a neuronal flash resolves the problem of Cartesian subjectivism within microseconds, revealing other persons and their motivation to share good company. (p. 577)

One cannot help but hear Reis's eschatological hope in the *neural basis of social identification* (Gallese, 2009), the *neurobiological implications of intersubjectivity* (Ammaniti & Trentini, 2009), and the *psychobiology of human meaning* (Trevarthen, 2009) as possessing the keys to the kingdom of a world redeemed from aggression and hostility. In philosophical parlance, Reis would appear to commit a category error in presuming that current science, which makes claims to resolve Cartesian mind-body dualisms, will also resolve the problem of evil.

A more comprehensive treatment of the problem of aggression and evil in the process of human development is the work of Hoffman (2011). Hoffman retains the intersubjectivity theory of Benjamin precisely because of its heuristic value for recognizing and not denying a human condition marred by a tendency to corrupt the good. Hoffman extends Benjamin's intersubjectivity theory by reclaiming the corpus of Hegel's theological constructs that refer to Jesus Christ's progression of intersubjective knowing that commences in *incarnation*, progresses to *crucifixion* and culminates in *resurrection*. Hoffman parses the resonance of the Christian meaning of incarnation and the relational psychoanalytic meaning of identification, then she parses the resonance of the Christian meaning of crucifixion with the relational psychoanalytic meaning of surrender. Her primary extension of Benjamin is in parsing the resonance between the Christian meaning of resurrection and the psychoanalytic meaning of gratitude, which she revives from its disuse in the psychoanalytic corpus. Hoffman posits a course of human development that understands identification, surrender and gratitude as three movements in intersubjective relating that cyclically repeat at every level of human existence from the lifespan of a person in relationship, to the rise and fall of nations and cultures, to a telos anticipated by Hebraic and Christian Scriptures that culminates in a new heaven and a new earth.

PERSPECTIVES ON PSYCHOPATHOLOGY

A reader of relational literature will be hard-pressed to find the language of psychopathology in the relational theory or practice. This missing psychopathological language should not be misunderstood as relational solipsism. Rather the concept of psychopathology is eschewed by some, if not many, relationalists because of the embedded meaning of a one-person psychology that is endemic to the meaning of the technical term *psychopathology*.[5] Since the inception of *Psychoanalytic Dialogues*, only three articles have contained the term *psychopathology* in the title.

That psychopathology is largely absent in relational literature also comes as no surprise when one recalls that the relational track at NYU Postdoc was formed by faculty from the interpersonal-humanistic track. This track's distinctions include counting Erich Fromm, a pioneer in the humanistic psychologies, as a faculty member.

There would be no overstatement in asserting that some relational psychoanalysts abhor diagnostics; in fact, some do not include the *Psychodynamic Diagnostic Manual* (PDM Task Force, 2006) in their library. A relational psychoanalytic sensibility is "experience near"; the analyst remains close to the phenomena emerging in the appointment and is committed to not foreclosing on what is spontaneously occurring in the space. A diagnostic category or a psychopathological understanding is avoided as a reified and limiting perspective about the other person in the psychoanalytic relationship.

Further, the perspectival epistemology of relational psychoanalysis understands that what might be experienced as undesirable (psychopathological symptoms) can also come to be recognized as necessary, even desirable. A relational iteration of this understanding may be found in Davies (2004), in which her transient hatred of her extremely difficult patient was instrumental in accessing tenderness in the patient. Likewise, Aron (2005) examines the biblical narrative of the tree of good and evil through utilizing Fromm and Solovetchik, explicating

---

[5]Please refer to "Perspectives on Therapeutic Change" in this chapter for an explanation and discussion of "one-person" and "two-person" psychologies.

the nuances of whether the evil could also contain the good.

Mitchell (1988) pursued a constructive critique regarding oversim-plified developmental perspectives that understood psychopathology as accretions of developmental arrest. He followed a dialectical approach to the possible effects of the past in the present. Seligman (2003) states that Mitchell on the one hand took very seriously "the essential effects of af-fective and cognitive immaturity" and did not neglect "concepts such as fantasies, drives, or primitive needs and states of mind" (p. 489). Mitchell understood events of childhood as the most influential in psychopa-thology. On the other hand, Mitchell's approach to psychopathology did not "rely on a conception of child psychology as organized by endog-enous, infantile givens that might be preserved directly into adulthood if development goes badly" (Seligman, 2003, p. 489).

Mitchell distanced from a developmental-arrest conception of adult psychopathology that is mediated by an infantile self. His relational-conflict perspective understood disturbances formed in early relation-ships and manifesting in adulthood not in the framework of fixations of infantile needs but rather as complex processes through which an inter-personal world (or world of object relations) has been created out of what was available in the developmental environment.

Moreover, Mitchell avoided preconceived systems of psychosexual or psychosocial stages leading to normative development, and privileged a reality-based attention to psychopathology as emanating from the prob-lematic childhood experiences of "what really happened." Bowlby's (1969, 1980, 1988) emphasis on attachment and loss, Kohut's (1977) self-object conception of recognition and the vicissitudes of failures of recognition, and Davies and Frawley's (1994) and Bromberg's (1998) attention to the spectrum of post-traumatic pathologies form the basis of much of the relational meanings of psychopathology. Additionally, dissociation as a defensive structure (Bromberg, 1998; Davies, 1996), multiple self states (Bromberg, 1998) and dissociation as unformulated experience (Stern, 1997) are relational perspectives on the genesis and maintenance of psy-chopathological relationship patterns.

PERSPECTIVES ON THERAPEUTIC CHANGE

With the radical recognition of a new paradigm in psychoanalysis, relational psychoanalysts came to understand relationships as what motivate and form psychic meaning. The dynamic in psychoanalysis was conceived to be more interpsychic and less intrapsychic. Classical psychoanalytic drive-instinct models of individualistic psychic structure and development, psychopathology and clinical practice were relinquished, and two-person systems were recognized as basal and primal units of psychic organization that substantiated within and without each person, as well as in the intersubjective space between persons. Each person's self-understanding is formatted as he or she is seen by others, and each person imagines him- or herself within the social context of knowing others. In this shift from a one-person to a two-person psychology, the analyst's authority was reconceptualized as residing within the analytic relationship rather than deriving from a positivist science that could unravel the complexities of a patient's intrapsychic world.

Perhaps the most significant implication of the new paradigm for clinical technique was the relational psychoanalyst's sensibility toward the analyst's action. The classical psychoanalytic stance of the analyst's neutrality and abstinence was vacated as practically untenable. Patient and analyst are a self-with-other unit that mutually influences each other in a moment-to-moment engagement that is desirable. Instead of contaminating the treatment, countertransference is a necessary and ubiquitous element of the treatment. As in a parent-child dyad, an analyst's interaction is potentially both regressive and progressive.

An analyst's interaction is regressive when he or she is caught in an enactment that is a constricted relational pattern repetitively reenacted by the patient in his or her relationships, including the analytic relationship. The analyst falls into these enactments because his or her own relational patterns contain a "valency" for the patient's maladaptive patterns. Because enactments are spontaneous actions within the therapy, which therapist and patient are unconsciously drawn into, a critical activity is required of the therapist. The therapist must provide an oscillating function called self-reflexivity, a capacity to be present with the patient in the moment while tracking concurrent dynamics in the analytic space. Aron describes this function of self-reflection as "based on the [analyst's] capacity for internal division, healthy dissociation, 'standing in the spaces' between realities (Bromberg, 1998), building bridges (Pizer, 1998), the transcendent oscillating or dialectical function" (2000, p. 677). This capacity for self-reflexivity gives rise to the "analytic third." The third is an alternative relational sensibility that permits the therapist to perceive that he or she is locked into an enactment with the patient. The third gives rise to the awareness that an enactment is occurring and offers a way out of the enactment. One of the actions of therapeutic change in a relational treatment is the transformation of these enactments. When an analyst becomes aware of an enactment in which he or she has been caught for minutes, days, weeks, months or even years, he or she achieves the possibility of changing the outcome of the enactment. Mitchell (1998) has succinctly described this process of transformation:

> The analysand enters treatment with a narrowed relational matrix; he seeks connections by projecting and recreating familiar, constricted relational patterns, experiencing all important relationships (especially the one with the analyst) along old lines. He continually reinternalizes and consolidates these relational configurations. The *central process* in psychoanalytic treatments is the relinquishment of ties to these relational patterns, thereby allowing an openness to new and richer interpersonal relations. (p. 170, emphasis added)

The relational crucible of therapeutic change comprises (1) reflection upon formative relational experiences in the patient's early parental/ significant other relationships, and (2) the transformative action of the "now moment" (Stern et al., 1998) in the analytic dyad. An analyst's progressive interactions are not conceived as "reparenting" in order to ameliorate developmental arrest; the focus of treatment is the relinquishment of old relational patterns that constrict freedom and "to find a way to be with patients that gives them the greatest opportunity, despite the odds, to make better lives for themselves" (Hoffman, 1998, p. xxxi). These ways of progressive interaction include containing and holding negatively charged affect, working through disruptions in the therapeutic relationship, enhancing reflective functioning and many others.

Aron (1996) describes the relational analytic relationship as "mutual though asymmetrical." There are multiple meanings implicit in Aron's conception of the analytic relationship, including the division of roles, responsibility and ethical obligations that are not the same for patient and analyst. For the present consideration, there is asymmetry with regard to the analyst's authority. The analyst's authority is negotiated and renegotiated in the fluid, developing analytic relationship. The analyst's training and experience draw the patient to seek such a relationship, but it is the transference-countertransference interaction that beckons the patient *into* the relationship.

While Mitchell (1998) eschewed the epistemic certainty of a positivist psychoanalysis, he also avoided the absurdity of an absolute relativism that never disagreed or argued with a patient. He asserted that it is "crucial both that the analyst not pull rank and that he also hold his ground when necessary" (Mitchell, 1997, p. 228). He approvingly quoted Wilfred Bion, "As a psychoanalyst I do not claim to know the answer, but I do not mean, therefore, that those who come to me for analysis know better" (Mitchell, 1993, p. 67).

Attention to dissociative processes is a significant focus of treatment in a relational approach. Dissociation is understood not only as the antecedent of severe trauma but also as a defensive organization that is present in a panoply of configurations. Dissociation is as widely presumed by relationalists as the presumption of repression is assumed by Freudians. Dissociation can result in "unformulated experience" (Stern, 1997) and is implicated in multiplicity within self-organization. Bromberg (1998) has proposed the presence of multiple self-states that are conceived as dissociated "selves," which remain unintegrated due to the perturbations and traumata associated with unreliable caregivers during early development. Bromberg (1998) advocates for an analyst "standing

in the spaces" of these dissociated selves by holding in mind the dissociated painful and anxiety-ridden experiences of the patient.

One further consideration concerning therapeutic change in the relational context is the burgeoning integration of Sandor Ferenczi's early
contributions in the history of psychoanalysis (Aron & Harris, 1993). Ferenczi wrote in 1932 that "being loved . . . is the natural emotional [desire]
of the baby. . . . The first disappointments of love . . . must have in every
case, a traumatic effect. . . . All subsequent disappointments, later on in
one's love life, may well regress to this wish fulfillment" (Ferenczi, 1995).
For Ferenczi, the paramount goal of therapy was overcoming the disintegration of "suffering people [who need] a quantity and a quality of love
of an extraordinary kind" (Ferenczi, 1995). Ferenczi enjoined analysts to
offer "tremendous patience and self-sacrifice . . . [in order to bring the
patient's] dead ego-fragments back to life" (Ferenczi, 1995). He wrote,
"Only sympathy heals. . . . Understanding is necessary in order to employ
sympathy in the right place (analysis), in the right way. Without sympathy: there is no healing. . . . [But] can one love everyone? Are there no
set limits to it?" (Ferenczi, 1995).

The Christian Scottish analyst Ian Suttie, in agreement with Ferenczi,
wrote in *The Origins of Love and Hate* that the analyst "shows by his understanding and insight that he too has suffered [the patient's] experiences, so that there is a 'fellowship of suffering' established. . . . I fully
accept Ferenczi's dictum, 'The physician's love heals the patient'" (Suttie,
1935, pp. 212-13). Zvi Lothane states that Ferenczi's many contributions
are best "recombined into a new synthesis guided by a new principle of
integration. That new principle is the concept of love, a containing and
encompassing concept within which dwells life and its various psychological processes, including the analytic process" (Lothane, 1998, p. 37).
This section on therapeutic change is fittingly summarized by a return to
the contributions of Lew Aron. Of all of Aron's considerable influences
in the emerging relational tradition, I believe that the greatest of these
influences is love, the return of the repressed legacy of Sandor Ferenczi
to relational theory and practice.

Christian Critique

Specific Christian traditions are themselves not fixed systems of belief but fluid organizing perspectives within which people of like sensibilities congregate. Christian traditions over the centuries have evolved and waned within the contexts of contemporaneous cultural tensions that sculpt theological assumptions. Historically, these traditions have cohered around such tensions as law and grace, divine sovereignty and human responsibility, sacramentalism and faith, and scholasticism and pietism. Within orthodox Christianity, theological traditions are presently reconfiguring along individualistic and communal/relational theological considerations. The individualistic emphasis of justification by faith focuses on personal salvation (I am saved from destruction and am going to heaven when I die), while the communal/relational emphasis of gospel focuses on God and God's purposes for all people (the kingdom of God is near, the kingdom of God is here, the kingdom of God is coming).

I situate myself within the emerging tradition of gospel, which intentionally acts to embody a present and coming kingdom of God and reconstitute the world (a new heaven and new earth).[6] I believe that Jesus finished the job of justification when he came to earth the first time. I believe that I am to work in concert with the acts of Jesus to bring into being the consummation of the realm or kingdom of God. I am to do this by loving God and loving my neighbor in the hope that I, with many others, will do "greater works" than those of Jesus, and achieve the restoration of the family of God—that, as Jesus prayed, "we all will be one, just as you [Father] and I [Jesus] are one" (Jn 17:21 NLT).

My Reformed theology, which was fortified during my theological studies at Westminster Theological Seminary, understands that personified evil was bound and globally restricted by Jesus' redemptive achievements. To the extent that personified evil continues to exert an influence in the world, this occurs through accretions of evil in the self-states of a person and within the relational matrices of interpersonal human re-

---

[6]I am most indebted to the Christian thought of the theologians Jürgen Moltmann and N. T. Wright, and the philosophers Paul Ricoeur and John MacMurray.

lating. This perspective of evil finds resonance in Mitchell's relational-conflict model, which understands that disturbances in early relational matrices (in a biblical understanding, the sins of one's parents) severely distort and impair subsequent relationships.

I understand relational theorists, including Reis (2009), who dismiss "a social context filled with tense antagonism and negation of others" (see "Perspectives on Development") as also rejecting Mitchell's relational-conflict understanding of development and preferring a Kohutian and earlier Winnicottian understanding of human nature that does not consider a berth for the presence of evil. A fully orbed relational theory follows Mitchell's spirit, which was committed to holding tensions even though they may be contradictory or even objectionable to one's personal sensibilities. Relational psychoanalysis embraces paradox and mystery, and will not collapse tensions that are humbly recognized as containing more complexity than one is capable of explaining. Relational theory is essentially agnostic toward God—neither affirming nor denying God's personal existence, influence and autonomy—but it is a benign agnosticism that might posit God as a null hypothesis whom one could be compelled to recognize in the face of numinous personal experience.

A relational sensibility that emphasizes mutual recognition as a desirable occurrence in the intersubjective space, for me, resounds with the Judaic and Christian understandings of each human person being "made in the image of God" and on this basis alone being due unqualified respect. A relational understanding of enactments emphasizes the necessity of finding a third, a way of relating that permits more freedom. Jessica Benjamin's (2009) "moral third" offers a berth for Judaic and Christian narratives that encourage prayer as a way of beckoning the presence of a loving and affirming God in a difficult time. Additionally, a relational approach recognizes love of the patient as a significant and even necessary active ingredient of an effective therapy. A relational analyst can enjoy the freedom to love a patient without fear of collegial disapproval.

I find much resonance between my preferred Christian understandings and the relational perspective in psychoanalysis. Areas of dissonance between my Christian perspective and relational perspectives pertain more to individual tilts of some relational authors. I prefer relationalists who follow the spirit of Stephen Mitchell, who was determined to not collapse tensions. When a relationalist tilts toward a mostly optimistic Kohutian understanding or a mostly pessimistic Kleinian or Fairbairnian understanding, I experience a dissonance with how I situate myself within Christian gospel. Like Ricoeur, I believe humans are capable of justifying and perpetrating radical evil; also like Ricoeur, I believe those same humans possess the potential to achieve and enjoy superabundant goodness.

Case Study: Tony

A relational treatment is a one-of-a-kind relationship of two unique persons. There is not a unique relational model for psychoanalytic work other than that the analyst be authentically him- or herself. There is no prescribed relational therapeutic frame with the possible exception of an assumed two-person psychology, and that the analyst be observant of the ethical principles and guidelines of his or her licensure. I will discuss the case of Tony within the context of my own uniqueness as a relational psychoanalyst.

Tony is talkative and engaging during the initial appointments; consequently, I anticipate that the therapy will begin as a cooperative alliance for learning about Tony's life with the possibility that emergent transference-countertransference dynamics can be experienced from the commencement of appointments. Because I am male, my initial consideration is that transference-countertransference dynamics will emerge more readily regarding Tony's relationship with his father. I understand this consideration is my own expectation and will attempt to not foreclose upon what Tony shares by expecting, and more likely influencing, what Tony chooses to talk about. I am ambivalent about Tony's choice to use the couch. I respect Tony's preference and accept Tony's wish to focus on his internal experiences. This wish could mean both that Tony wants to avoid competitive tensions like those he has with his father and avoid the intrusion of my gaze, which could lead to him becoming quiet like he does with his mother. At the same time, I am concerned that Tony's use of the couch will impede the development of mutuality in our therapeutic relationship and that Tony's preconceptions about practicing free association could belie a one-person psychology expectation that could foreclose upon a more relational self-with-other unit. I defer to Tony's choice of reclining on the couch with a self-understanding that I anticipate revisiting Tony's use of the couch as the therapy progresses.

I encourage and appreciate all that Tony offers regarding his developmental history and ask questions that invoke Tony's present feelings about experiences with significant others. I also express interest in Tony's present relationships and his perceptions regarding himself in these relationships. I am detailed in my inquiry into Tony's subjective experience of boredom and passivity in his romantic relating to females and his competitiveness and mistrust in his male relationships. I begin to talk about Tony's current constricted relational patterns as familiar recreations of family-of-origin relationships that he reinternalizes and consolidates in his present relationships.

Also significant are Tony's affective states and actions when he is alone. Symptoms of anxiety and depression, ruminative mentation and boredom, and compulsive acting out of these self-states is explored with compassion and sincere curiosity to understand. I anticipate that over the course of the analysis, Tony will reexperience with me dissociated, severely distressing affective self-states which, at earlier times in Tony's life, he could not perceive, express, process and resolve. I am careful to not reify the masturbation as an addiction, and also to clarify that when Tony masturbates in public settings, he is not placing himself or others at risk. I understand Tony's dreams as uncensored dramatic depictions of Tony's affect-laden self-states and invite Tony to talk about his dreams during appointments so that they can be explored.

I understand and experience my relationship with Tony as an authentic relationship in which I am enveloped in Tony's narrowed relational matrices of being with another. My therapeutic approach anticipates that I will unconsciously become enmeshed in Tony's restricted relational patterns time after time. I attempt to practice a relating presence that listens to what is emerging in Tony, what is emerging in me and what is emerging in the space between Tony and me. Tony's desperate longing for approval will likely expect agreement from me about his father's uneducated and old-fashioned religious perspectives. I can profess agreement (perhaps because of my own experiences that resonate with Tony), but in doing so, I can become embroiled in an enactment with Tony of his seeking a restricting experience of refuge from father with mother. Or I can ask a question about Tony's perceptions of his father's religion and become just as embroiled in an enactment that replicates his father being disapproving and disappointed with Tony. In such enactments I look for a third to disentangle from the narrowed relational matrix that Tony and I are presently suffering in together. In finding a way out of this and many more enactments, Tony and I are cocreating a new and richer relational matrix. This process of rupture and repair is anticipated to occur throughout the course of our therapeutic relationship. In order for Tony to benefit from working through the enactments, he will need to relinquish ties to old and limiting relational patterns. Throughout the treatment, I will listen for and become enjoined with Tony's hopes and dreams, and hold in my mind the person that Tony longs to become.

Tony initially requested psychotherapy appointments at a frequency of one time each week. I will in time offer the opportunity to meet two times or three times a week. Multiple appointments each week both deepen the transference-countertransference intensity and thereby enhance the poignancy of working through enactments, and create sufficient space for Tony to more profoundly experience my love for him, and hopefully in a time to come, our love for each other.

8

Attachment-Based Psychoanalytic Therapy and Christianity

Being-in-Relation

Todd W. Hall *and*
Lauren E. Maltby

In the history of psychoanalytic theory, two broad relational traditions split off from Freud's "drive/structure model." One can be traced through the transitions of ego psychology to the many strands of the "relational/ structure model," such as object relations theory, that proliferate today (Greenberg & Mitchell, 1983). Fairbairn's theory of object relations, along with several other key theories, formed the foundation for the development of relational psychoanalysis by contemporary theorists. For myriad reasons, attachment theory developed along an independent though parallel theoretical trajectory as that of the relational/structure model. For years these relational cousins were estranged from each other. They developed in separate sociopolitical groups of academicians, each with their own language, training programs, journals and conferences. Because of this "broad schism," as Mitchell (2000) put it, attachment theory developed more as a research tradition in academic psychology departments.

In recent years, however, we have seen a rapprochement between these two lines of theory, partly spurred on by major developments in infant research (Beebe & Lachmann, 2002; Stern, 1985; Tronick, 2007), affective neuroscience and narrative psychologies in the past several decades, which has significant clinical implications (Fonagy, 2001; Holmes, 1993; Mitchell, 2000). The implications of these developments have application to therapy and have also informed theory development. In this chapter, as background for the main theory, we provide an overview of the emergence of attachment theory, the leading theorists (John Bowlby and Mary Ainsworth), and contemporary innovations since the original pillars of attachment theory were laid. Following this, we review the main tenets of attachment theory under the headings of motivation, development and psychopathology. We then discuss our take on how attachment theory interacts with our "theologically traditioned" version of evangelical Christianity. Finally, we close the chapter by discussing the process of therapeutic change and apply our attachment-based approach to therapy to the case provided by the editors.

THE EMERGENCE OF ATTACHMENT THEORY

As post-Freudian psychoanalysis unfolded, controversy abounded within the British Psychoanalytic Society as Anna Freud and Melanie Klein, and their respective followers, each claimed the right to Freud's theoretical throne. In addition to these two groups, a third group of *independents*, also called the *middle group*, consisted of theorists such as W. R. D. Fairbairn, John Bowlby, D. W. Winnicott and Michael Balint, who were pioneers in developing early relational theories. The object relational ego psychology traditions that grew out of Anna Freud's group (e.g., Margaret Mahler and Rene Spitz), as well as Klein, both paved the way for a full relational/structure theory, albeit in radically different ways. The object relational ego psychologists developed the profoundly new idea that the ego is dependent on early (object) relationships for its development, whereas Klein radically redefined the Freudian notion of drives as being fundamentally psychological in nature, and as having internal objects built into to them.

Building on the shell of Klein's theory of internalized objects, Fairbairn entered the discussion. He combined his clinical experience, in which he saw his patients carrying with them the residues of early relationships, with the notion that there are structures in the mind with which we relate (Fairbairn, 1952). In doing so, he developed his central theoretical principle—that we internalize not phantasized images but *experiences of real relationships*. He was one of the first theorists to develop a theory of personality and development based on the notion that relational connection is our primary motive and need. His theory was also one of the first to develop a vision of the mind as being *structured* not by drive forces but by the subjective experiences of relational meanings. It is difficult to overestimate Fairbairn's impact on the theoretical developments that have ensued since the 1940s. Though they never appeared on the conceptual radar screen before him, now Fairbairn's basic ideas about relationality are a mainstay of research and theory.

LEADING THEORISTS: JOHN BOWLBY AND MARY AINSWORTH

At the same time, a British psychiatrist, John Bowlby, began his own reformulation of drive theory. Bowlby borrowed methodology from neighboring disciplines and in doing so went outside the psychoanalytic epistemology; the result was an independent tradition of relational theory—that of attachment theory.

Bowlby's theory was forged in the context of his work on maternal deprivation, in which he saw connections between the responses and processes stemming from maternal deprivation among children and those of older individuals still suffering from the effects of maternal separation in early life. He observed two distinct patterns of relational disturbances: one group made excessive demands on others and were anxious and angry when the demands were not met, as is often seen in

2

dependent-type personalities, and a second group did not develop deep relationships and made "strenuous attempts to claim emotional self-sufficiency and independence of all affectional ties" (Bowlby, 1980, p. 202). Later, Bowlby (1980) identified a third pattern in the context of discussing loss, one he called "compulsive caregiving" (p. 206).

These patterns, which covered a wide spectrum of psychopathology, seemed to mirror the patterns he had observed in children who had been separated from their mothers. Bowlby saw continuity in the effects of maternal deprivation, an insight that would lead to his concept of *internal working models* (IWMs). All the evidence from his studies clearly indicated that the social-emotional need for a primary caregiver is not reducible to lower-order needs, an idea that contradicted the Freudian psychoanalytic theory of his day.

While Bowlby originated attachment theory, Mary Ainsworth did more than anyone else to put attachment theory on solid empirical footing. In 1950, Ainsworth took a position working in Bowlby's research unit in London. Ainsworth worked primarily on analyzing James Robertson's observational data on young children. She was greatly impressed with the naturalistic observation method, which she applied in Uganda to her studies of mother-infant attachment in 1953. Ainsworth's results were revealing, about not only the quality of mother-infant interaction but also maternal sensitivity to infant signals. Ainsworth observed three distinct attachment patterns in the Ganda infants (Ainsworth, Blehar, Waters & Wall, 1978). Securely attached infants exhibited minimal crying and enjoyed exploring in the presence of their mothers. Insecurely attached infants, in contrast, cried frequently and showed minimal exploratory behavior. Infants who had not yet become attached showed no differential behavior toward their mothers. Ainsworth also found that indicators of maternal sensitivity correlated positively with secure attachment.

Ainsworth went on to develop the "strange situation" in 1963, a standardized behavioral observation in which mother-infant behavior is closely observed during experiences of separation and reunification. Observing infants' behavior through the "strange situation" led to the identification of three attachment classifications (Ainsworth, Blehar, Waters & Wall, 1978). *Securely attached* infants showed a pattern of actively playing and exploring, seeking contact with mother when distressed after the brief separation, being easily comforted by mother and quickly returning to their play. *Anxiously attached and avoidant* (anxious-avoidant) infants showed disinterest when mother left and avoided her upon reunion, while engaging in activities to actively distract themselves from their distress (Rholes & Simpson, 2004). Finally, *anxiously attached and resistant* (anxious-resistant, or anxious-ambivalent) infants vacillated between seeking contact and resisting contact with their mother. Later, a fourth classification labeled *disorganized attachment* was discovered in which infants exhibited bizarre and dissociative-type behaviors, reflecting that they did not have an organized strategy for achieving proximity to mother (Main & Solomon, 1986).

Attachment theory was initially rejected by psychoanalysis, thus Bowlby's theory did not lead to a new school within psychoanalysis. Consequently, while there is an attachment theory today, currently there is not a mature modality of *attachment-based therapy*. Because of Bowlby's bent toward systematic observation and empirical research, attachment theory caught on in the empirically oriented academic community (e.g., Mary Ainsworth), and has become a major theoretical paradigm within the field of developmental psychology and the research tradition within clinical psychology. In recent years attachment theory has become more clinically focused, giving contour to an emerging attachment-based psychoanalytic therapy (e.g., Eagle, 2013; Wallin, 2007). This emerging clinical modality that overlaps with relational psychoanalysis, to which we will return, has developed largely due to contemporary innovations in attachment theory in which theoretically driven research and psychoanalytic therapy have reengaged in significant dialogue.

CONTEMPORARY INNOVATIONS

Since the original formulation of attachment theory by Bowlby and Ainsworth, several innovations have refined and expanded the theory and methods to the point that it is probably fair to consider attachment theory to be a family of theories. These innovations have included (1) assessing adult attachment and the development of the "adult attachment interview," (2) assessing adult attachment using self-report measures, (3) the development of the "dynamic maturational model" of attachment and adaptation, and (4) mentalizing as integral to secure attachment.

ASSESSING ADULT ATTACHMENT

Mary Main and the adult attachment interview. In the early 1980s Mary Main (a former student of Mary Ainsworth) and her colleagues moved attachment theory to the "level of representation"—a development that would turn out to be a major innovation in attachment theory (Main, Kaplan & Cassidy, 1985). As part of a longitudinal study of attachment among infants and children, Main and her then-students Nancy Kaplan and Carol George discovered that the way a parent told her story allowed them to predict the strange-situation classification of that parent's child (George, Kaplan & Main, 1996). This led to the development of the adult attachment interview (AAI), a semistructured interview designed to prime the attachment system by probing attachment-related memories, including experiences of loss, rejection and separation. The AAI coding system assesses an adult's state of mind with respect to attachment, which reflects an ingrained pattern of emotional communication (Main, Goldwyn & Hesse, 2003). In essence, the AAI evaluates not so much the content of individuals' attachment stories but rather the *coherence*, or lack thereof, of the way they tell their story.

Several studies have conducted AAIs with mothers *before* the birth of their children, and have found a strong correspondence (approximately 75% for secure versus insecure) between mothers' *prenatal* AAI interviews and their children's strange-situation classification at one year of age (Fonagy, Steele & Steele, 1991). This rules out the possibility that the association could be due to some influence of the child's interactions with the mother. In short, researchers using the AAI have advanced the field by discovering that IWMs—ingrained patterns of emotional communication—are passed down intergenerationally. These findings have enormous implications for clinical work, suggesting that therapists can pass down more secure IWMs to their clients through emotional communication that relies heavily on nonverbal channels.

Mary Main's contributions—both substantive and methodological—arguably represent the most significant innovations in attachment theory since the foundational work of Bowlby and Ainsworth. Substantively, Main and her colleagues refined and advanced our understanding of the characteristics of adult attachment classifications. Methodologically, Main and her colleagues developed the first implicit, nonself-report measure of adult attachment, which has become more significant over time as a self-report tradition has developed independently.

The self-report tradition and measurement controversy. Following Bowlby's lead, Hazan and Shaver (1987) hypothesized that romantic relationships were a type of attachment relationship and thus should yield the same basic attachment IWMs as in infants and adults in general. They developed a self-report measure of adult attachment style (secure, anxious or avoidant) based on the infant strange-situation classifications. Their original three-scale measure has been revised and expanded by several researchers, most notably being expanded to a four-category model that added *fearful* attachment (Bartholomew & Horowitz, 1991). Based on an extensive factor analysis of all existing English-language dimensional measures of attachment style up to that point, Brennan, Clark and Shaver (1998) found two underlying dimensions: <u>attachment-related avoidance</u> and <u>attachment-related anxiety</u>.

Four adult attachment styles can be generated from the two underlying dimensions. Secure attachment is represented by low anxiety and low avoidance on self-report measures. Anxious attachment is represented by high anxiety and low avoidance. Avoidant attachment is represented by low anxiety and high avoidance. Fearful attachment is manifested by high anxiety and high avoidance, and may combine features of anxious/preoccupied and avoidant/dismissing attachment. Although this tradition has a different approach to measuring attachment than the AAI/interview tradition, and has been motivated by different research questions (Mikulincer & Shaver, 2007), it clearly represents a major innovation in attachment research that has significantly advanced our understanding of adult attachment, particularly in the domain of romantic relationships. However, it has raised some controversy as to what self-report attachment measures assess in comparison to implicit interview-based measures such as the AAI. Attempting to sort this controversy out has advanced our understanding and assessment methods of adult attachment.

The dynamic maturational model of adult attachment. Since its inception in the mid-1980s, the AAI (George et al., 1996) combined with the Main and Goldwyn scoring method (M&G–AAI; Main et al., 2003) has been the most widely used interview-based measure of adult attachment. As noted above, the M&G–AAI pioneered a line of research that has been instrumental in corroborating the central tenets of attachment theory, most notably the intergenerational transmission of attachment (Fonagy et al., 1991). However, it is not without its limitations.

In response to some of the limitations of the M&G–AAI and to new developments in cognitive neuroscience, a former student of Mary Ainsworth, Patricia Crittenden, developed a new approach to the discourse analysis (scoring method) of the AAI based on a revised model of attachment—the dynamic-maturational model (DMM) of attachment and adaptation (Crittenden, 1995, 2008; Crittenden & Landini, 2011). The DMM offers a way to understand the meaning underlying unclear communication and a theoretical model of distorted communication and dysfunctional behavior (Crittenden & Landini, 2011). Interestingly, the DMM approach particularly resonates with a mentalizing approach (see next section); that is, it seeks to understand the mental states, intentional structure and meaning underlying behavior and communication (particularly of the disordered kind) that appear on the surface to be dysfunctional and therefore meaning-less. In fact, the authors stated that what is needed to understand psychological disorder is a "language of shared meaning" (Crittenden & Landini, 2011, p. 3).

In general, research on the DMM–AAI suggests that it (1) differentiates adaptive and maladaptive individuals, (2) differentiates among disorder types in clinically meaningful ways, (3) can formulate disordered behavior in terms of psychological functions, and (4) may be able to identify subgroups of psychiatric diagnoses in terms of information processing patterns. Although the DMM–AAI research is still in the early stages, it shows promise to significantly advance the field in theory and clinical work. The combined theoretical and methodological advancements of the DMM may prove to be as groundbreaking as the AAI was some twenty-five years ago.

Mentalizing as Integral to Secure Attachment

In the last decade Peter Fonagy and his colleagues have expanded Mary Main's work on metacognition by developing the interrelated concepts of mentalizing and reflective function (Fonagy, Gergely, Jurist & Target, 2002). Whereas Main focused on how adults monitor their own thinking during the AAI, Fonagy's broader view includes adults' attention to mental states in general, even the mental states of others (Wallin, 2007). The concept of mentalizing has "flourished in the framework of attachment theory," and thus represents a significant innovation in attachment theory that has important clinical implications (Allen, Fonagy & Bateman, 2008, p. 8).

Mentalizing is an unfamiliar term to most clinicians but, arguably, is not a new concept or new type of therapy (Allen et al., 2008). In fact, the general idea harkens back to Freud's notion of transforming nonmental bodily processes into mental/psychic experience, and it resembles Bion's (1962a, 1962b) concept of containment, in which mentalizing modulates strong emotions. Rather than introducing a new concept, Fonagy and colleagues are sharpening the focus on a process so fundamental to human development and psychotherapy that they boldly claim that mentalizing is "the most fundamental common factor among psychotherapeutic treatments" (Allen et al., 2008, p. 1). Fonagy and colleagues refer to mentalizing as "the process by which we realize that having a mind mediates our experience of the world" (Fonagy et al., 2002, p. 3). In the broadest conceptual sense, then, the capacity to mentalize is based on the process by which individuals develop a psychological self in relation to others, which both engenders secure attachment and is developed in the context of a secure, intersubjective attachment relationship. While the general idea of mentalizing may not be new, Fonagy and colleagues' refinement and elaboration of the concept enriches the framework of attachment theory and therapy.

MOTIVATION, DEVELOPMENT AND PSYCHOPATHOLOGY

Given this brief overview of the origins, founders and key developments in attachment theory, we turn our attention to its main tenets. We have organized our discussion around three distinct yet overlapping domains: motivation, development and psychopathology.

Motivation. In the broadest sense the attachment system is an innate motivational system that influences and organizes motivational, emotional and memory processes with attachment figures (Siegel, 2012). An attachment relationship is a relationship with an emotionally significant or preferred caregiver (attachment figure), based on an invisible attachment bond. In these relationships, children (and adults have their own version) exhibit four interrelated types of attachment behavior, which together define an attachment relationship (Bowlby, 1982).

First, children seek proximity to their attachment figures, which is one class of "attachment behavior" (Bowlby, 1982, p. 180). This can be done through numerous mechanisms, such as crying, following and clinging, all of which are part of a goal-corrected, attachment behavioral system that has as its set goal increasing physical and psychological proximity to the attachment figure. The flip side of this motivational coin is that children protest separation from their attachment figures and show frustration when they are separated. Both related attachment behaviors serve to protect children from harm, and thus the attachment system is highly responsive to danger (Crittenden & Landini, 2011; Siegel, 2012). Third, children seek a *secure base* and *safe haven* (Ainsworth et al., 1978; Bowlby,

1982, pp. 337-38). The function of the secure base is to enable the child to explore his or her environment, and the safe haven refers to the child's seeking out the caregiver in the face of distress. Fourth, there is evidence that children seek *primary intersubjectivity* (Trevarthen, 1979), which is a sense of intimacy and belonging that is related to emotional communication. Broadly speaking, intersubjectivity refers to the interaction between two subjectivities or two minds (Wallin, 2007). As such, it is centrally important to the development of attachment relationships and to psychotherapy.

The term *attachment style* (sometimes called orientation or "state of mind with respect to attachment") is used in a general sense to refer to the overall state and quality of an individual's attachments (Holmes, 1993). More specifically, attachment style refers to relatively stable individual differences in people's (1) tendencies to seek comfort and support from attachment figures, and (2) implicit expectations about how responsive attachment figures will be to bids for connection (Rholes & Simpson, 2004). The quality of attachment is divided into two main classifications: secure and insecure. Insecure attachment is further divided into three subclassifications (preoccupied, dismissing and disorganized/unresolved), resulting in four major attachment classifications in both childhood and adulthood.

These classifications can be thought of as strategies for connection even though these strategies are predominantly nonconscious. This is consistent with Bowlby's (1973) later emphasis on the child's appraisal of his or her attachment figure's emotional availability, and the notion that felt security is the ultimate goal of the attachment system (Sroufe & Waters, 1977). Securely attached caregivers make connection easy and fluid for the infant by being responsive to bids for connection and comfort, and by being emotionally available. Insecurely attached caregivers make this more difficult as they are not as responsive or emotionally available in different ways. Consequently, in relating to such attachment figures, infants nonconsciously develop strategies to work around their caregivers' lack of responsiveness and availability, and to maximize the connection, given the less-than-ideal relational environment. This "workaround" strategy is what Mary Main (1991) called "secondary felt security."

A caveat about categories is in order here. Since the research literature emphasizes attachment categories, it is important to clarify that people do not easily fit into categories. Though oversimplifications of clients' relational styles, these categories still help to capture a real and meaningful picture of how they manage emotions with respect to emotionally significant people in their lives. In discussing attachment categories in the context of psychotherapy, David Wallin (2007) reminds us that as we get to know clients better, "we often feel less clear about exactly who the patient is—or, at any rate, that clarity is no longer reducible to a single classification" (p. 97). As we develop clarity on the particulars of our clients' stories, their particulars may fit less and less well into a categorical box. While the categories are helpful heuristic mechanisms, it is important that we not think of clients as fitting neatly in a category.

Development. Considering lifespan psychological development through an attachment lens, Bowlby (1973) articulated two primary theses regarding the developmental roots of adult attachment patterns: (1) attachment patterns stem from real (as opposed to fantasized) relational experiences in one's family of origin during childhood, and (2) attachment patterns are fairly stable across the lifespan, although they can and do change, usually due to new relational experiences.

Bowlby rejected the Freudian notion of a series of sequential stages on a single track during which an individual can become developmentally arrested. Instead he used the analogy of a complex railway system— similar to the one in Great Britain when he was writing—to suggest a model of *multiple* developmental pathways, integrating the two already mentioned theses. Bowlby argued that early experiences with parents (and other attachment figures) heavily influence which of many developmental pathways individuals take early in life, which in turn influences which attachment pattern(s) they exhibit in close relationships as adults.

Research supports the general continuity of attachment patterns throughout the lifespan (Grossmann, Grossmann & Waters, 2005). However, Bowlby (1973) also theorized that at any point in life, new circumstances can lead to attachment experiences that challenge current attachment patterns, thereby revising them. There is a growing literature addressing changes of attachment patterns during childhood and the impact of attachment-related experiences during childhood on later adolescent and adult attachment (Mikulincer & Shaver, 2007).

Over thirty studies have examined the stability of attachment patterns during adulthood (Mikulincer & Shaver, 2007). Bowlby (1973) argued that while these patterns are always open to change, they become more stable over time. The average test-retest concordance for attachment classifications across numerous studies was approximately 70% (Mikulincer & Shaver, 2007). These results indicated a fairly high level of stability, which was similar across varying durations. A meta-analysis of twenty-four of these studies showed that the overall stability of attachment patterns within adulthood (.54) was higher than in childhood (.39). Consistent with this, the longitudinal studies highlighted earlier generally provide evidence for "lawful discontinuities" between attachment patterns at infancy versus adulthood. In most cases attachment-relevant stressful life events (e.g., death of a parent, parental divorce, abuse, parental substance abuse, maternal depression) could be linked to the change in a person's attachment style (Grossmann et al., 2005).

Psychopathology. Attachment theory has been concerned with psychopathology from its inception. Bowlby (1944) developed the framework for attachment theory in an effort to explain the link between early emotional deprivation and later psychopathology among thieves. It is fundamentally a theory of both normal development and psychopathology. Normal development and psychopathology are both conceptualized as dynamic processes that turn "at each and every stage of the journey on an interaction between the organism as it has developed up to that moment and the environment in which it then finds itself" (Bowlby, 1982, p. 364).

Bowlby's (1973) railway model of multiple developmental pathways provides a conceptual framework for his ideas about how prior experience and current events interact to shape psychopathology. Several ideas embedded in this railway model are relevant to understanding psychopathology from an attachment theory perspective (Egeland & Carlson, 2004). First, there is a lot of variation within normal functioning. Second, certain developmental pathways represent failures to adapt, which increase the likelihood of later psychopathology. These pathways, associated with variations of insecure attachment, are not defined as psychopathology per se, but rather function as risk factors for psychopathology. The outcomes of a given pathway are multidetermined; some individuals may develop psychopathology and others may not. Early pathways do not determine the final outcome (such as a particular form of psychopathology) but rather initiate a set of possibilities with certain constraints. Third, psychopathology results from a series of maladaptations that center around deficits in affect regulation (Schore, 2003). Fourth, as noted earlier, change is possible at any point along the developmental pathway, although it is constrained by prior maladaptation. Thus, future psychopathology can never be perfectly predicted solely on the basis of an individual's developmental trajectory, because that trajectory is a complex dynamic process that unfolds over time in a nonlinear manner.

Still, there are deep associations between attachment, maladaptation and specific psychopathologies. In addition to research that consistently demonstrates a relationship between higher levels of attachment security and lower levels of negative affect and psychiatric symptoms, a significant literature now exists linking attachment patterns to specific psychopathologies. Studies have investigated the association between attachment patterns and (1) affective disorders, (2) trauma, PTSD and dissociation, (3) antisocial behavior, (4) personality disorders, (5) schizophrenia, (6) suicidal tendencies and (7) eating disorders. In general, the research has shown theoretically meaningful associations between attachment insecurities and all these forms of psychopathology (Mikulincer & Shaver, 2007). Moreover, the research generally supports the risk factor model; that is, specific attachment insecurities do not lead directly or inevitably to particular disorders. Rather, they increase an individual's vulnerability for a certain range of disorders. However, many other factors (e.g., genetic predisposition, relational environment) play a role in whether a certain disorder ensues.

THE PROCESS OF THERAPEUTIC CHANGE

Before addressing a specific case, we address here the process of therapeutic change from an attachment perspective. First and foremost, attachment-based psychoanalysis assumes that the patient's attachment to the therapist is foundational in the change process. A major difference between classical (e.g., Freudian and ego psychology approaches) and attachment-based psychoanalysis is Bowlby's conviction that the real relationships of early childhood—not internally driven fantasies about them—fundamentally shape personality. Consequently, attachment-based psychoanalysis posits that the real relationship with the therapist, not the patient's fantasy about the therapist, produces change. The relationship with the therapist becomes dyadically regulating, and "by virtue of the felt security generated through such affect-regulating interactions, the therapeutic relationship can provide a context for accessing disavowed or dissociated experiences within the patient. . . . Overall, the relational/emotional/reflective process at the heart of an attachment-focused therapy facilitates the integration of disowned experience, thus fostering in the patient a more coherent and secure sense of self" (Wallin, 2007, pp. 2-3). This manifests, clinically, in the therapist's emphasis on the client's experience of the therapist, and at times the therapist's affective self-disclosure as it pertains to the client. For example, if a client were to tell the therapist that the client felt the therapist was angry at him or her, rather than interpreting this as a projective fantasy about the therapist, the therapist would first consider whether he or she was in reality angry at the client. The therapist would then consider sharing his or her felt sense of the situation with the client.

Another key concept of attachment-based psychoanalysis is the concept that psychological health is the ability to fully experience emotions so that their adaptive contributions to functioning can be maximized. In order to fully experience emotions, one must be able to use significant relationships to help regulate strong affect. Infants and young children, however, do not yet have the affective regulation capacities (either neurologically or mentally) to regulate experiences that are intense or painful. Instead, they use the power of the dyad to coregulate these experiences. Gradually, infants and children learn that others are reliably available to help them regulate strong affects and that they are capable of doing so, and can therefore engage fully in the world, both intra- and interpersonally, with confidence that they will not be overwhelmed.

This concept is manifested very clearly in situations where the presenting problem is depression and the primary symptom is amotivation. From an attachment-based psychoanalytic perspective, the inability to experience all emotions, including positive ones (as in the case of depression), inhibits the patient from utilizing the adaptive contributions of those emotions (e.g., a patient who is unable to fully experience her anger is likely to also have a difficult time finding the energy to set and maintain healthy boundaries). Attachment-based psychoanalysis assumes that children learn that it is safe to experience all of their emotions, and that they will not be overwhelmed by their affective states, through the consistent coregulation in significant attachment relationships.

In contrast, infants who develop insecure attachment relationships are unable to harness the power of the attachment relationship to regulate strong affect. Instead, they must learn to disavow or dissociate certain affective states or experiences to avoid being overwhelmed. From an attachment-based psychoanalytic perspective, pathology is the inability to fully experience emotions or to use significant relationships to regulate affective experiences. Therefore, the goal of therapy from this perspective is to help patients use the therapeutic relationship to regulate strong affect, thereby eliminating the need to avoid or disown certain affective experiences. When patients are able to use the therapeutic relationship for this purpose, they can then safely access all emotional states and maximize the adaptive contributions of such emotions. This experience transforms their attachment style of relating to others, and patients are then able to use other relationships, outside the relationship with their therapist, in a similar way. In turn, this promotes secure, intimate relationships with others.

CHRISTIAN CRITIQUE:
OUR CHRISTIAN THEOLOGICAL TRADITION

Both of us have fairly similar church and theological backgrounds. We will describe our theological tradition in order to provide readers a view of the broad theological vantage point from which we evaluate attachment theory and therapy. Both of us identify as evangelical Christians. Within the evangelical movement, Todd grew up attending Baptist churches and Lauren grew up attending both Baptist and Evangelical Free churches. While Todd has attended a range of conservative evangelical churches, including Presbyterian and community churches, his current church affiliation is Baptist. Lauren considers the Evangelical Free Church to be her current ecclesiological home.

Of course, there is much debate about what it means to be an evangelical Christian, and there are theological differences both between and within the hundreds of denominations that make up the movement. We follow church historian Douglas Sweeney (2005) in his description of evangelical Christianity as "a movement that is rooted in classical Christian orthodoxy, shaped by a largely Protestant understanding of the gospel, and distinguished from other such movements by an eighteenth-century twist" (the eighteenth-century twist referring to the Great Awakening) (p. 24). We are committed to orthodoxy as expressed in the ancient Christian creeds and developed by Reformers such as Luther, Zwingli and Calvin.

As part of the evangelical movement, we are linked to (1) the Reformation in emphasizing salvation through faith in Christ and the authority of Scripture over the institutional authority of the church itself, as in Roman Catholicism, (2) the eighteenth-century Great Awakening in emphasizing a personal conversion experience and sense of identification across denominational lines with anyone who has had a similar conversion experience and holds to a core set of common beliefs, and (3) the modernist-fundamentalist split in maintaining the middle ground (that existed prior to the split) by holding together a conservative doctrine of Scripture on the one hand and engagement in the broader culture and intellectual pursuits on the other hand.

The center of the evangelical movement comprises a number of core theological convictions. There are numerous taxonomies that summarize these core convictions, but we resonate with Alister McGrath's (1995) six "controlling convictions": (1) the supreme authority of Scripture, (2) the majesty of Jesus Christ as incarnate God and Savior, (3) the lordship of the Holy Spirit, (4) the need for personal salvation, (5) the priority of evangelism, and (6) the centrality of the Christian community for spiritual nourishment, fellowship and growth. While evangelicals emphasize their common convictions and corporate mission, there is a broad spectrum of theological views on secondary issues within the very diverse movement that is evangelicalism. Informed by our particular traditions, we hold to the inerrancy of Scripture and to a generally Reformed view of original sin (that because of Adam's sin, all people are born with a corrupted nature and are guilty before God) and soteriology, although we do not hold to the notion of limited atonement. While the image of God is thoroughly marred due to original sin, we believe it is retained after the fall, and is being renewed into the likeness of Christ among believers.

We would also note that neither of us grew up in the Holiness, Pentecostal or charismatic traditions within evangelicalism. Thus, our sensibilities are more oriented to a model of progressive or gradual sanctification, and to God working through natural relational processes that we believe are spiritual in a very real sense. At the same time we would not reduce "spiritual" mechanisms of growth as being strictly psychological (Coe & Hall, 2010). We believe that Christians have very real experiences of God (and not just of internal working models of God) through the Holy Spirit that are transformative. Nonetheless, our belief in an Augustinian-Reformed view of original sin and our psychodynamic background have led us to a depth view of sin (see Coe & Hall, 2010, chap. 14), that is, the view that our sin is pervasive and that we are not always aware of our own sin patterns. Sanctification is, in our view, a very difficult process because it centers on transforming our relational patterns that are not always under our direct control. We see God at work in transforming these relational patterns in human relationships and believe that psychotherapy can play a key role in this endeavor.

Having stated this, we profoundly resonate with the call to personal holiness in this life and to the pursuit of sanctification. Moreover, while we do not hold to the notion of a supernatural "second blessing" from God, and do not personally practice speaking in tongues, we do believe in the importance of *experiencing* God, something that is sometimes underemphasized in our branch of the conservative evangelical movement. All relationships involve experiencing the person with whom you are in relationship. In our view, this holds true for relationship with God as well as with fellow humans. This stems from our particular theological sensibilities, which are oriented broadly toward a trinitarian-relational theological paradigm (Leupp, 2008), which we draw on in the following discussion. This emphasizes a relational view of the *imago Dei* (e.g., Brunner, 1939; Grenz, 2001; Gunton, 1998) as having three components: (1) relational nature of humanity, (2) relational process of sanctification as the renewal of the *imago Dei*, and (3) a relational telos of sanctification as love of God and neighbor. We might then call our theological perspective "relational evangelical theology."

In sum, we are certainly in some sense products of our background in the conservative evangelical movement. This undoubtedly shapes our engagement with attachment theory in general as well as our Christian critique of attachment theory. We hope this will help the reader better understand and evaluate our Christian critique of attachment theory. Our theological tradition brings with it some baggage that we do our best to become aware of and overcome, but it also brings with it the blessing of a rich diversity across cultural and denominational lines held together by a common legacy and spirit that flows from the good news of Jesus Christ.

We turn our attention now to areas of resonance and dissonance between attachment theory and our particular evangelical Christian perspective.

RESONANCE BETWEEN ATTACHMENT THEORY AND
OUR RELATIONAL EVANGELICAL THEOLOGY

We believe that numerous areas of attachment theory and therapy resonate with a Christian worldview and with the relational outlook particular to our evangelical background, including relational nature and the image of God, internal working models, and growth and healing as a relational process.

Relational nature and the imago Dei. The first area of resonance is the most foundational. Attachment theory, taken as a whole, contends that people are fundamentally motivated by and develop in the context of emotionally significant (i.e., attachment) relationships. While Bowlby (1982) adopted an evolutionary psychology framework emphasizing attachment *behavior* that provides selective advantage, he also emphasized the importance of a warm, secure relationship with attachment figures. The scope of subsequent research on attachment theory attests to the centrality of relationships for healthy development in early life and throughout the lifespan.

This relational paradigm of attachment theory resonates deeply with a rich trinitarian theme in Christian theology suggesting that relationality is at the core of what it means to be created in the image of God. An explicitly trinitarian-informed view of the *imago Dei* goes back to Augustine (1991) who described the image of God in human beings as an *imago trinitatis*—an image of the Trinity. The great Reformers Luther and Calvin adopted a generally more relational view of the *imago Dei*, departing from the longstanding view of the *imago Dei* as rationality (Cairns, 1973). With the revival of trinitarian theology during the second half of the twentieth century (Leupp, 2008), a trinitarian-relational view of the *imago Dei* is receiving increasing attention.

The general shift from the rational to the relational view of the *imago Dei* involves a move from finding the image in an analogy of being (i.e., essence, nature, capacities that reside in a person, such as rationality) to an analogy of relation. This line of thought has been carried forward by contemporary theologians such as Stanley Grenz (2001) and Colin Gunton (1998). Gunton, for example, articulates this analogy of relation in a poignant way that has clear connections with attachment theory:

> We are in certain ways analogous to the persons of the Trinity, in particular in being in mutually constitutive relations to other persons. Who and what we are derives not only from our relations to God, our creator, but to those others who have made and continue to make us what we are. Just as Father, Son and Holy Spirit constitute the being of God, so created persons are those who, insofar as they are authentically personal . . . are characterized by subsisting in mutually constitutive relations with one another. . . . To be in the image of God is therefore to be in necessary relation to others so made. . . . The doctrine of the image thus places us in a layered network of relationships, first to God the creator, then to one another, and then to the world in its diversity. (pp. 208-11)

As we can see, a trinitarian-relational view of the *imago Dei* articulates from a theological perspective much of the relational nature we see expressed in attachment theory. Attachment theory has shown that infants who do not become attached experience "failure to thrive" and 10 to 20 percent of these children die (Karen, 1998). Clearly, there is a profound way in which humans need, and are constituted by, relations to attachment figures as well as God. Attachment relationships, more than any other type, shape our identity, sense of self, agency, development and well-being.

The shift to an analogy of relation in the last half of the twentieth century has, almost without exception, been pitted against an analogy of being. W. Norris Clarke (2008) noted that this rich development of the relational aspect of the person has been "suspicious of, or even positively hostile toward the notion of person as *substance*" (p. 4). This represents an understandable but misguided reaction to the classical Aristotelian conceptualization of relations as being *accidental* to human nature rather than *essential*. However, rather than positing the analogy of being and of relation as mutually exclusive, we would suggest that both are intricately

intertwined in a relational view of the *imago Dei* as *being-in-relation*.
Douglas John Hall (1986), for example, contends that just as the triune
God is "Being-in-relationship," humans are "beings-with-God" and
"beings-with-humankind." Extending the thought of Thomas Aquinas,
W. Norris Clarke (2008) developed this line of thought more fully, con-
tending that to be fully human means to be *substance-in-relation*. He
stated that "relationality is a primordial dimension of every real being,
inseparable from its substantiality, just as action is from existence. . . . It
turns out, then, that relationality and substantiality go together as two
distinct but inseparable modes of reality" (p. 14).

On one side of the being-in-relation coin, human beings, as image
bearers, have a nature or essence. Substance is the primary mode that
grounds all else, including relationships. A relationship itself is not iden-
tical to the people who have that relationship. However, rather than ne-
gating human relationality, it turns out that the nature that inheres in the
person-as-substance—the "in-itself" dimension of being—is fundamentally relational. Being-as-substance, in other words, naturally flows into
being-as-relational since relationality is intrinsic to the human substance
(Clarke, 2008). As Hall puts it, "We cannot cease to be beings whose lives
are intended for relationship with God" (p. 144).

On the other side of the being-in-relation coin, it is equally clear that
a person who lacks attachment relationships and other forms of meaningful human connection does not manifest the fullness of what God
intended personhood to be. Research linking insecure attachment and
loss of attachment to all kinds of psychopathology demonstrates this with
painful clarity. Relating to other persons, if given the opportunity, flows
from the very nature of a person as an existent being. While particular
relations with particular people may be "accidental," some form of relations, and especially attachment relationships, are not "accidental" to
personhood, to use Aristotelian language. Rather, relationality constitutes the very nature of the human substance just as the relations of pro-
cession between the three persons of the Trinity are not accidental but
constitutive of the nature of the divine substance (Clarke, 2008). The

reason for this likeness in relational substantiality is that humans are made in the image of the triune God.

We would contend that attachment theory is not only consistent with this view but actually provides a more in-depth understanding of human image bearers as being-in-relation. Attachment theory provides a powerful picture of the innate "toward others" dimension of being that constitutes the in-itself dimension of being (Clarke, 2008). For example, infants inevitably respond to loss of an attachment figure with a predictable sequence of protest, despair and detachment (Bowlby, 1980) because of the in-itself dimension of being. They do not respond in randomly different ways, because humans have a substantive nature that dictates this general response. Losing contact with an attachment figure is painful because the longing for an attachment figure constitutes the very nature of our being. At the same time, this response to loss is equally due to humankind's relational, toward-others dimension of being. If God did not create our being with the impulse to attach to others, loss of physical or emotional contact with an attachment figure would not result in psychological pain. In short, attachment theorists may have put their finger on the most profound aspect of what it means to be made in God's image—*being-in-relation.*

Internal working models. The second point of resonance with our particular evangelical Christian perspective pertains to attachment patterns. The notion that we internalize models of self-in-relation as internal working models parallels numerous relational emphases in Scripture, including the interconnectedness of the body of Christ (1 Cor 12), marital union (Eph 5), abiding in Christ (Jn 15) and the notion that the Holy Spirit takes up residence within believers. The scope of attachment-related research showing that relational experiences become a part of the self as implicit memories, which then influence perception without awareness, fleshes out our vision of the interconnectedness and union in human relationships and the human-God relationship. This human interconnection points to an even more profound union with God as the Holy Spirit resides within the person of the believer. This union goes beyond human relationality (Coe & Hall, 2010), but certainly attachment theory points us in the right direction.

Growth and healing as a relational process. The next three points of resonance are interrelated in addressing development, growth and healing. Attachment theory resonates with a biblical view of sanctification in depicting growth and healing as relational processes. Just as secure attachment develops from responsive and emotionally available caregiving, psychological growth and healing from painful attachment-related experiences also result from secure, responsive and available attachment relationships. Robert Karen (1998) captured this idea beautifully in his summary statement of attachment that we are loved into loving. This parallels the big picture Scripture presents of sanctification as a relational process.

In a foundational sense, sanctification is the renewal of the *imago Dei*, which we believe has been pervasively damaged by the fall. If the image of God signifies being-in-relation, as we have suggested, then sanctification is the renewal of being-in-relation (to God and others). Being-in-relation can only be renewed by relational currency. This is made eminently clear by attachment theory and research indicating that implicit relational knowledge (Process of Change Study Group, 1998) can only be directly impacted by this same kind of relational knowledge or experience (Bucci, 1997). The mechanism of growth and healing is not only relational; it is also a *process*. The scope of the New Testament paints a picture of sanctification as a relational process of conforming to the image of Christ, which is the renewal of the *imago Dei*.

DISSONANCE BETWEEN ATTACHMENT THEORY AND RELATIONAL EVANGELICAL THEOLOGY

When attachment theory is brought into contact with our tradition of evangelical Christian theology, some areas of dissonance also become evident: internalization and original sin, and the naturalistic worldview of attachment theory.

Internalization and original sin. Given the historical context in which he was writing, it is understandable that Bowlby may have underemphasized the role of the child in internalizing experience. Against the dog-matic overemphasis on internal "phantasy," he proposed that infants and children rather straightforwardly internalize their experience of parents (Bowlby, 1980). This emphasis on the relational environment in devel-opment and psychopathology leaves little room for the role of original sin. While it is impossible to isolate the "variance" in development due to original sin, our Christian worldview would suggest all humans are in-clined toward sin from the very beginning of life. As such, it stands to reason that infants and young children bring their proclivity to sin to the processes involved in experiencing, internalizing experience and re-sponding to attachment figures, even if unknowingly. Therefore, even in a perfect relational environment, infants would still develop less-than-perfect internal working models. This relates to the more general trend in psychodynamic psychologies of ignoring the role of sin and moral culpa-bility altogether (Jones & Butman, 2011). In short, an overall shortcoming of attachment theory is its lack of accounting for original sin and sinful acts in the development of insecure attachment and psychopathology.

Naturalistic worldview of evolutionary psychology. Bowlby's (1982) understanding of attachment is rooted in his view of instinctive behavior within an evolutionary framework. Bowlby argued that humans' innate behavioral patterns (instinctive behaviors) resemble that of subhuman species and represent a prototype of other animal species. He concluded that the preponderance of evidence indicates that instinctive behavior, homologous with other species, exists in humans. This naturalistic worldview, in which attachment theory was originally embedded, creates a theory in which relationality is extrinsic. Relationality is, at the end of the day, a means to survival of the species. There is no teleology of which to speak. This is, of course, what we would expect from a theory built on a naturalistic worldview—if it is internally consistent. It is interesting to note that Bowlby explicitly distances himself from a teleological theory in favor of evolutionary theory, and yet throughout his writings he uses the language of design. Moreover, the fact that Bowlby is recurrently led to use teleological language suggests that it is difficult to explain the co-

herent behavioral systems apart from the notion of a relational design
and teleology of human nature. In explaining that function stems from a
system's structure, he notes that this "still leaves the problem of understanding how in living organisms such ingenious structure comes into
existence" (1982, p. 126). This is indeed a problem, and one that we believe
a Christian worldview explains better then a naturalistic worldview.

CASE STUDY: TONY

Given the minimal information provided about Tony, we want to note up
front that we make numerous assumptions in discussing the case. In reality, conceptualizations are always a starting point and should be held
with some measure of tenuousness, constantly subject to reinterpretation
based on new data. For the sake of brevity, we will not articulate the
competing hypotheses that could be generated about Tony within an
attachment-based perspective. Instead, we will identify the major themes
and the most likely hypotheses from an attachment-based perspective.

Conceptualization. Most commonly, the first step of any case conceptualized within an attachment-based psychoanalytic framework is to
identify the patient's attachment style. This is helpful to the clinician in
that it provides a lens through which to understand the patient's present
symptoms and past history, facilitates the identification of relevant
treatment goals, and guides decision making in the room when faced with
complex situations. However, as Wachtel (2010) has pointed out, attachment is always dimensional despite the heuristic value of categorical
language. Therefore, it is not uncommon for patients to present with one
overarching attachment style, but to have a secondary style that emerges
with certain people or when their primary style of relating fails to help
effectively manage strong affect. This appears to be the case with Tony.

Based on the information in the vignette, Tony appears to have a
primary preoccupied style of attachment. Preoccupied attachment in
adults is marked by hyperactivation of the attachment system (including
abandonment threats and signs of distress) and a fear of abandonment.
Tony was spending time monitoring his therapist's reactions, likely

scanning for signs of potential relational abandonment (a demonstration of the hyperactivation of the attachment system). Preoccupied attachment is also marked by difficulty regulating strong affect. Tony's experience of distress is also consistent with a preoccupied attachment style, in that he experiences negative affect as overwhelming and has difficulty regulating it (e.g., "he would collapse into depression and a vague sense of hopelessness"). There is also some indication that Tony experiences a fear of abandonment ("In relationship to others he reported high levels of anxiety as he wondered if he fit in and was acceptable"). This is consistent with a preoccupied style of relating, in which one "feels" rather than "deals" with thoughts and situations (Fosha, 2000).

Tony's history is likewise consistent with a preoccupied attachment style. Inconsistent caregiving has been shown to predict preoccupied attachment (Ainsworth et al., 1978). Tony's mother was only inconsistently available to him; she was sometimes intrusive, thereby creating an overwhelming experience for Tony rather than helping him regulate overwhelming experiences. However, Tony's mother was not always intrusive, and at times it appears that Tony did experience some comfort and regulation from her ("he would frequently seek refuge with her from his father"). Her inconsistent availability likely taught Tony that the most reliable way to get his emotional and relational needs met was by amplifying his signs of distress. Additionally, her intrusion disregarded Tony's developing needs for autonomy, and likely resulted in the implicit belief that he was incapable of being independent, as well as creating an implicit association of independence with relational isolation. Children who develop preoccupied attachment "are filled with self-doubt and fearful of being too independent" (Wallin, 2007, p. 224). Tony's amplification of signs of distress, coupled with his sense of dependency and incompetence, create the overwhelming affective states into which he collapses.

Although Tony wants more closeness in his relationships ("His primary complaint was a sense of disconnection from friends and romantic relationships"), his preoccupied attachment style has made him hypervigilant to possible signs of abandonment. Therefore, Tony tries to rely on himself in isolation to regulate his overwhelming feelings through compulsive masturbation, which he finds self-soothing. Unfortunately, Tony experiences guilt following engagement in masturbation, further reinforcing his belief that he is inadequate to regulate his own feelings and returning him to an overwhelming affective state from which he wishes to escape. This pattern of regulating strong affect with an isolating behavior is understandable but ultimately self-defeating. Tony is not able to get the help he legitimately needs to manage his feelings in relationship, and the negative feelings he experiences after attempts at self-regulation (i.e., masturbation) reinforce his belief that he is incapable of soothing himself appropriately or effectively, further increasing his shame and isolating behavior.

Although Tony's core attachment style seems to be preoccupied, at times he seems to draw upon a more dismissive style, particularly with men. Tony's relationship with his father lacked emotional closeness and created feelings of shame and inadequacy. In order to cope with these feelings, Tony learned to deactivate his relational needs for intimacy with his father and other men, and instead seek connection through displays of power (Tony takes a competitive stance toward others, particularly men). Unfortunately, his competitive stance often serves to drive others away, further reinforcing his belief that men are not available for connection.

Treatment goals. Broadly speaking, the goal of any attachment-based psychoanalytic therapy is to increase the patient's ability to access emotional states and to use significant relationships to regulate those emotional states that are too overwhelming or intense to face alone. In other words, helping patients develop a secure attachment through corrective emotional experience is the ultimate goal of attachment-based psychoanalysis. However, the means to achieving this broad goal varies with the patient's unique attachment style and includes shorter-range goals specific to the various attachment categories. Treatment goals for Tony, or for others with preoccupied attachment styles, would include strengthening his capacity for emotional balance, self-esteem and trust. Hyperactivation of the attachment system is a hallmark of preoccupied attachment, and therefore treatment with Tony should focus on offering him a relationship that offers an alternative to this hyperactivating strategy, namely, a developmentally facilitative relationship (Lyons-Ruth, 1999).

Developmentally facilitative relationships are marked by inclusiveness and a developmental gradient. In other words, they aim to encourage patients to connect to as much of their experience as possible—especially experiences for which original attachment relationships made no room. For Tony, these experiences likely include feelings of anger and rage, autonomy and independence, and a desire for intimacy with men. Developmentally facilitative relationships also have a developmental gradient; the therapist must expect more of patients than they initially feel capable. "Of course we have to meet the patient where [he] is. Yet we usually fail the patient when we're too ready to assume that's as far as [he] can go. Far more helpful is the assumption that the patient is actually capable of feeling and thinking in greater depth than [he] appears to be" (Wallin, 2007, p. 230).

Therefore, it would be important in Tony's treatment to gently encourage him to think about his overwhelming emotions and to refrain from the assumption that Tony is incapable of doing so. Over time, a developmentally facilitative relationship will render Tony's current preoccupied style of relating unnecessary. As he finds that the relationship with his therapist has room for all of his emotional experiences, and that the relationship is capable of helping him regulate those strong feelings, Tony will no longer need to constantly scan his environment for signs of rejection and abandonment, or amplify his signs of distress to ensure his therapist is responsive. Instead, Tony will begin to internalize the felt sense of this therapist as consistently available and attuned to him, and ultimately Tony will have access to this felt sense even outside the physical presence of his therapist.

A second treatment goal pertains to Tony's attachment to God and ability to experience God as personal. Given the frequent casting of God as male and the (often exclusive) use of male pronouns, Tony's image of God is likely to be distinctly male. A significant body of research has demonstrated that attachment to God tends to parallel human attachment relationships (Hall et al., 2009). Therefore, it is unsurprising that Tony experiences a disconnected, distant relationship with God, as it seems to parallel his experience of male relationships, such as the relationship with his father. Tony's history of experiences with his father as rigid and fundamentalist, with little room for grace or differences in the midst of connection, seem to have transferred into his attachment to God. Tony's intense distress following acts of masturbation may indicate feelings of guilt stemming from his experience of male figures as rigid and demeaning. By helping Tony gain access to all of his emotional experiences, including his firsthand, subjective emotional experiences with God, Tony is likely to begin to experience God differently than he currently does, that is to say, as more available for intimacy and connection, and less demeaning and judgmental.

Countertransference. In treatment with Tony the therapist is likely to feel a strong desire to rescue, particularly in light of Tony's overwhelming affect and feelings of helplessness and hopelessness. Tony, associating independence and autonomy with rejection or abandonment, has been unwilling to utilize his own internal resources to regulate his feelings. With such patients the therapist must remain aware of his or her own desire to rescue and be idealized. If this dynamic is enacted, the therapist then has the opportunity to reflect on this with Tony, thereby illuminating new facets of Tony's experience in the context of the relationship with the therapist. Additionally, some countertransference with Tony is also likely to vary by therapist's gender. Tony is more likely to incite feelings of competition in a male therapist and a desire to intrude upon and rescue him in a female therapist as he recreates his initial attachment experiences. This is not to say, however, that Tony would not be capable of experiencing a female therapist similarly to how he has experienced his father, and vice versa.

Attachment-based interventions. While attachment-based psychoanalysis was slower to articulate clinical interventions specific to its perspective, more and more lucid articulations are emerging as more clinicians describe the ways they apply attachment theory. Wallin's (2007) book *Attachment in Psychotherapy*, Fosha's (2000, 2009) Accelerated Experiential-Dynamic Psychotherapy model (AEDP), Lieberman and Van Horn's (2008) Child-Parent Psychotherapy (CPP), and the work of the Process of Change Study Group (1998) are good examples of the burgeoning development of a language to describe the clinical application of attachment theory.

Drawing on such work, we identify five categories into which most interventions in treatment fall in our practice of attachment-based psychoanalysis. Some interventions are common to other forms of psychodynamic psychotherapy, and some are unique to attachment-based psychoanalysis. These are attunement/empathic interventions, relational interventions, reflective interventions, appropriate use of interpretation, and affective self-disclosure.

In treatment of Tony, attuning to his affect may initially seem easy as he presents with "a number of anxiety and depressive symptoms." However, the challenge with preoccupied patients is to empathize with underlying emotions that remain unexpressed verbally. Because of Tony's strong fear of abandonment and implicit belief that autonomy leads to abandonment, Tony is likely to be compliant on the surface, only expressing, for example, emotions that he believes his therapist would be comfortable discussing. However, if the therapist can create a relationship with Tony that includes all of Tony's feelings, even anger and frustration with the therapist, he or she will be providing Tony with the developmentally facilitative relationship needed to transform his attachment style. Thus, while empathy with verbalized statements matters, attunement to Tony's implicit and nonverbalized affective states also matters, perhaps more. It will assure him that the therapist can tolerate all of his emotions and that expression of these states will not result in loss of the relationship. The result will likely be what Fosha calls "positive relational affect" (Fosha, 2000), the positive feeling that results from attunement with an attachment figure, even in the midst of experiencing core painful affect about the self.

Attunement to Tony's underlying emotions presents a rich opportunity for relational interventions through reflection on his relationship with the therapist. Processing interactions between Tony and the therapist will not only help Tony and his therapist understand Tony's behavior in other relationships, but it will also help Tony experience his therapist as tolerant of all of Tony's feelings and affective states, even when Tony perceives them to be potentially threatening to the therapist (e.g., feeling angry at the therapist, disappointed with him or her, etc.).

Because of Tony's preoccupied attachment style, reflective interventions, or helping Tony mentalize about his experience, will likely be more difficult. Tony's tendency toward heightened experiences of distress contributes to his difficulty "harnessing the linguistically oriented left brain's ability to make orderly sense of disorderly experience" (Wallin, 2007, p. 224) and may prevent him from briefly stepping outside of his experience to observe it with the therapist. Since mentalizing requires attention to both one's own mental states and those of others, this is yet another place where balancing Tony's needs for empathy with confidence in his ability to do something new is essential.

The use of interpretation in attachment-based psychoanalysis may be less emphasized than in other forms of psychodynamic psychotherapy. Still, it is important in helping clients make sense of their experience. The therapist offers interpretations mainly in the service of helping Tony develop empathy toward himself and facilitating connection with the therapist. In other words, attachment-based psychoanalysis adopts the view that "the patient needs a relationship more than a reason why" (Wallin, 2007, p. 126). For example, interpretations connecting Tony's inconsistent experience with caregivers to his expectation of abandonment and compulsive coping (i.e., masturbation) would be offered only when they will increase Tony's connection with himself and his therapist. In attachment-based psychoanalysis, interpretations are not offered for their own sake, as insight alone is not sufficient to transform the patient's implicit relational knowledge (Process of Change Study Group, 1998).

Finally, the use of affective self-disclosure in therapy is a hallmark of attachment-based psychoanalytic therapies. Affective self-disclosure involves the explicit and appropriate expression of the therapist's own emotional experience. This type of intervention is particularly critical in creating attunement to the patient's experience. For example, a therapist may share that he or she gets a pit in the stomach whenever Tony describes his interactions with his father at the dinner table that felt demeaning to him. This is an example of a self-disclosure that is affectively resonant with the client's own experience. When the therapist shares his or her experience of Tony's narrative like this, Tony can become more aware of his own internal reactions and increase his confidence that the therapist truly understands and experiences the depth of his pain.

Affective self-disclosure may also take the form of the therapist sharing his or her own experience of the client at a given point in time. For example, as treatment progresses and Tony begins to feel attached to his therapist, he may wonder implicitly whether his therapist ever thinks about him between sessions. In attachment-based psychoanalysis, the therapist, after making the implicit question explicit, would answer the question after exploring the meaning of the question to Tony (e.g., "I do think of you between sessions; I keep you in mind even when you are not here"). The more traditional psychoanalytic response of only exploring Tony's fantasies of what the therapist may be thinking of him (the imagined relationship) is considered less important than exploration of the real relationship between patient and therapist.

In summary, the goal of the therapy with Tony, from this perspective, would be to help Tony experience the therapist as consistently attuned, available and open on an emotional level. All of this requires the development of an attachment relationship by attuning to Tony's affect moment-to-moment, maintaining positive relational affect, facilitating discussion of the relationship (between the therapist and Tony), offering empathic interpretations that simultaneously help Tony make sense of his experience and "feel felt" (Siegel, 2012), and using affective self-disclosure. All of these let Tony know he affects the therapist, who is attached to Tony as a caregiver. The hope is that Tony would develop an increasingly secure internal working model, intimate relationships, and an overall sense of emotional and spiritual well-being.

CONCLUSION

Attachment theory has grown tremendously since its inception in the 1940s and has recently been applied more explicitly to the therapeutic process. Now that the theoretical model has been adopted within clinical practice, a distinct modality is beginning to emerge. Within attachment theory, psychological health is the ability to fully experience emotions so that their adaptive contributions to functioning can be maximized. In order to fully experience emotions, one must be able to use significant relationships to help regulate strong affect. Pathology, on the other hand, is the inability to fully experience emotions or to use significant relationships to regulate affective experiences. Therefore, the goal of therapy from an attachment perspective is to help patients use the therapeutic relationship to regulate strong affect, thereby eliminating the need to avoid or disown certain affective experiences. When patients are able to use the therapeutic relationship for this purpose, they can then safely access all emotional states and maximize the adaptive contributions of such emotions.

With this understanding of pathology/health, an attachment-based psychoanalytic modality believes that the patient's attachment to the therapist is primary in the change process. The common interventions implemented by therapists therefore focus on the patient-therapist relationship and include attunement/empathic interventions, relational interventions, reflective interventions, appropriate use of interpretation and affective self-disclosure. Examples of these interventions were given in the context of the case of Tony, which also demonstrated application of adult-attachment categories (e.g., dismissive, preoccupied).

Although it is our belief that attachment-based psychoanalysis can be easily and deeply integrated with Christian beliefs, there remain some points of dissonance, including the exclusive emphasis on environmental factors in the development of pathology (i.e., no discussion of original sin), the naturalistic worldview that is assumed, and the location of relationality as extrinsic rather than intrinsic to personhood. Despite these points, we believe the points of resonance between attachment-based

psychoanalysis and Christianity are much more significant. These include the essentially relational paradigm of attachment theory, which
corresponds well to the image of God in human beings and the view of
growth and healing as a relational process. It is our hope that we have
described and then demonstrated these points in our case study, and we
are eager to see the new directions that will emerge as Christian scholars
continue to engage with attachment-based psychoanalysis.

9

Psychoanalytic Couples Therapy

An Introduction and Integration

Earl D. Bland

Couples therapy takes courage! Wading into the morass of conflicted relational experience is often daunting, even for the most seasoned clinicians. The contrasting force of divergent individual priorities in the midst
of mutual longing for connection and understanding strains the immediacy of therapist empathy and highlights the acute pain associated with
witnessing two people hurt each other. Alternatively, patients find it difficult and often shaming to seek help from a therapist. Inviting a stranger
into the intimate machinations of a relationship exposes the interpersonal
inadequacies of both partners and tacitly concretizes the realization of
failure. The sweat of couples work underscores the complicated relational
dynamics involved in maintaining an intimate partnership. Being a couple,
notwithstanding its developmental and evolutionary imperative context,
is the relational fount of profound love, devotion and sacrifice coexisting

with the potential for unmitigated selfishness, domination and derision.

Drawing from more contemporary understandings of self and relational theory, this chapter briefly outlines a psychoanalytic vision of couples work. While there is no singular pathway for conjoint treatment, our field has advanced to the point where we can specify clinical insights and therapeutic strategies that are likely to enhance outcomes. From the psychoanalytic perspective these successful therapeutic approaches purposefully engage patients in the realm of unconscious mental processing and seek to understand the impact of past experience, emotional expression, defensive response patterns, relational/attachment organizations and transference phenomena (Gabbard, 2010; McWilliams, 2004; Shedler, 2010). In the context of couples treatment we enlarge our consideration of these psychoanalytic concepts to include the notion of couple transference enactments, the need for increased therapist activity in treatment sessions, sensitivity to triadic relational patterns, and complex defensive schemes that activate in the object relational fields unique to each couple (Bagnini, 2012; Gerson, 2001; Greenbaum, 1983; Pizer, 2008; Ringstrom, 2012; Scharff & Scharff, 1991; Zeitner, 2012). Using case material, two coexisting and interrelated priorities for couples treatment are considered in this chapter: (1) the need to understand and address emotional processing within the couple interactions, and (2) the nature and function of defensive activities that emerge from these transactions. Following this orienting discussion is a more pragmatic outline of strategies one might use in psychoanalytically oriented couples work. Before ending I discuss the aim of marital work within the Christian imagination of marriage as wholeness and surrender.

Before jumping into our main discussion I want to identify a few assumptions I make about the couple/marital therapy process. These are underlying value assumptions that help set general parameters for my work with couples. Rather than reason through the validity of these underlying assumptions I offer them simply as markers of the cultural, religious and philosophical perspectives that shape my clinical work and theoretical preferences. To begin, I assume that humans were created for relational engagement, not just as social beings requiring communal association but a deeper connective intimacy that is primarily achieved in the fidelity of dyadic monogamy. Moreover, this intrinsic relationality carries distinct properties that challenge, alter, enhance or degrade our psychological processes and experience of self. Second, I lean toward broad gender egalitarianism. I see no essential ontological distinction between men and women despite unique biological characteristics. Notwithstanding the inextricable influence of biology on the shaping of one's psyche and behavior, ascribed or prescribed cultural roles do not exist as indispensible categories. These sociohistorical and ingrained psychological, behavioral and relational identity patterns are subject to alteration and correction depending on particular demands of a given sociocultural context. Finally, I expect and embrace the dialectical tension inherent in intimate relationships between self-oriented motives and those that emphasize the other. There is no hard line clearly demarcating self-oriented from other-oriented intentions and actions, because most relational exchanges contain a plurality of motives. However, the assumption holds that the vicissitudes of relational engagement require a reasonably stable sense of self that is able to sustain a fair amount of psychological and relational flexibility if one expects to experience enduring and satisfying intimate connections (Blatt & Luyten, 2009; Luyten & Blatt, 2013). As James Fisher (1999) argues,

> The capacity to pursue the truth of one's own experience and also tolerate the truth of another's experience, acknowledging and taking in the meaning of the other's experience without losing the meaning of one's own, especially when these experiences not only differ but conflict, is a major developmental achievement. (p. 56)

RON AND BETH

Ron was angry, lost, depressed and scared. He began treatment after seeing a therapist one time with his wife, Beth.[1] The therapist promptly

---

[1] In any case discussion one must decide which aspects of the total treatment narrative are most relevant to the discussion at hand. At some risk, I present an incomplete story of my work with Ron and Beth and hope it will serve as a useful illustration for the ideas contained in the chapter. Ron and Beth have graciously allowed me to discuss their marriage and treatment in hopes that it may help other couples. I have deep respect and affection for both of

diagnosed him as narcissistic and referred him for individual work. Initially Ron masked his inner turmoil and talked with animation about his life experiences and successes in an engaging, funny and loquacious manner. Sessions were a mixture of stories about his daily life and past accomplishments punctuated by expressions of frustration and anger at his wife. His intermittent admissions of loneliness, helplessness and uncertainty about his worth and importance reflected an inner self-doubt he strived hard to conceal. Ostensibly in therapy to work on his marriage of thirty-two years by fixing his own emotional life, Ron quickly formed an alliance and seemed to enjoy having a place to talk about his inner world without being edited or demeaned. Although many topics highlighted the initial treatment, one of the main dynamics that emerged was Ron's reluctant fear of vulnerable emotional engagement. He desperately wanted to be closer to his wife, but often approached her in a contradictory controlling or denigrating style mixed with frustration and timid acquiescence, which belied any desire to connect. Conversely, he repeatedly felt attacked, blamed and unappreciated, feelings that left him searching for external validation from friends or even random acquaintances with whom he would engage in conversation or flirtatious banter. "How come all these other people think I'm great? They really want to spend time with me, but my wife doesn't want to be around me." Statements like this were frequent in the first years of treatment as Ron struggled to understand his emotional life in relation to his wife. Why was she so scary and difficult to talk to?

In many ways Beth was indifferent. After years of emotional ups and downs she had found a sense of detachment that allowed her greater freedom to live life on her own terms. The veteran of two bouts with major depression, Beth tended to be wary of emotional sentiment and chose to impound feelings of sadness, loss and vulnerability behind a somewhat dispassionate attitude that served to protect her from hurt and disap-

---

them, and it is important to note that Ron and Beth, individually and as a couple, are much more complex, dynamic and compelling than I am able to portray in the two-dimensional world of the printed page. I have altered identifying information and details, although their story essentially remains intact.

pointment. Tired of the endless self-sacrifice she experienced in her efforts to maintain family cohesion amid the emotional turmoil in her marriage, she warily joined Ron in marital therapy. Unsure about the prospects for change, Beth was matter-of-fact in her exchanges with Ron and with me. She viewed Ron as self-centered and was reluctant to feed his hunger for affirmation and sex, especially because she experienced his attempts at intimacy as one-sided, with little attention paid to her needs for tender affection and shared time. Beth also harbored feelings of hurt and anger regarding Ron's past behavior, in particular several years when Ron was drinking heavily, ignoring or verbally injuring the family, and blatantly flirting with other women. In treatment Beth consciously resisted moving from her self-protective stance, or even exploring the nature of her hurt and distress for fear of reawakening her loneliness and longing for connection. She did not want to be hurt by Ron again. Although the insulated safety of her detached emotional stance was not satisfying, it was better than unrequited need and vulnerability.

EMOTIONS AND PSYCHOANALYTIC COUPLE THERAPY

Encompassing cognitive, behavioral and physiological processes, emotions are the currency of relationships and psychological life (Siegel, 2012). Specifically for couples, we are interested in the function of emotions within two interrelated and coacting relational dynamics associated with attachment—security and intimacy. Developmentally, our first psychic response to perceptual input involves the embodied emotional appraisal system that automatically discriminates a bad or good emotional valence and the determination of danger and safety. Dedicated neurobiological and motivational systems then allow us to mobilize a complex web of meaning and value discriminations using information from the body, external sensory input and representations of prior experience (Lindquist, Wager, Kober, Bliss-Moreau & Barrett, 2012). Relationally mediated, these primary or core affective arousal experiences are regulated and categorized into discreet emotional states through intersubjective developmental engagements (Lyons-Ruth, 2006; Porges, 2009;

Siegel, 2012). More specifically, in childhood the quality of relational attachments and affective attunement interacts with contextual factors and biogenetic proclivities to organize emotional experiences into predictable response configurations involving unconscious evaluations, conscious emotional awareness, behavioral and physiological responses, and procedural/episodic memory patterns (Fonagy, Gergely, Jurist & Target, 2002; Sroufe, 2005; Thelen & Smith, 1994; Tronick & Beeghly, 2011). The degree of emotional sophistication and effective regulation is largely shaped by the quality of these early attachments (Blair & Raver, 2012). In addition, a fundamental sense of self emerges through the patterns of our affect regulation (Schore, 2003). We come to know ourselves and experience a sense of intimacy, security and resilience through self-regulating strategies and the tempering effects of caring relationships (Beebe & Lachman, 1988, 1998). In couples, depending on relationship longevity and the nature of individual and shared dynamics, these early patterns are reinforced, elaborated, modified or extinguished by the complex relational situation, not totally dissimilar to processes found in the early attachment environment (Dicks, 1967; Feld, 2004). Difficulties arise in couple connectedness when one or both partners fail to understand and regulate their own negative emotional experience or repeatedly fall short of empathic attunement to their partner's emotional life, both critical skills in interpersonal exchanges (Lavner & Bradbury, 2011). In times of distress partners seek safety and comfort. For positive experiences, it is a shared amplification of euphoric emotion that one desires. Spouses who fail to provide and sustain adequate responsiveness for the purpose of strengthening, moderating or holding the emotional life of their partner experience significant gaps in emotional intimacy and relational safety. Couples' sense of connectedness (Giest, 2008) or "feeling felt" (Siegel, 2012, p. 176) may diminish and trigger longstanding procedural responses in the form of entrenched behavioral repertoires or couple states involving escalated conflict, painful withdrawal or protective attacking.

To work with Ron and Beth we recognize that couples treatment has moved beyond the simple application of behavioral and communication strategies as the primary means for solving intractable conflict and fractious relational bonds. While it is true that both Ron and Beth need to engage with direct communication, harness reflective listening skills, use soft startups, improve timing, be open to influence, and avoid assumptions of intent, these more apparent relationship skills are stultified, not because of gross ignorance or lack of skill, but due to emotional regulation failure and troublesome latent emotional organizing tendencies of which neither was aware. For Ron the difficulty was not just understanding his emotions but managing them in a manner that allowed him to stay grounded, flexible and self-aware in his conversations with Beth. Ron and Beth both faced the repetition of primary attachment wounds intermixed in a long relationship of ingrained response patterns that elaborated and solidified early destructive patterns. Much of the therapeutic process involved understanding, distinguishing, communicating and altering these confused emotional dynamics.

For Ron, the third of five children, self-regulation of emotion was always a dicey undertaking. Saddled with an overactive sense of curiosity and a tendency toward impulsive action, extroversion and attention seeking, Ron was a high-spirited child. Devoid of energy and time, Ron's parents provided sufficient resources but struggled to sustain an atmosphere of emotional warmth. His mother tended to react with controlling criticism, and his father was prone to frightening rages and physical violence. Ron was punished and frequently shamed regarding his perceived lack of self-control and impulsive tendencies. His kinetic activity was further heightened by a pervasive sense of anxiety regarding his needs for closeness and affirmation. He recalls moments of terror watching his brothers and mother being abused. Expressions of anger were common, intermixed with irregular islands of connection in a sea of emotional neglect. Emerging from this environment Ron found it difficult to manage his emotional life in a manner that allowed for flexible and adaptive responses to intimate relational situations. He acknowledged strong desires to be close to his wife, but primarily saw this as an expression of physical or sexual intimacy. He struggled to adequately read his wife's feeling states and frequently saw her as antagonistic and overly stern. He would often misinterpret her emotional need and respond with jokes or demeaning statements that created an effective distance, and thus recapitulate the experiences of longing and frustration he had during childhood.

For Beth, the youngest of three, emotional safety was achieved by the diminishment of self-desire, need and expressiveness. Bookended by a mother who both directly and implicitly communicated her preference for her other two children, and a father whose affection and care were achieved through active mirroring and an abdication of self-expression, Beth learned to shut out her distinctiveness. In many ways Beth experienced a sheltered and neglectful childhood where male dominance and importance was assumed, and the service of women taken for granted. Cautious and yet charmed by her father, whom she saw as a respite from the more obvious disdain shown by her mother, Beth was a good Catholic girl who reflected the socially proscribed innocence, despite her inner longing for acceptance and connection. Initially captivated by Ron's gregarious and demonstrative nature, Beth was enlivened by his attention and passion. Her well-rehearsed pattern of losing herself and reflecting the other's grandiosity in hopes of some reciprocal recognition of her need for connection and love was once again enacted and unanswered. Over the years Beth's experiences of neglect and hurt fueled a self-protective caution that Ron interpreted as uncaring and abrupt. She was reluctant to move toward Ron with any vulnerability, preferring detached management of his needs in an effort to contain any extreme emotional expression or disruption from Ron.

Ron and Beth's relational difficulties highlight two interrelated areas of emotional processing in couples that are frequent culprits in sustaining intractable conflict: problematic self-regulation of intense emotion and difficulty providing adequate attunement or selfobject responsiveness to the partner's emotional experience (Finkelstein, 1988; Leone, 2008; Livingston, 2007; Shaddock, 2000; Zeitner, 2012). As previously discussed, it is widely accepted that empathy and attunement to the emotional processing of others requires a developmental environment of adequately established affective attachment with a caring other. One learns to distinguish and organize emotional self-states and the feelings and intentions of others through a mutually validating and elaborating affective exchange in the first years of life. Further, the dyadic nature of emotional processing allows for some "mutual mapping" of the other's states of consciousness which in turn influences meaning making (Tronick et al., 1998, p. 296; see also Schore, 2003). Couples need the ability to mutually anticipate, read and empathize with the emotional experience of the other. When this selfobject function works effectively, each person in the couple feels a sense of connection or "felt presence in the other's subjective world" (Geist, 2008, p. 131).

This self-sustaining emotional function of the other within a couple is elaborated and particularized by Zeitner's (2012) concept of the *selfdyad,* which captures the "relationship system—an extension of two individual personalities who have now evolved into an amalgam of revised parts of two selves" (p. 39). Properly understood the selfdyad is an emergent intersubjective psychic reality that reflects patterns of emotional organization unique to each couple. It is not just the selfobject function but also encompasses the relationally derived and maintained attachment features of the couple system that lead to experiences of self-transformation and wholeness. Greater than *you* or *me*, the selfdyad is the *us* that reveals the modification of *you* and *me* as *we* sustain a committed connection over time. As Zeitner points out, a primary psychological reason people enter into committed relationships is that the self is transformed in connection—we experience desired aspects of ourselves in relationship with others, and our partner's self-attributes offer to complete inadequate and underdeveloped aspects of our self-experience. Essentially, we feel like a better version of ourselves when in relationship with a loved and desired other.

To offer an illustration, Ron and Beth were originally attracted to important features of the other that held desired visions of the self, which provided a sense of and hope for completeness. Ron found the admired self in Beth's eyes and a container for his emotional chaos. Beth responded to these projections and needs with aplomb. Not only was she able to help Ron feel desired, but in responding to his attachment style she too felt enlivened by his energetic and positive demeanor. Her depressive calmness felt stable to Ron, while she in turn felt desired and chosen. Further, each belonged to an urban, mid-twentieth-century Catholic community with similarly prescribed idealized role expectancies. For both, imagined and unconscious understandings of marriage were largely in sync.

DEFENSIVE DYNAMICS IN COUPLES TREATMENT

Among the numerous factors that contribute to the deterioration of healthy couple functioning, the main intersubjective culprits are the failure of emotional regulation processes and the activation of insidious defensive or protective organized patterns of relating. Often dormant or consciously suppressed during courtship and commitment phases of a relationship, in the continued pursuit of intimacy and connection, certain relational sequences inevitably trigger deficits in self-functioning and ways of relating (Dicks, 1967; Fairbairn, 1952). As many have pointed out, when you activate a developmental need—say the desire for emotional closeness or tender affection—the forward-edge longing is accompanied by a dread of repeating disappointments and failures that existed in formative relationships related to the experience of the specific longing (Mitchell, 1993; Ornstein, 1991; Tolpin, 2002). These conscious and unconscious relational expectancies continually operate within the relational exchanges of each couple. Depending on the response of each spouse, dread is avoided through various defensive operations marshaled to achieve the desired longing and protect the self from vulnerability

When we talk about these defensive or self-protective processes in couples, we are addressing psychological phenomena that emerge from intersubjective emotional states to produce specific thoughts, perceptions, memories, behavior and verbal responses. Couples ward off painful vulnerability, fears and experiences of fragmentation by withdrawing, detaching or attacking their partner. Of course, all the usual suspects are present when it comes to defensive maneuvers. To varying degrees partners can isolate affect, project internal states onto their partner, deny untoward wishes or motivations, disavow aspects of the self, act out, and engage many other avoidances of emotional or relational interactions. Therapists who treat couples need a deft understanding of the various reasons each partner engages in these strategies and to what end.

More pervasive, however, especially in couple relationships, is the relationally organized entanglement historically described as projective identification. Although the controversy and confusion over this term is well documented and beyond the scope of this chapter, for our purposes I want to remove the moniker "psychological defense" and discuss the phenomenological aspects of this process absent the more controversial and *experience distant* theoretical complications. Essentially, psychoanalytic couple therapists have been trying to figure out the intrapsychic and relational process whereby the *joint marital personality* (Dicks, 1967) or *selfdyad* (Zeitner, 2012) forms and becomes a relatively resilient entity. Beyond the notion of shared interests and similar values or cultural background, what is it that creates so much intimacy and connection as well as anger and conflict? How can these ways of relating coexist over a long period of time in the same couple? I first outline the relational experience and then demonstrate how it applies to Ron and Beth.

In the development of the self there are always unrealized developmental potentials and problematic states of self-expression that may hinder growth and progress. Each person in a couple approaches the relationship with a unique combination of strengths, weaknesses and vulnerabilities related to self-expression and relational functioning. As a person self-organizes vis-à-vis the other, he or she expects certain self and relational experiences. Both partners tend to selectively attend and draw meaning from interactions and internal emotional states that confirm what one presumes will occur. The degree to which these expectancies and self-states are conscious varies significantly, but it is the implicit or unconscious and underdeveloped, deficient or dissociated aspects of the self that tend to create the most problems.

In the formation of a couple, all the previously mentioned factors are at play. When the couple commits to a sustained relationship, various needs, strengths and vulnerabilities are maintained in some form intersubjectively, and interactions are often structured to confirm expectancies. To be more specific, as each couple brings the totality of their self-experience to the relationship, aspects of this experience are enlivened and enhanced in the couple interactions, resulting in greater feelings of closeness and connection. Parts of the self that are desirable find a home in the couple interactions as each person resonates with the other's desired parts. Further, in what feels like an invitation, each spouse exhibits dispositions and attributes that act to complete or compensate for their partner's self-inadequacies or vulnerabilities. For instance, early in the relationship, Ron's social ease and engaging style made him a lively and interesting companion. He was confident and funny, able to see the bright side of almost everything, and he had boundless, optimistic energy. Beth, seeking refuge from a home where acceptance and liveliness were questionable, readily attached to these parts of Ron, especially because they echoed the experience of specialness she felt with her father. Ron wanted to be with her and felt responsible for her. She felt chosen and desired, a prime relational home where she could beat back the fears of undesirability and loneliness. For Ron, Beth's enchantment with his personality and gregarious, active pace was a fresh and self-enhancing answer to the inner rejection and shame he carried from his early caretaking environment. She desired him and reflected his needs for dominance and mastery, and he liked having a person who reflected his need to be desired. In addition she seemed stable and steady, a sharp contrast to his sometimes-chaotic inner emotional experience. Both Ron and Beth were able to accept, hold and enact the projected image of the other. In a positive sense this unconscious relational process binds a couple together with mutuality and a strong sense of completeness, belonging and being known. What was experienced as a deficit or weakness in the self is transformed through the empathic acceptance of the partner, who acts to positively redeem what was once seen as detrimental. Further, each person's strengths are confirmed and admired, increasing one's sense of efficacy and esteem.

Conversely, in a more negative and insidious way, there are aspects of one's self that, when enacted or projected in the relationship, are "experienced as incongruent with aspects of the receiving partner's self" (Zeitner, 2012, p. 38). In other words partners are not able to take in, absorb or reflect certain expectancies of their spouse because they are experienced as alien, too painful and shaming, or resurrections of their own past relational trauma. Often conflict or a retraumatization of each spouse occurs due to this selfobject failure, and the experience of dreaded relational exchanges is repeated. Again, as each person in the couple self-organizes relative to the other, implicit fears and inadequacies are activated through internal and external triggers. Once set in motion the resulting self-state organizations selectively attend and engage in such a way that couple interactions begin to evoke and provoke in each other actions that confirm negative expectancies. Critical to the altercation is each partner's unconscious willingness to enact or participate in the painful exchange. Usually this occurs because spouses embody, to a greater or lesser degree, an echo of the characteristic or relational style so dreaded by their partner. Despite the negative affective valence, each spouse feels justified in his or her self-experience and can't understand why their spouse is acting so hurtful or unreasonable. In many ways these troublesome conflicts that plague so many couples are enacted self-fulfilling prophecies because each unconsciously behaves in a manner that virtually guarantees the replay of old relational scripts (Ringstrom, 2012).

The destructive iteration of this process for Ron and Beth was powerful and acted to undermine their positive linkages. Over time their obstructive relational sequences stabilized and dominated the relationship, serving as a recognizable, albeit painful, intersubjective home. Ron and Beth had been there before; as time progressed and each became involved in the duties of raising a family and establishing a career, life did not seem that abnormal—despite the unhappiness and longing that still existed in the relationship. Beth's routine need for consistent relational connection and stability felt like criticism and nonacceptance to Ron. He felt she was unable to have fun or join him in his enthusiastic search for success and belonging. For her part, Ron's need for affirmation and take-charge style morphed in such a way that Beth now experienced him as self-centered and domineering. She began to see herself as alone again, undesirable to the one who mattered most. In a painful dance Beth's aloofness and Ron's unseasoned empathy protected vulnerable self-states but blocked intimacy and connection.

SUGGESTIONS FOR TREATMENT

In response to the critical function of emotional regulation and defensive processes in the formation of couple distress, the following two thera-peutic strategies are held, inter alia, as springboards for developing a psychoanalytic approach to couples work. These strategies are not tech-niques per se, although they may involve some directive actions. Rather these approaches to the couple should be considered a priori therapeutic outcomes, which, if achieved to an adequate degree, serve to perpetuate healthy couple functioning. Following is an overview of each.

Empathic connection within transference dynamics. Establishing and maintaining a triadic sense of empathy in work with couples is of primary importance. By *triadic* I am referring to the flow of empathy between the therapist and the both persons in the couple, between the therapist and the couple as an entity that emerges from the intersubjective activity of the partners, and the development of empathy between each partner in the couple relationship. As many have pointed out (Brody, 1988; Leone, 2008; Ringstrom, 1994, 2012; Shaddock, 2000; Trop, 1994) couple thera-pists use empathy to gain a perspective from inside the couple. Beyond understanding the subjectivity of each partner, as transferences are en-acted between the couple and therapist, both corporately and individ-ually, the therapist is able to understand and articulate the felt experience of both partners as they function as a couple. Moreover, the tricky problem of overidentification or taking sides is avoided if the therapist is able to empathize with both partners' experience as well as what it is like to feel pulled to one side or the other in the enactment of couple dynamics. To be more specific, couples must believe they are going to get a fair hearing and that no one version of reality is sufficient (Ringstrom, 2012). However, because the pull for taking sides is often significant, I find it useful to explicitly identify the dynamics at play in this fight to win, and to help articulate each partner's experience of vulnerability and dread if their version of truth does not trump.

It is also important that therapists empathically hold the couple as an intersubjective entity that can survive and transcend the high levels of conflict and emotional distancing so prevalent in distressed couples. This is both implicitly communicated through the primacy of joint sessions for treatment and explicitly by communicating to the couple that the relationship is the focus of treatment. Specifically, I see this as a function of the therapist's ability to access and sustain the couple's initial hope and believe that the often-faint glimmers of connectedness can be restored to luminance. While many factors contribute to the success or failure of marriage therapy, I am inclined to agree with Buechler (2004) that a therapist's empathy and relentless desire to understand his or her patients instills a hope that change in the future is possible. Yes, couples must come to grips with disappointment, uncertainty and mystery, especially in the middle phases of therapy where change is incremental if not invisible, but a therapist's indefatigable faith in the therapeutic process encourages couples to experiment with new and more beneficial ways of relating.

The final leg of triadic empathy is the encouragement of mutual attunement and understanding between the partners. The restoration of an empathic selfobject function for each partner is a key objective of any marital treatment. When couples are able to feel understood and sustained by their partner, many conflicts are easier to negotiate (Leone, 2008). Following Trop (1994) I believe this starts during the initial assessment as the therapist models empathy for each person's perspective. During couple assessment and history taking, I want both partners present in order to model empathy for each person's story and to gauge each partner's insights and ability to hold concern and care for the other as he or she talks. The type and degree of emotion activated in each partner while listening to the other's story is important in terms of prognosis and treatment course. Zeitner (2012) believes it is also vital to grasp the courtship narrative of each couple in order to understand the rewarding features of the *selfdyad* that are often responsible for initial attraction and commitment. Within the context of the initial relational exchanges one can measure how and to what degree the relationship has deteriorated. I often find it necessary to offer some suggestions to allow for the development of relational empathy. Depending on the couple, many or few of the following suggestions are communicated at various points in the treatment:

1. Use reflective listening techniques. (Sometimes these must be taught.)

2. Stay on topic without attacking, and limit associations to past events as a means of building a case.

3. Assume your mate is benevolent—don't read intention into his or her actions. (Clearly, when a mate is not benevolent in intention this needs to be addressed.)

4. Avoid absolutist language (always, never) and preferably use *I* statements.

5. Take time-outs to calm emotions. (Awareness training is sometimes necessary.)

6. No turning tables on complaints by accusing the other of similar actions (Pizer, 2008).

7. Practice soft startups and develop repair rituals (Gottman, 1999).

The teaching and encouragement of relationship virtues is not because improved communication is the linchpin to couple change. Rather, in agreement with recent work in the area of emotion-focused therapy (Johnson, 2004) couples must be able to understand and articulate their own feelings at multiple levels and engage the other partner in a manner that allows both to feel understood at multiple emotional levels. This mutual attunement and respect acts to regulate and contain powerful feeling states. The fostering of this deep intimacy and attachment creates the safety needed to sustain vulnerable and honest communication.

Mentalizing the couple. Our second strategy addresses the impaired mentalization many distressed couples experience, making it difficult for spouses to reflect on and apprehend subjective self-states (Fonagy, Gergely, Jurist & Target, 2002). Couples with faulty emotional processing must learn how to psychically represent and communicate the meaning of powerful internal affective experiences. A key feature of marital treatment identified by Ringstrom (2012) is the capacity to reflect on one's own experience in the presence of a partner. As each partner begins to feel accepted and safe within the therapeutic frame, the partners can begin to explore the ways in which each contributes to the perpetuation of conflict and distress. Reflection and reappraisal of the sources of intense emotion act to increase emotional regulation (Webb, Miles & Sheeran, 2012). Further, this perspective taking is a relational act, where players in the relational exchange (therapist, couple and couple-as-selves) are able to look at something (e.g., a relational sequence or emotional state) "where they stand side by side to look at a 'third' thing" (Boston Change Process Study Group, 2010, p. 200). However, effective reflection is only possible by slowing down psychological and emotional processing as a way to thoroughly examine what factors are at play in conflict and distress. Therapists often need to model and encourage curiosity about emotion states to open a pathway for emotions that link with previously unexplained behavior or thought processes. As partners experience this holding of the marital tension, the therapist can encourage a reappraisal of the frustrating spouse and the identification of self-related contributions to the marital problems. Holding each other's view with equal grace and respect is crucial. The goal is to articulate the way in which the couple's interactions evoke and provoke styles or patterns of relating that end up frustrating desires for intimacy and connection.

In many ways this calls for a more active therapeutic style than is characteristic of individual psychoanalytic treatment. Because of the ease and rapidity of conflictual exchanges, therapists must be willing to interrupt couples for the purpose of reflection. In so doing therapists also enter the intersubjective space and willingly reflect on the meaning, timing and nature of their active insertion into the couple system. I often find myself supporting a reflective function and promoting perspective taking when my own emotional state or reaction to the therapeutic material runs counter, or to a different degree of intensity, than one or both members of the couple. Critical to this process is the maintenance of what family therapists have called multidirected partiality (Boszormenyi-Nagy & Krasner, 1986), or the mutual and simultaneous expression of empathy for each person's experience (including the therapist's) while holding its partiality in the total understanding of the couple. If the therapist is successful, partners will feel safe to loosen their grip on the certitude of their own perspective in order to consider the possibility of holding the other's thoughts and experiences as valid and worthy of note. For Sells and Yarhouse (2011), critical to gaining perspective on protracted conflict is the capacity to recognize one's own pain (often unconscious) and how this gets enacted as a "pain between" (p. 93). When couples identify something broken or troublesome in their own and their partner's past or current behavior, reflection and curiosity about its meaning for the relationship can loosen entrenched patterns of blame and attribution.

An excerpt from a session with Ron and Beth will illustrate. This small exchange is taken from a session in the middle stages of our work together. We had been working on Beth identifying what she needs from Ron for her to let down her guard, forgive past actions and reengage him in his pursuit of intimacy. Beth had identified two things: a small gift to symbolize a change in their relationship, and more effort on Ron's part to treat her differently. Ron was hurt that he needed to do anything besides just apologize ("Why can't she just accept me?") and proceeded to question the validity of the whole relationship. Beth responded with a clarification and need:

> BETH. In the past your actions were not loving nor honoring. Our vow has been broken, dismissed, put aside, whatever word you want to put to it. That is extremely hurtful to me. If you can't understand the depth of that hurt, that's good because then you haven't been hurt that badly, I would

guess, but it was an extremely hurtful thing. The fact that it was repeated makes me very hesitant to believe that things will change. I believe you are sorry. I have no problem believing you are sorry, I believe that. I have to believe that things are going to be different; in order for me to believe things will be different I need to see things being different. What you did was wrong, but that doesn't mean your person is wrong.

Ron struggled with this account; he became protective with statements that were intended to minimize the intensity and severity of his previous actions. I briefly intervened and helped him identify his shame and the anxiety about being rejected; he went on to identify some of his fears:

> RON. The problem I have is one I've had for a long time with you. I feel that you predicate our love by external signs and all the things I've bought you. I think things make you happy, but that I don't as a person make you happy, as a husband, as the one you are supposed to be involved with in a relationship. I don't make you happy, but things, external signs apparently make you happy and that's what you desire.

> BETH. Well, let me explain to you what makes me happy. I am happy being married to you, when we are on the same page, when you are affectionate, when we have sex, when you are nice, when you are spontaneous, when you are fun, I'm happy then. I like getting nice things, yes, I like having the gifts that you have given me, that makes me happy, but that's not the only thing that makes me happy. I'm like a little kid, I like Christmas. That doesn't mean that I love you only because you buy me presents.

> RON. Feels like it to me.

> BETH. Well, I don't know how to answer that, but if that were true, why would I stick around when we were broke? If I only wanted you because you could buy me things, why didn't I just say "So long, you have no money and I don't think you ever will, so I'm out of here"?

> RON. Where would you have gone? What would you have done?

> BETH. I could have gone home with my mom and dad.

> RON. Well, the things you said earlier are the things that have died off in me, just all of that stuff has just died, and it's dead.

BETH. Maybe you could revive them.

RON. I don't even feel like I should approach you about sex, because there will be some condition: "Well, if you do this then we can have sex." I say to myself, *I don't want it; I'm not going to buy sex*, and it just drives a wedge between us.

BETH. If the way you feel is true, then why wouldn't I have left, because we were certainly broke.

RON. I don't know. You are the only one who can answer that question. Why didn't you leave?

BETH. Because I love you; I want to be with you.

RON. The way I am now?

BETH. Well, I'm hoping you'll change. (*smiles and chuckles lightly*)

RON. For what? I was bad then, and I'm bad now.

BETH. You are not bad, I keep telling you this.

RON. It'll get worse later.

BETH. You keep thinking because you do something that I don't like, that I don't like you. You can do something wrong without being wrong as a person.

RON. Well, a gift, a symbol? I mean, I can do it. It's not going to mean that much to me to go out and buy you whatever this gift is; I'm not sure what the price tag on the symbolism is that you need. Do you have a price tag or an object?

BETH. No, but I told you, you didn't even have to do that. You can draw a picture, cut out a picture.

RON. I wrote you a love letter but I think you lost it.

BETH. I bet not.

RON. I can write you another one.

BETH. That would be nice.

RON. I'll have to build up to it.

BETH. I'm sorry for that.

RON. That's how I feel.

BETH. Then maybe you have some issues you need to discuss with Earl, because I can't solve those issues.

RON. Maybe. So you are clear in your mind, huh, where you want to go?

BETH. I'm clear in my mind. I'm on my path.

RON. Right, your mind is clear; you want to continue on in this relationship, or you want me to change, some which way or another?

BETH. I would like to be happy in this relationship.

RON. That would be nice.

EARL. Where are you at, Ron? What are you feeling?

RON. There may be hope . . .

EARL. There may be hope . . .

This short excerpt highlights the delicate negotiation of intimacy. Ron wrestles his fears of rejection and self-disparagement in light of Beth's desire to shift her way of engagement. Clearly the distance between them was mutually created and mutually preserved, and the road to intimacy is tentative as each mobilizes underutilized relational skills for affection and vulnerability. This reflective conversation between Ron and Beth allows them to talk about desire and fear, even doubts about the viability of the relationship. What emerges from this brief dialogue is a new possibility for tenderness and connection—a hoped-for future.

As a point of clarification, my work with Ron and Beth had many such exchanges as each attempted to test the possibilities of a new relational dynamic. It was a long road, and important to their eventual success was not just the technical aspects of their communication style or their emotional resilience. Both Ron and Beth are Christians who emerged from a Catholic tradition that views marriage as sacramental. Talk of God and his action in their lives and marriage was not uncommon. At key points in the treatment each was able to identify significant spiritual experiences that helped shift self-protective enactments and liberalize their experience of generosity for the other. As each began to appreciate the other's experience as valid and worthy of note, forgiveness, grace and tenderness increased.

SURRENDER AND WHOLENESS AS THE CHRISTIAN IMAGINATION OF MARRIAGE

I have argued elsewhere (Bland, 2010) that therapeutic marital work is a vehicle for virtue development. The very nature of intimate human interaction calls for vocabularies of kindness, patience, love, courage, forgiveness and many other relational qualities that are necessary if one is to have a successful marriage or intimate partnership. As a spiritual formation process, deep intimacy involving emotional and sexual union is a pathway to betterment and greater developmental wholeness. Couples embody a trinitarian understanding of the *imago Dei* as fundamentally relational. As Westermann (1974) argues, humans do not find the true meaning of life in their mere existence. The creation narrative, which specifically identifies the relational need of human beings: "it is not good for the man to be alone" (Gen 2:18), sets the intimate bonding of two people as a core analogue of the divine image. Moreover, two persons joined in a committed marital attachment reveal the manner of God's pursuit and care for his human creation (Grenz, 2001). Marriage and sustained intimate partnerships enact and reflect the nature of God and his action in the world. To be more specific, surrender to the relational core of one's self is to surrender to the image of Christ. As a model, marriage or couple relationships of a deep, intimate variety activate the inner relational capacities needed for the ability to lose one's self in Christ. Marriage is an identification with both sides of the divine-human exchange: the power to love in a way that echoes divine love, and the opportunity to experience grace and love as transformative acts when shared in the manner of our Creator. When enacted in couple relationships, the image of God surges with forgiveness and perseverance through conflict, the unyielding optimism of redemption in the face of failure and error, the surrender of domination, the pursuit of peace as a relational home, and a loving celebration of the other.

For its part, psychoanalytic couples therapy provides a needed corrective to the sustained pressures couples face in modern life. This form of treatment creates opportunities to examine the privation of virtue in couple relationships and to explore the Christian imagination of an intimacy where each is fully surrendered to the other. Following after Christ in one's relationship is not about the assertion of rights or self but the mutual loss of self to the wholeness and completeness of relational connection, which reflects the *perichoretic* entanglement of our God, "of endless mutuality of relationship between equals" (Holmes, 2012, p. 26).

But how do we get there? In this psychoanalytic contribution to marriage literature, I have sketched a path to greater relational fulfillment through the attainment of effective management of emotions and a capacity to meaningfully reflect on one's relational process for the combined purpose of increased freedom regarding one's actions in a relationship and the advancement of mutual respect and dignity. Lasting relationships that have the potential for deep intimacy and the fulfillment of one's deepest attachment longings can only be achieved within a mutually committed relationship where self-differentiation and distinction finds its zenith in the surrender of its right to exist. This is not a utopian vision, because its achievement requires attention to the granular, moment-to-moment interactions of the couple, who must come to wrestle with their own conscious and unconscious relational expectations and fears, many of which run counter to deep connectedness. Obdurate conflict occurs within the activated terrors of reprisal, alienation or destruction, and is only resolved when both partners surrender their *rightness* to allow sufficient room to reflect on their partner as a subject. The task is to understand and manage emotion for the purpose of building a "nascent curiosity about their mate's subjectivity (their unique way of experiencing the world and their unique perspective on it)" (Ringstrom, 2012, p. 89). As each partner's curiosity blossoms to the point of mutual recognition, both partners can experience the spouse not only as a selfobject—one who provides needed connectedness for the sustenance and enhancement of self—but as "another mind who can be 'felt with,' yet has a distinct separate center of feeling and perception" (Benjamin, 2004, p. 5; see also Zeitner, 2012).

Yet there can be no mutual recognition without mutual surrender (Hoffman, 2011). In couples the difficulty with mutual surrender is often related to confusion with what Ghent (1990) calls submission or the subordination of self to the dominance of another. For mutual surrender to be transformative there must be open authenticity and clear expression, a sense where each partner in the couple is allowed full access to their own self-experience. The emerging confidence in these exchanges allows each person to be fully present without the threat of losing the self when their partner's self asserts temporary prominence. A continual stream of grace supplants worries about hierarchy; the goal is *knowing* and *being known.*

10

Brief Dynamic Psychotherapy

Michael W. Mangis

If one were to build an understanding of psychoanalysis from undergraduate textbooks and introductory courses, it would be easy to assume that psychoanalytic psychotherapists are like buffalo: they certainly exist somewhere but not in the strength of numbers that they once enjoyed. Much of the reason for this misconception comes from the false assumption that psychoanalytic psychotherapy is always an open-ended, long-term process available only to the wealthy.

Fortunately, in this age of managed care and evidence-based treatments, psychoanalytic psychotherapy has matured so that strong models of brief psychodynamic psychotherapy are available for the practitioner. Shedler (2006) has traced the changes in psychoanalytic therapies from the classical five-times-a-week-on-the-couch, long-term, structural model to contemporary, more realistic models. He has noted the disservice that undergraduate textbooks and professors do by introducing psychoanalysis in its most archaic form.

HISTORY AND THEORISTS

Although brief models of psychoanalytic psychotherapy are not a separate school per se, they do warrant attention, especially in light of the previously mentioned stereotypes. Several authors have provided excellent summaries of the history of brief psychodynamic psychotherapy (e.g., Bauer & Kobos, 1987; Horowitz, Marmar, Krupnick, Wilner, Kaltreider & Wallerstein, 1997; Levenson, 2010). Most histories begin by mentioning that several of Sigmund Freud's first cases were short-term, though not necessarily by design. Freud's intimate friend Sandor Ferenczi provided the first step toward brief models by advocating an active and directive role for the therapist as opposed to Freud's passive, open-ended approach. In Freud's original thinking the analyst was an objective scientist, an archaeologist painstakingly uncovering and addressing the patient's problems of infantile sexuality and unresolved Oedipal conflicts. This process necessarily required multiple sessions per week extended over several years. As the assumptions about these purposes of analysis evolved, so did the assumptions about its length and intensity. Although the terms *psychodynamic* and *psychoanalytic* are often used interchangeably, *psychodynamic* has generally evolved to mean treatments that do not rely on a couch or on multiple sessions per week over several years. The evolution of brief psychodynamic therapy can be seen as the gradual breaking of these and other psychoanalytic taboos (Levenson, 2010).

The most significant movement toward brief dynamic models of psychotherapy came with the advent of attachment theory and its impact on psychotherapy in general. The movement away from classical drive theory toward relational and interpersonal theories has been, in part, motivated by the simple fact that most patients do not want and cannot afford to see an analyst several times a week for several years. In response, various psychoanalytic practitioners have developed more focused processes to benefit patients who want to address specific problems in lieu of extended analysis (Chernus, 1983; Ornstein & Ornstein, 1997). Contemporary, brief-model theorists such as Basch (1995) and Levenson (2010) would argue that by forsaking long-term intensive psychoanalysis patients are not missing out on the benefits of psychodynamic psychotherapy. Meta-analysis of the research literature supports this conclusion, first by showing that virtually all psychodynamic therapists do short-term therapy, and second by demonstrating that patients receiving short-term psycho-dynamic therapy maintain their therapeutic gains and, in fact, continue to improve after therapy ends (Safran, 2002; Shedler, 2010).

While many aspects of brief dynamic psychotherapy differ from classical psychoanalysis, the biggest difference is probably in the attitudes of the therapist toward the process. This brief model moves away from any idea of detached therapeutic neutrality toward an active and involved attachment. This move is not simply a function of the postmodern hermeneutic turn from objective neutrality to intersubjectivity, but it also reflects an attitude change in the role of the therapist and in the very principles that define psychotherapy.

Contemporary brief psychodynamic psychotherapy does not simply give lip service to the current intersubjective zeitgeist; it fundamentally relies on it. A brief dynamic model starts with the assumption that every person, and therefore every patient, is motivated not by drive satisfaction but by the desire for attachment to healthy objects. This is of central importance because, whereas the drives of infantile sexuality and unresolved Oedipal conflict are hidden in the deep recesses of the unconscious, invulnerable by direct assault, an individual's patterns of relationship are current and open to observation, insight and experiential change. While more classical models of psychoanalysis sometimes required the analyst to frustrate the patient's desire for comfort, encouragement and mirroring, brief dynamic therapy allows for greater mutuality between therapist and patient.

Developmental maturity, in this perspective, is measured by the individual's patterns of relating. Although patients may be resistant to seeing and changing them, these cyclical relational patterns are quite evident in their current lives and in their history. Healthy, loving attachments provide the individual with an image of the self as seen through the eyes of the object: valued, competent and supported by caring relationships.

Patients come to therapy because this healthy sense of self has been hindered by early attachment failures that have led to the compulsive repetition of those failures through cyclical patterns of relating to others. Change comes in therapy when these maladaptive cycles are broken, enabling the patient to internalize a new sense of self as valued, competent and supported, which then leads them to develop more healthy relationships, forming new relational cycles.

The roles of transference and countertransference are dramatically different in brief dynamic psychotherapy from what they are in psychoanalysis. Whereas transference was previously something to be interpreted and eliminated, following contemporary relational models transference is now both expected and welcomed as the only reliable means by which the patient can teach the therapist about his or her internal world (Safran, 2002). Likewise, countertransference, once considered a taboo sign of the analyst's own uncompleted analysis, is viewed by brief dynamic therapists as an inevitable and invaluable guide to the internal world of the patient. While therapeutic objectivity was traditionally defined as the absence of the therapist's own experience corrupting the sterile surgical field of analysis, the brief dynamic therapist defines therapeutic objectivity as the capacity not to eliminate or step completely clear of his or her own experience, but to step beside it with just enough distance to observe it and to be curious about it. In other words, the brief therapist seeks a new kind of objectivity, not the ability to be free from feelings, fantasies or reactions in relation to the patient, but rather the capacity to be fearless, honest and thorough in observing, recording and understanding these reactions.

TECHNIQUE

Brief psychodynamic psychotherapy differs from psychoanalysis in its techniques.

Metacommunication. While all psychoanalytic psychotherapies seek to bring the patient's unconscious into consciousness, brief psychodynamic psychotherapies go further, bringing the unconscious and nonverbal communication of both the therapist and the patient to light. Empathic interpretation of needs, emotions and experience broadens the perspective as the therapist actively and consistently shares his or her understanding of what experiences and emotions mean to the patient (Gardner, 2000).

Immediacy. The therapist frequently uses immediacy to talk about the patient's life and relationships through the lens of what is happening in the office at the current moment. For example, in accelerated experiential-dynamic psychotherapy (AEDP) Diana Fosha (2000) argues for the intensification of the therapeutic relationship, both positive and negative elements, to allow for collaborative processing of here-and-now relational experiences. Asking patients: "How do you feel here with me? and What's your sense of me? (or How do you experience me?)" (p. 220) are standard questions that aim to enhance immediate reflection on the patient's explicit and implicit emotional processes.

Use of patient's strengths. Even though most patients do not feel very strong when they enter a therapist's office, brief psychodynamic models count on the presence of healthy sectors in the patient's sense of self that can be accessed to encourage growth and problem resolution. A patient's ability to "self-right" (Fosshage, Lachmann & Lichtenberg, 1992) plays a key role in addressing problems within time-limited therapy. Along with understanding a patient's struggles, brief-oriented therapists look for ways the patient has adapted to problems or difficult circumstances in the past. Identifying relationship resources or healthy ways of thinking and emotional processing that already exist for the patient allows for the creative exploration of how these strengths can be applied to current situations (Basch, 1995; Gardner, 2000).

Self-disclosure. Self-disclosure, anathema to some models of psychoanalysis, is necessary from a brief psychodynamic perspective. While therapists do not necessarily disclose personal information about themselves, they do disclose their experience of the patient and of the relationship, enabling the patient to experience empathic attunement and to develop insight into cyclical relational patterns that have been reproduced in the therapeutic relationship. The therapist is particularly attentive to these repetitions in order to break from the patient's usual maladaptive cycle, providing the patient with the new experience of how satisfying relationships can be.

Brief psychodynamic psychotherapy is more eclectic than psychoanalysis, allowing for techniques from other theoretical perspectives to assist in the process of change. In this way, a distinction is made between conceptualization and treatment. While the therapist understands the patient's problems of living in light of attachment difficulties and unhealthy cyclical relationship patterns, the therapist does not assume a passive, nondirective role, and may use methods outside the traditional psychoanalytic toolbox. Other evidence-based treatments can easily be utilized to bring both relief of symptoms and lasting change.

Time limitations. Whereas psychoanalysis remains open-ended, continuing until the analysis is "complete," brief psychodynamic psychotherapy relies on time constraints to condense the process. Some theorists set the termination date from the very beginning (e.g., Strupp & Binder, 1985; Bauer & Kobos, 1987), while others adapt to the limitations established by managed healthcare or the patient's expectations. For Mann (1973) brief psychoanalytic treatment assumes the power of a short termination horizon to drive the treatment. He proposes we use the limited time to highlight conflicts related to separation/individuation. Mann suggests four neurotic conflicts common to all patients (independence versus dependence, activity versus passivity, adequate versus inadequate self-esteem, and unresolved or delayed grief), each requiring a mastery of the separation/individuation process. A predetermined number of sessions heighten the likelihood such core conflicts will quickly be demonstrated, allowing the therapist and patient to move toward understanding and resolution in a shorter period of time. While all psychoanalytically oriented therapies trust the process to bring about the patient's necessary healing, brief psychodynamic psychotherapy trusts that the patient's unconscious motivation for change and healthy attachment will lead the patient to fit the process into the time frame that is available. With these brief therapies, patients are seen to develop the necessary transference more quickly than with open-ended therapies. This enables them to quickly reproduce their maladaptive relational patterns within the therapy context. The therapist may then observe this repetition and provide the patient the opportunity to both insightfully take note of the cycle and experientially choose a new way of relating. As termination approaches, patients in brief psychodynamic therapy experience optimal anxiety, motivating them to both consciously and unconsciously resolve their attachment expectations with the therapist.

CHRISTIAN CRITIQUE

Contemporary psychodynamic theory has proven to be a rich field for the integration of psychology and Christian faith, as evidenced by the fact that much, if not most, of the integration literature of the past several decades has been from a psychodynamic perspective. As noted in chapter two, it is important to articulate an integrative perspective and its roots in a particular theological tradition.

My own theological tradition is evangelicalism, with roots in the very Arminian, even semi-Pelagian, fundamentalist church of my upbringing. I have gravitated from those roots to a much more Reformed perspective and a greater appreciation for the sovereignty of God. I will articulate what I believe to be points of resonance and dissonance of this theological perspective with contemporary psychodynamic theory.

Evangelical theology resonates with contemporary psychodynamic theory in its relational view of humans. The *imago Dei*, the image of God in which humans are created, is generally thought by evangelical theologians to be our relational nature, just as God the Trinity is relational. Just as a therapist helps the patient to trace her relational history back to early attachments, the relational history between God and humanity can be traced back to the disharmony caused by sin in the Garden of Eden.

Evangelical theology comes to dissonance with psychodynamic theory in several areas. The first point of dissonance occurs around the postmodern hermeneutic of suspicion. Evangelical thought is founded in the authority of Holy Scripture and in the access of individuals to the truths of Scripture without an ecclesiastical intermediary. The psychodynamic supposition that all human experience is filtered through lenses that are distorted by unconscious fears and desires does not sit well with evangelical thought. Many within this tradition would like to believe that these limitations do not apply to an individual's interpretation of Scripture, and to suggest otherwise sounds to them like a slippery slope leading to relativism. Such extremes are not necessary. It is possible to humbly acknowledge the limitations of our perspective without abandoning our confidence in an authoritative truth (Mangis, 1999).

Integrative tension for evangelical theology and psychodynamic thought is also found in the contrast between sin and sickness. Psychodynamic theory looks for the source of human foibles in unmet relational needs and disrupted attachment dynamics, which can lead to a diminished sense of personal responsibility. An evangelical theological perspective is resistant to the placement of responsibility for sin upon anything but the individual will. The psychodynamic understanding of psychological defenses and their impact on individual choice, however, actually has much to contribute to a theological understanding of sin. Elsewhere, I have discussed the contribution of an intrapsychic understanding of sin to Christian spiritual formation (Mangis, 2008).

Finally, in regard to Christian critique, many evangelical Christians are resistant to psychodynamic theory's insistence that, because of the power differential caused by transference, the therapist must refrain from disclosing personal values that the patient might then adopt out of fear of rejection or abandonment. The heart of evangelicalism lies in the belief that all people should hear the gospel, and restraints from such sharing are resisted. This struggle is not unique to psychodynamic theory, however, and remains an ethical dilemma for Christian therapists of any theoretical orientation.

CASE STUDY: TONY

Tony's case presents several interesting points for elaborating on brief psychodynamic psychotherapy. First, Tony seems to be a good candidate for brief psychodynamic therapy: he is in sufficient distress to be motivated for the work, he identifies the primary source of his problems as relational in nature, and he seems to be able to invest in a meaningful mutual relationship with the therapist. The first area of concern comes with his preconceived desire to use the couch, suggesting both that he has misconceptions about the nature of psychotherapy, perhaps expecting it to be psychoanalysis, and that he may be beginning the relationship with significant defenses against the process or against the mutuality and intersubjectivity that brief psychodynamic therapy requires (cf. Goldberger, 1995).

Tony seems to have had a rather ambivalent attachment with his mother due to his fear of her intrusiveness. He seems to have developed a cyclical maladaptive pattern in which he expects others to want too much from him. To prevent this, Tony takes a passive, noncommittal stance in his relationships. He seems to expect that he will "not measure up" and that he will be shamed for his inadequacy. Because his response is to be limp and uncommitted, other people he relates to become frustrated and push him away, fulfilling his prophecy. This makes him feel even less competent and more likely to avoid manning up in a relationship, thus perpetuating the cycle. Since this cycle seems quite pervasive in his life, it is likely that he will quickly bring it into the therapy office. The therapist should be attentive for countertransferential feelings of frustration and impatience with Tony, as these will be the first signs of the recurrence of Tony's relational cycle. In particular, it is likely that the therapist will make an unintentional error or failure of empathy, such as a scheduling error, which Tony will experience as rejection. It is important for the therapist honestly and openly to acknowledge this failure and seek to repair the attachment relationship, helping Tony to see the pervasiveness of his cyclical relational style and giving him a significant attachment relationship that does not end in the usual painful abandonment. Tony may then be helped to see concrete ways in which he might intervene to break that cycle in other relationships.

In light of Tony's attachment difficulties with his father, it is likely that his transference attachment will increase with a male therapist. If he seeks the approval or praise of the therapist, the expression of warmth and encouragement should not be withheld, but the connection of these feelings with his unmet needs from his father may gently be pointed out to facilitate his insight. As Tony begins to carry these new attachment experiences into other relationships with success, these successes should be noticed with positive affect from the therapist. The rewards of these more fulfilling relationships should be self-sustaining, but if the therapist notices reports of any relationships that are falling into Tony's previous maladaptive cycle, Tony should be reminded of the steps they had taken before to break that cycle.

As termination approaches, Tony will likely experience heightened anxiety and some regression. This may be normalized as a common experience nearing the loss of such a significant relationship, and the history of successes may be rehearsed to facilitate the solidifying of Tony's new sense of self. Termination regression often causes brief psychodynamic psychotherapists to doubt the wisdom of their short-term strategy; however, the patient usually needs to draw confidence from the therapist's assurance that he or she still has the tools that have been gained and the competence to use them. Postponing termination runs the risk of communicating an expectation of failure, but if the therapist has significant concerns about patient safety, clinical wisdom and professional judgment should prevail over rigid maintenance of the termination deadline. Similarly, when the termination date has been arbitrarily set by an insurance company and not by the therapist's assessment of this unique patient, it may be necessary to fight for an extension of the termination deadline.

11

Christianity and Psychoanalysis

Final Thoughts

Brad D. Strawn and
Earl D. Bland

As we come to the final chapter of this volume, a question may linger: What is the overall goal of this project? In the first chapter we argued for a reconsideration of psychoanalysis and Christian theology in light of the relational renaissance in contemporary understandings of psychoanalytic theory. The constructivist/hermeneutical turn in the human sciences has made possible a new rapprochement between psychoanalysis and theology, absent the burdensome trappings of Enlightenment scientific inquiry that shackled both disciplines (Burston & Frie, 2006; Cushman, 1995; Grenz & Franke, 2001; Murphy, 1996; Orange, 2011). To appreciate the diversity of post-Freudian psychoanalysis we asked six authors to outline six different psychoanalytic models that are prominent in today's clinical landscape. Recognizing the changing world of therapeutic practice we also included one chapter on psychoanalytic marital therapy and a chapter on short-term psychoanalytic treatment. In chapter two Wright, Jones and Strawn outlined our integration strategy, calling for the necessity of Christian clinicians to *tradition* themselves in terms of their particular theological specificity, and we asked each of the various contributors to do just that in the context of the six different schools of psychoanalysis. But has this volume simply been a theological survey of psychoanalysis, or has there been an end to our means? In this final chapter we will endeavor to explicate that end.

REVISITING CHRISTIAN TRADITIONING

Chapter two argued that Christian integrators and integrative clinicians need to specifically tradition themselves within their historical theological specificity. This argument is important for a number of reasons. Assuming therapy is foremost an ethical dialogue between two individuals related to the *good life*, we contend that all therapies contain within them implicit religio-ethical systems and that therapists may unwittingly adopt the ethics of their theoretical orientation while being unaware of how that orientation's ethics may conflict with their own more privately held assumptions. Further, it is only from within a particular tradition that ethics can be advanced. The Enlightenment project attempted to disconnect individuals from tradition in an attempt to find universal truth. This project failed and left individuals at the whim of an individual emotive ethic (MacIntyre, 2007). Feelings became important considerations in ethical actions. On a broad scale psychoanalysis embraced aspects of this system and may be best understood as espousing an expressivist ethic based on "empathic mutual recognition" (Summers, 2013, p. 43), a significant departure from the historical prominence of religion and philosophical knowledge as the starting point for ethical reasoning (Taylor, 1989, 2007). The various chapters have been an attempt to highlight how the different psychoanalytic theories may dialogue with various theological traditions, and what clinical-ethical conclusions might be drawn from this conversation.

Key to the argument forwarded in chapter two is that clinicians cannot keep themselves out of the work—especially when doing psychoanalytic therapy where transference and countertransference are integral to effective treatment. For this reason it is far more ethical and helpful for patients if therapists own their irreducible subjectivity, especially emotional information, and find ways to utilize their unique personhood therapeutically. This is not an excuse for therapists to say or do whatever they want. We must always practice in disciplined ways, but we must move away from Enlightenment ideas regarding the objectivity of therapist's perspectives. No longer can therapists conceive of themselves as blank screens or clear reflecting mirrors who hold therapeutic authority and truth.

To own one's tradition is an invitation not to a debate about which tradition is better but to reflect on how that tradition shapes and forms one's "seeing." It is likewise not a denunciation of more objective methods for discovering truth. Traditions function as *horizons of meaning*, much like one's theoretical orientation (Orange, 2010b; Taylor, 2011). But because traditions become so deeply ingrained in us, they are often outside our conscious awareness (i.e., implicit knowledge). They operate in the background—offline. We advocate taking the theological horizon of meaning out of the background and moving it to the foreground. How is theology shaping what the therapist sees, values and imagines? What ethical and theological implications come with this tradition? How and when should this be worked with overtly, and when should it remain as a quiet but helpful guiding force—like theory? It is our belief that we need more examples of how therapists work overtly with their theological presuppositions. Hopefully we moved in this direction as each clinician interacted with the case of Tony. Because our case material is static, we undoubtedly limited each author in demonstrating how theological issues would be taken up in actual dialogue. What we see in the chapters is more of how each clinician theologically conceptualized the case. This too is a helpful and important addition to the literature: How do Christian clinicians think theologically about cases?

A final challenge to traditioning oneself is the influence of a religiously diverse society. In cultures like North America many Christians find themselves to be theological "mutts." They demonstrate a kind of theological pluralism, sometimes not even recognizing the contradictions this may incur. We believe that as theological concepts emerge in therapy, clients will be the first to recognize these conflicts and discrepancies in their therapist (although we suspect they will go without comment), so it behooves Christian clinicians to be as clear about their theology as they are about their theoretical orientation.

PSYCHOANALYTIC TREATMENT IN THE CHRISTIAN TRADITION

Regarding theory, the point of this book has *not* been to advocate a kind of broad and inclusive psychoanalytic eclecticism. Sometimes individuals will speak of psychoanalytic pluralism using the metaphor of toolbox. Clinicians may conceptualize their work from one particular theory but reach into the toolbox of other orientations for what they need at any particular moment. While the toolbox metaphor may in fact be helpful at times, it can also lead to assumptions that disembody the tool from the therapist. Rather it is our hope that the reader can sense that we believe that the irreducible, subjective aliveness of the therapist is the *embodied operator* and that theories are language constructions meant to articulate and enhance a relational experience for the purpose of healing and restoration.

Good therapists are able to navigate various language traditions and the subtending presuppositional assumptions without losing their own grounding (i.e., identity, tradition and subjectivity). Flexibility with knowledge categories and divergent phenomenological descriptors allows a therapist choice and creativity in the use and application of different theoretical constructions, depending on situational demands. We assert that client-presenting problems, developmental diagnosis, the degree and intensity of trauma, cultural and gender considerations, faith traditions, unconscious processes, phase of treatment, and relational contexts are all mutually and reciprocally interactive forces that help differentiate the usefulness of particular theoretical insights.

This then raises the question, what do we mean by psychoanalytic psychotherapy? If each psychoanalytic model should preserve its uniqueness, how do they all qualify as psychoanalytic? In attempting to define psychoanalytic therapy McWilliams (2004) suggested that "It seems to me that the overarching theme among psychodynamic approaches to helping people is that the more honest we are with ourselves, the better our chances for living a satisfying and useful life" (p. 1). She points out that the various psychoanalytic therapies share the goal of increasing self-knowledge through "acknowledging what is not conscious—that is, to admit what is difficult or painful to see in ourselves" (p. 1).

From a religious perspective it is fascinating that McWilliams (2004) notes the moralistic tone of this, but acknowledges that she is not the first to identify it as such. Authors such as Philip Rief had suggested much earlier that Freud was essentially a moralist, and Thomas Szasz had defined psychoanalysis as "a moral dialogue, not a medical treatment" (cited in McWilliams, 2004, p. 2). She notes that even Wilfred Bion had noted that psychoanalysis consisted of a medical aspect (e.g., rational, technical procedures offered by an expert in an attempt to obtain repeatable results) and a religious aspect (e.g., existential, humanistic, romantic ways to seek answers).

> Bion did not go so far as to say so, but it is arguable that there is a rather substantial "theology" shared by psychoanalytic practitioners. Among its articles of faith are, as noted earlier, the belief that knowing oneself deeply will have complex positive effects; that being honest (relinquishing defensiveness or replacing the false self with authenticity) is central to health and especially to mental health; and that the best preparation for doing analytic therapy is to undergo an analytic therapy. (p. 4)

Yet is there anything that sets psychoanalytic psychotherapy apart from other therapies? As we stated in chapter nine, several authors (Gabbard, 2010; McWilliams, 2004; Shedler, 2010) have highlighted the key factors that differentiate psychoanalytic from cognitive-behavioral, family systems, humanistic/existential and other theory modalities. Within the realm of conscious and unconscious processes the distinctive of psychoanalytic treatment includes:

1. focus on affect and the expression of emotion

2. exploration of the patient's efforts to avoid certain topics or engage in activities that retard therapeutic progress (i.e., work with resistance)

3. identification of patterns in the patient's actions, thoughts, feelings, experiences and relationships (object relations)

4. emphasis on past experiences

5. focus on interpersonal experiences

6. emphasis on the therapeutic relationship (transference and the working alliance)

7. explorations of wishes, dreams and fantasies (intrapsychic dynamics)

These differences are dimensional, not categorical, both between various schools of psychoanalysis and psychoanalytic treatments as a whole versus other theoretical orientations.

McWilliams (2004) goes on to suggest that what really sets psychoanalytic psychotherapy apart from other forms of therapeutic treatment is not so much technique as it is "the nature of the assumptions that underlie the therapist's activity" (p. 4). In a similar vein, Stolorow (1994b) posits that intrinsic criteria rather than extrinsic criteria determine whether a therapy is psychoanalytic or not. To define this intrinsic criteria Stolorow proposes "that psychoanalysis is defined (1) by its central *aim*, (2) by its *investigatory stance*, and (3) by its distinctive *domain of inquiry*" (p. 150).

> My collaborators and I . . . have defined the fundamental aim of a psychoanalytic process as the *unfolding, illumination, and transformation of the patient's subjective world*. We further suggested that the investigatory stance most likely to create a therapeutic situation in which this aim can be maximally achieved is best characterized as an attitude of *sustained empathic inquiry*—one that consistently seeks understanding from within the perspective of the patient's own subjective frame of reference. Such inquiry must include the analyst's continual reflection on the involvement of his own personal subjectivity in the ongoing investigation. . . . [W]e assume that the distinctive domain of psychoanalytic inquiry, and the one

> in which its therapeutic action can be found, lies in the investigation of the patient's experience of the analytic relationship—the *analysis of the transference*. (pp. 150-51)

Therefore, it is not the external trappings, such as use of a couch or number of sessions per week, that define a psychoanalytic treatment. The intrinsic relational process factors clearly define a psychoanalytic method. This is important because as we have trained students interested in learning psychoanalysis, they often assume they must practice in a manner similar to what they read in analytic books and journals, often written by trained analysts seeing patients three to five times per week. We contend that how one practices varies based on issues such as diagnosis and frequency of session. However, this does not mean that a once-per-week treatment cannot be considered psychoanalytic. If the intrinsic factors define a treatment as psychoanalytic, then the person of the therapist and his or her relational connection to the patient are the critical markers of psychoanalytic psychotherapy and the fundamental ingredients to its ongoing success.

McWilliams (2004), who recently has done more for bringing psychoanalytic ideas to a wider audience than perhaps anyone, suggests that while there may not be one true or universal technique of psychoanalysis (extrinsic factor), perhaps there are "universal beliefs or attitudes" (p. 27) that undergird a psychoanalytic treatment (intrinsic factors). The following is a brief outline of these essential elements and our understanding of how the core of psychoanalytic treatment interlocks with our Christian theological tradition.

First, psychoanalytic practitioners share a sense of *curiosity* and *awe*. This idea suggests that much of the impetus for our behavior, feelings, perceptions and thoughts lies outside of our conscious awareness. Curiosity regarding the unconscious realm is not for simple intellectual gain or trivial gratification of banal inquisitiveness. In line with Thomas Aquinas, who saw studiousness (love of knowledge) as a virtue undergirded by temperance (Roberts & Wood, 2007), psychoanalytic psychotherapists are awed by the knowledge of unconscious mentation as a pathway to understanding and caring for a person. Remaining curious about what is hidden, and holding to a belief that one can never be sure what we know or will learn about a patient, pushes us to persistent inquiry and a lingering humility. This is why McWilliams (2004) likes the metaphor of therapist as travel guide. We may not know where we will end up with a patient; we need only be sure the journey is safe.

Second, psychoanalytic psychotherapists hold to a belief in the complex and conflicted nature of human psychological processes. As Jeremiah observed, "the heart is deceitful above all things" (Jer 17:9), and Paul admits to his own confused and conflicted motives in Romans 7 (multiple self-states, if you will). McWilliams (2004) elaborates these biblical examples by recognizing that any psychological problem or phenomenon will have more than one cause and fulfill more than one function. Her goal is to underscore the nature of human multiplicity but also to emphasize the sometimes-confusing and convoluted motivational processes that plague our psychic processes. We may wish to be close to others and afraid of it at the same time. We may long to trust in God and also avoid opportunities to live into this reality. We may claim we desire freedom but act in ways that keep others close in dependent ways. The psychoanalytic clinician is comfortable with complicated and diverse explanations. As Christians we believe that God made the world intelligible despite its confusions and contradictions. In light of this complexity we do not shy away from mystery or dampen its accompanying anxiety with spiritual inanities or generalities that do violence to the multifarious and intricate obscurities of God's creation—particularly the functioning of the human mind. We live in an ambiguous world, and the exploration of psychic life must be thoughtful and passionate. As Jens Zimmermann (2013) argues, "Christian living does not entail a mere 'aping' of Christ, asking naively 'what would Jesus do,' but a genuine interpretation—or even better, enactment—of the gospel for one's culture in the service of a common humanity" (p. 272). Nowhere is this sensibility more relevant than in the practice of soul (psyche) care.

Third, psychoanalytic psychotherapists acknowledge the importance of identification and empathy. Harry Stack Sullivan's comment that "we are all more simply human than otherwise" (cited in McWilliams, 2004, p. 34) recognizes the essential humanness of therapists and patients. Identification with a patient's humanity aids psychoanalytic psychotherapists to deeply empathize and make use of their countertransference or cotransference (Orange, 1995) in decisions regarding diagnosis and treatment interventions. We suggest the fundamental Christian motive of love is deeply communicated in a dialectical tension where the other is appreciated as wholly other in Levinasian terms (see Goodman, 2012), in coexistent tension with our own experience. Love is not the renunciation of self where the other dominates, yet in the process of treatment a level of asymmetry is necessary in the developmental progression of mutual recognition (Hoffman, 2011).

Transference in all its forms is an invitation to use information about the patient, ourselves as therapists, and the relationship we are constructing to advance healing and reconciliation. Empathy is the promotion of understanding and love, which involves the eradication of judgmental condemnation and blaming (Willard, 1998). When we understand our patients from an empathic perspective, a view from inside the patient, then we are better able to know what they need. It is not the imposition of an ought contained in so many Christian discussions of healing. Therapy is not based on a prejudgment about what the person needs—it is an experience-near communal participation in the life of the patient that allows for creative compassion and particularized interventions that fit the uniqueness of each person within their social, religious and cultural context. Psychoanalytic treatment is a participation in "God's ongoing work of caring" (Olthuis, 2001, p. 49), involving love as a fundamental way of knowing. N. T. Wright (1999) highlights this idea of love as a mode of comprehension:

> I believe we can and must as Christians within a postmodern world give
> an account of human knowing that will apply to music and mathematics,
> to biology and history, to theology and to chemistry [and psychoanalytic

treatment]. We need to articulate, for the post-postmodern world, what we might call an *epistemology of love*. (p. 195, italics added)

A fourth belief that psychoanalytic psychotherapists hold is the importance of subjectivity and attunement to affect (McWilliams, 2004). Subjectivity is not the lesser stepchild of objectivity but is an important window into realms of unarticulated and unformulated experience. There is an important place for objective knowing, but therapeutic subjectivity is related to a kind of feeling knowledge or attunement to affective experience that transcends explicit knowing. First evidenced in infants and caregivers, emotional connectedness becomes the lingua franca that is the intimate exchange of psychoanalytic psychotherapy. Jumping off this image, Old Testament scholar Walter Brueggemann (1999) sees early intimate relationships as prefiguring intimacy with the transcendent God. Even a cursory reading of the Psalms or the prophetic biblical literature demonstrates the critical function of emotion in our relationship to God. We weep and he listens, we mourn and he comforts, we dance and sing in celebration of his goodness. For Brueggemann the Psalms are a dialectic of complaint and praise, of self-assertion and self-abandonment.

> I have no doubt that theologically and emotionally, self-assertion precedes self-abandonment, for there is no self to abandon or to pledge loyalty unless that self has been claimed and valorized. . . . It is through urgent insistence that God can be bonded to my issues, so that I may be bonded to God's expectations. (p. 7)

Emotion is a relational teacher in its capacity to speak truth about our internal nature, our needs and the status of our intimate interactions. To the degree that Christian theology dismisses emotion as truth, we see psychoanalytic treatment offering the Christian community a curative balance to any tendency toward favoring rational knowledge and declarative approaches to suffering and change.

The languages of object relations and especially attachment theory have opened up the concept of "developmental deficit" as an important aspect of psychopathology and clinical treatment. McWilliams (2004) posits that a fifth belief for most psychoanalytic psychotherapists is that therapy is more than the imparting of new information or facilitating "aha" moments. Psychotherapy, for many patients, is a new experience in which developmental deficits can be worked through and individuals can psychologically and emotionally grow up. In this sense the therapist steps in as a new *good object* even as they also work through bearing the brunt of being an old *bad object*—this time with a different ending. This maturational process allows patients to see the world as it really is: easy and complicated, hopeful and tragic, frightening and joyous. As Christians we know that growth and maturity are complex processes that do not necessarily involve striving and doing. We are fundamentally abiders. "Abide in Me, and I in you. As the branch cannot bear fruit of itself unless it abides in the vine, so neither can you unless you abide in Me" (John 15:4 NASB). In psychoanalytic language we may look to Emmanuel Ghent's (1990) notion of surrender—the something-other-than submission whereby we move toward growth, not as action-based behavior but releasing in the context of a facilitative environment. As therapist and patient abide in the deeply immersive process of therapy—newness, clarity, unity and wholeness emerge.

McWilliams's (2004) sixth and last belief for a therapist practicing from a psychoanalytic sensibility is *faith*. Here she is referring to a conviction or trust that the therapist has in the process of therapy. This hopeful confidence does not just spring from theoretical or technical knowledge, but from a deep experience in the therapist who has traveled this exploratory pathway in his or her life. Even when the actual therapy gets difficult and stalemates or enactments occur, the psychoanalytically oriented therapist believes there is hope. Psychoanalytic therapists

> are loath to make predictions about just where the professional journey with an individual will go, but they trust it to take the therapist and the patient into areas that will ultimately strengthen the client's sense of honesty, agency, mastery, self-cohesion, self-esteem, affect tolerance, and capacity for fulfilling relationships. (p. 42)

Yet psychoanalytic treatment within the Christian tradition is not merely an expressivist exercise for the promotion of self-fulfillment and psychological health, regardless of the nobility of these outcomes. For the Christian in psychoanalytic treatment, something much deeper is occurring. Both therapist and patient are participating eschatologically in the redemptive and reconciling work of Christ. As Jens Zimmermann (2013) avers, "In Christ the cosmos regains its fundamental orientation towards the human" (p. 266). The highly subjective and humanistically focused frame of psychoanalytic treatment is not egoism. Psychoanalytic treatment is the search for truth about humanity that, when achieved, celebrates the work of our Creator.

We believe, with McWilliams, that these six sensibilities of psychoanalytic psychotherapy are the ground that underlies all the different theories of psychoanalysis. We believe these are the important characteristics, values, beliefs or even virtues that reflect Christ and make this kind of work so powerful in the lives of patients. In the world of empirically validated treatments psychoanalysis has sometimes taken a hit on the chin. Yet we affirm, with McWilliams (2004), that these sensibilities are a helpful corrective to the "intellectual passivity, opinionated reductionism, emotional distancing, objectification and apathy, personal isolation and social anomie, and existential dread [that have often] been lamented by scholars and social critics as the price we pay for our industrialized, consumer-oriented, and technologically sophisticated cultures" (p. 45).

While there is an increase in sophisticated outcome studies demonstrating the positive clinical impact of psychoanalysis (Leichsenring & Rabung, 2008; Shedler, 2010), arguing for the efficacy of psychoanalysis has not been the goal of this volume. Rather than arguing for which theory is better, we have, in part, been advocating for a "practical psychoanalysis" (Renik, 2006).

> Practical clinical psychoanalysis is a treatment that aims to help the patient feel less distress and more satisfaction in daily life through improved understanding of how his or her mind works. . . . Practical psychoanalysis means remaining open-minded with regard to theory, holding nothing as

axiomatic; and it means retaining an experimental approach to technique—that is, searching for whatever way of working together with a given patient seems to make progress toward the desired goals of treatment. (p. 3)

As noted earlier, we believe that theories are language constructions meant to articulate and enhance a relational experience for the purpose of healing and restoration. Of course, as Christians we believe that our faith, as articulated both explicitly and implicitly, is an essential aspect of this process. In one sense, theology is also a language construction that attempts to articulate a relational experience between humans and God. It is our hope that in some small way this book has captured a dialogue between praxis theology and the language construction of psychoanalysis with the ultimate goal being the restoration of human persons toward the image and likeness of Christ.

References

Ainsworth, M. D. S., Blehar, M. C., Waters, E., & Wall, S. (1978). *Patterns of attachment: A psychological study of the strange situation.* Hillsdale, NJ: Erlbaum.

Allen, J. G., Fonagy, P., & Bateman, A. W. (2008). *Mentalizing in clinical practice.* Arlington, VA: American Psychiatric Publishing.

Altman, N. (1995). *The analyst in the inner city: Race, class and culture through a psychoanalytic lens.* Hillsdale, NJ: Analytic Press.

Altman, N. (2010). *The analyst in the inner city: Race, class, and culture through a psychoanalytic lens* (2nd ed.). New York: Routledge.

Ammaniti, M., & Trentini, C. (2009). How new knowledge about parenting reveals the neurobiological implications of intersubjectivity: A conceptual synthesis of recent research. *Psychoanalytic Dialogues, 19,* 537-55.

Armistead, K., Strawn, B., & Wright, R. (Eds.). (2010). *Wesleyan theology and social science: The dance of practical divinity and discovery.* Cambridge, UK: Cambridge Scholars Publishing.

Aron, L. (1991). The patient's experience of the analyst's subjectivity. *Psychoanalytic Dialogues, 1*(1), 29-51.

Aron, L. (1996). *A meeting of minds: Mutuality in psychoanalysis.* Hillsdale, NJ: Analytic Press.

Aron, L. (2000). Self-reflexivity and therapeutic action of psychoanalysis. *Psychoanalytic Psychology, 17,* 667-89.

Aron, L. (2004). God's influence on my psychoanalytic vision and values. *Psychoanalytic Psychology, 21,* 442-51.

Aron, L. (2005). The tree of knowledge, good and evil: Conflicting interpretations. *Psychoanalytic Dialogues, 15,* 681-708.

Aron, L., & Harris, A. (Eds.). (1993). *The legacy of Sandor Ferenczi.* Hillsdale, NJ: Analytic Press.

Aron, L., & Harris, A. (Eds.). (2005). *Relational psychoanalysis: Vol. 2. Innovation and expansion.* Hillsdale, NJ: Analytic Press.

Aron, L., & Harris, A. (Eds.). (2012a). *Relational psychoanalysis: Vol. 4. Expansion of theory.* New York: Routledge.

Aron, L., & Harris, A. (Eds.). (2012b). *Relational psychoanalysis: Vol. 5. Evolution of process.* New York: Routledge.

Aron, L., Harris, A., & Suchet, M. (Eds.). (2007). *Relational psychoanalysis: Vol. 3. New voices.* Mahwah, NJ: Analytic Press.

Atwood, G. E., & Stolorow, R. D. (1984). *Structures of subjectivity: Explorations in psychoanalytic phenomenology.* Hillsdale, NJ: Jason Arenson.

Atwood, G. E., & Stolorow, R. D. (1993). *Faces in a cloud: Intersubjectivity in personality theory.* Lanham, MD: Jason Aronson.

Augustine. (1991). *On the Trinity.* (E. Hill, Trans.). Brooklyn, NY: New City Press.

Bacal, H. A. (1985). Optimal responsiveness and the therapeutic process. *Progress in Self Psychology, 1,* 202-27.

Bacal, H. A., & Carlton, L. (2010). Kohut's last words on analytic cure and how we hear them now—a view from specificity theory. *International Journal of Psychoanalytic Self Psychology, 5,* 132-45.

Bacal, H. A., & Newman, K. (1990). *Theories of object relations.* New York: Columbia University Press.

Bagnini, C. (2012). *Keeping couples in treatment: Working from surface to depth.* Lanham, MD: Jason Aronson.

Balint, M. (1933). *Primary love and psychoanalytic technique.* London: Hogarth.

Balint, M. (Ed.). (1949). Sandor Ferenczi. *International Journal of Psychoanalysis, 30,* 4.

Balint, M. (1959). *Thrills and regressions.* London: Hogarth.

Balint, M. (1968). *The basic fault: Therapeutic aspects of regression.* Evanston, IL: Northwestern University Press.

Balswick, J. O., King, P. E., & Reimer, K. S. (2005). *The reciprocating self: Human development in theological perspective.* Downers Grove, IL: InterVarsity Press.

Bartholomew, K., & Horowitz, L. M. (1991). Attachment styles among young adults: A test of a four-category model. *Journal of Personality and Social Psychology, 61,* 226-44.

Barton, J., & Haslett, T. (2007). Analysis, synthesis, systems thinking and the scientific method: Rediscovering the importance of open systems. *Systems Research and Behavior Science, 24,* 143-55.

Basch, M. F. (1990). Further thoughts on empathic understanding. *Progress in Self Psychology, 6*, 3-10.

Basch, M. F. (1995). *Doing brief psychotherapy*. New York: Basic Books.

Bauer, G. P., & Kobos, J. C. (1987). *Brief therapy: Short-term psychodynamic intervention*. Northvale, NJ: Jason Aronson.

Beebe, B., Jaffe, J., & Lachmann, F. M. (1992). A dyadic systems view of communication. In N. J. Skolnick & S. C. Warshaw (Eds.), *Relational perspectives in psychoanalysis* (pp. 61-81). Hillsdale, NJ: Analytic Press.

Beebe, B., & Lachmann, F. M. (1988). Mother-infant mutual influence and precursors of psychic structure. *Progress in Self Psychology, 3*, 3-25.

Beebe, B., & Lachmann, F. M. (1998). Co-constructing inner and relational processes: Self and mutual regulation in infant research and adult treatment. *Psychoanalytic Psychology, 15*, 480-516.

Beebe, B., & Lachmann, F. (2002). *Infant research and adult treatment*. Hillsdale, NJ: Analytic Press.

Benjamin, J. (1988). *The bonds of love: Psychoanalysis, feminism, and the problem of domination*. New York: Pantheon.

Benjamin, J. (1990). An outline of intersubjectivity: The development of recognition. *Psychoanalytic Psychology, 7*, 33-46.

Benjamin, J. (1995). *Like subjects, love objects: Essays on recognition and sexual difference*. New Haven, CT: Yale University Press.

Benjamin, J. (1998*). Shadow of the other: Intersubjectivity and gender in psychoanalysis*. New York: Routledge.

Benjamin, J. (1999). Recognition and destruction: An outline of intersubjectivity. In S. A. Mitchell & L. Aron (Eds.), *Relational psychoanalysis: The emergence of a tradition* (pp. 181-210). Hillsdale, NJ: Analytic Press.

Benjamin, J. (2004). Beyond doer and done to: An intersubjective view of thirdness. *The Psychoanalytic Quarterly, 73*, 5-46.

Benjamin, J. (2009). A relational psychoanalytic perspective on the necessity of acknowledging failure in order to restore the facilitating and containing features of the intersubjective relationship (the shared third). *International Journal of Psychoanalysis, 90*, 441-50.

Benner, D. G. (1983). The incarnation as a metaphor for psychotherapy. *Journal of Psychology and Theology, 11*, 287-94.

Benner, D. G. (2011). *Soulful spirituality: Becoming fully alive and deeply human*. Grand Rapids, MI: Brazos.

Bettelheim, B. (1982). *Freud and man's soul.* New York: Alfred A. Knof.

Bingaman, K. A. (2003). *Freud and faith: Living in the tension.* Albany, NY: State University of New York Press.

Bion, W. R. (1962a). *Learning from experience.* London: Heinemann.

Bion, W. R. (1962b). The psycho-analytic study of thinking, II: A theory of thinking. *International Journal of Psychoanalysis, 43,* 306-10.

Bion, W. R. (1977). *Seven servants.* New York: Aronson.

Black, D. M. (1993). What sort of a thing is a religion? A view from object-relations theory. *International Journal of Psycho-Analysis, 74,* 613-25.

Blair, C., & Raver, C. C. (2012). Child development in the context of adversity: Experiential canalization of brain and behavior. *American Psychologist, 67,* 309-18.

Bland, E. D. (2010). Finding self and forming virtue: The treatment of narcissistic defenses in marital therapy. *Journal of Psychology and Christianity, 29,* 158-65.

Bland, E., Strawn, B., Tisdale, T., Hicks, M., & Hoffman, L. (2012, March). *Integrating traditions: Christianity and psychoanalysis in conversation.* Symposium conducted at the International Conference of the Christian Association for Psychological Studies, Washington Dulles Airport Marriott.

Blatt, S. J., & Luyten, P. (2009). A structural-developmental psychodynamic approach to psychopathology: Two polarities of experience across the lifespan. *Development and Psychopathology, 3,* 793-814.

Bornstein, R. F. (2001). The impending death of psychoanalysis. *Psychoanalytic Psychology, 18,* 3-30.

Boston Change Process Study Group (2010). *Change in psychotherapy: A unifying paradigm.* New York: W. W. Norton.

Boszormenyi-Nagy, I., & Krasner, B. (1986). *Between give and take: A clinical guide to contextual family therapy.* New York: Brunner/Mazel.

Bowlby, J. (1944). Forty-four juvenile thieves: Their characters and home life. *International Journal of Psychoanalysis, 25,* 1-57.

Bowlby, J. (1969). *Attachment and loss: Vol. 1. Attachment.* New York: Basic Books.

Bowlby, J. (1973). *Attachment and loss: Vol. 2. Separation: Anxiety and anger.* New York: Basic Books.

Bowlby, J. (1980). *Attachment and loss: Vol. 3. Loss: Sadness and depression.* New York: Basic Books.

Bowlby, J. (1982). *Attachment and loss: Vol. 1. Attachment.* 2nd ed. New York: Basic Books.

Bowlby, J. (1988). *A secure base: Parent-child attachment and healthy human development.* New York: Basic Books.

Brandchaft, B. (1983). The negativism of negative therapeutic reaction and the psychology of the self. In A. Goldberg (Ed.), *The future of psychoanalysis* (pp. 327-59). New York: International Universities Press.

Brandchaft, B. (1986). Self and object differentiation. In R. F. Lax, S. Bach & J. A. Burland (Eds.), *Self and object constancy* (pp. 153-76). New York: Guilford Press.

Brandchaft, B. (2007). Systems of pathological accommodation and change in psychoanalysis. *Psychoanalytic Psychology, 24,* 667-87. doi:10.1037/0736-9735.24.4.667.

Brandchaft, B., Doctors, S., & Sorter, D. (2010). *Toward an emancipatory psychoanalysis: Brandchaft's intersubjective vision.* New York: Analytic Press.

Brennan, K. A., Clark, C. L., & Shaver, P. R. (1998). Self-report measurement of adult attachment: An integrative overview. In J. A. Simpson & W. S. Rholes (Eds.), *Attachment theory and close relationships* (pp. 46-76). New York: Guilford Press.

Brenner, C. (1982). *The mind in conflict.* Madison, CT: International Universities Press.

Brody, P. R. (1988). Couples psychotherapy: A psychodynamic model. *Psychoanalytic Psychology, 5,* 47-70.

Brokaw, B. F., & Edwards, K. J. (1994). The relationship of God image to level of object relations development. *Journal of Psychology and Theology, 22,* 352-71.

Bromberg, P. M. (1998). *Standing in the spaces: Essays on clinical process, trauma, and dissociation.* Hillsdale, NJ: Analytic Press.

Bromberg, P. M. (2004). More than meets the eye: A professional autobiography. *Psychoanalytic Inquiry, 24,* 558-75.

Bromberg, P. (2006). *Awakening the dreamer: Clinical journeys.* Mahwah, NJ: Analytic Press.

Bromberg, P. M. (2011). *The shadow of the tsunami.* New York: Routledge.

Brown, W. S. (1998). Cognitive contributions to the soul. In W. S. Brown, N. Murphy & H. N. Malony (Eds.), *Whatever happened to the soul? Scientific and theological portraits of human nature.* Minneapolis: Fortress Press.

Brown, W. S. (2004). Resonance: A model for relating science, psychology, and faith. *Journal of Psychology and Christianity*, 23(2), 110-20.

Brown, W. S., Murphy, N., & Malony, H. N. (Eds.). (1998). *Whatever happened to the soul? Scientific and theological portraits of human nature*. Minneapolis: Fortress Press.

Brown, W. S., & Strawn, B. D. (2012). *The physical nature of Christian life: Neuroscience, psychology, and the church*. New York: Cambridge University Press.

Browning, D. S. (1987). *Religious thought and the modern psychologies: A critical conversation in the theology of culture*. Philadelphia: Fortress Press.

Browning, D. S., and Cooper, T. D. (2004). *Religious thought and the modern psychologies* (2nd ed.). Minneapolis: Fortress.

Brueggemann, W. (1999). *The covenanted self: Explorations in law and covenant*. Minneapolis: Augsburg Press.

Brugger, C. E. (2009). Psychology and Christian anthropology. *Edification*, 3(1), 5-18.

Brunner, E. (1939). *Man in Revolt*. (Olive Wyon, Trans.). London: Lutterworth Press.

Bucci, W. (1997). *Psychoanalysis and cognitive science: A multiple code theory*. New York: Guilford Press.

Buechler, S. (2004). *Clinical values: Emotions that guide psychoanalytic treatment*. Hillsdale, NJ: Analytic Press.

Burston, D., & Frie, R. (2006). *Psychotherapy as human science*. Pittsburgh: Duquesne University Press.

Cairns, D. (1973). *The image of God in man* (2nd ed.). London: Collins.

Carlton, L. (2009). Making sense of self and systems in psychoanalysis: Summation essay for the 30th annual international conference on the psychology of the self. *International Journal of Psychoanalytic Self Psychology*, 4, 313-29.

Carter, J. D., & Narramore, B. (1976). *The integration of psychology and theology: An introduction*. Grand Rapids, MI: Zondervan.

Catechism of the Catholic Church with modifications from the Editio Typica. (1995). New York: Doubleday.

Chernus, L. A. (1983). Focal psychotherapy and self pathology: A clinical illustration. *Clinical Social Work Journal*, 11, 215-27.

Chessick, R. D. (1983). *How psychotherapy heals: The process of intensive psychotherapy*. New York: Jason Aronson.

Chodorow, N. (1978). *The reproduction of mothering: Psychoanalysis and the sociology of gender.* Berkeley: University of California Press.

Chodorow, N. (1991). *Feminism and the psychoanalytic theory.* New Haven, CT: Yale University Press.

Chodorow, N. (2011). *Individualizing gender and sexuality: Theory and practice.* New York: Routledge.

Clarke, G. S. (2011). Suttie's influence on Fairbairn's object relations theory. *Journal of the American Psychoanalytic Association, 59,* 939-60.

Clarke, W. N. (2008). *Person and being.* Milwaukee: Marquette University Press.

Clayton, P. (2006). Conceptual foundations of emergence theory. In P. Clayton & P. Davies (Eds.), *The re-emergence of emergence: An emergentist hypothesis from science to religion* (pp. 1-34). New York: Oxford University Press.

Clayton, P., & Davies, P. (Eds.). (2006). *The re-emergence of emergence: The emergentist hypothesis from science to religion.* Oxford, England: Oxford University Press.

Clement, C. (2010). Commentary on paper by Philip A. Ringstrom. *Psychoanalytic Dialogues, 20,* 219-23.

Coe, J., & Hall, T. W. (2010). *Psychology in the Spirit: Contours of a transformational psychology.* Downers Grove, IL: InterVarsity Press.

Coen, S. J. (1988). How to read Freud: A critique of recent scholarship. *Journal of the American Psychoanalytic Association, 36,* 483-515.

Colburn, W. J. (2011). Recontextualizing individuality and therapeutic action in psychoanalysis and psychotherapy. In R. Frie & W. J. Colburn (Eds.), *Persons in context: The challenge of individuality in theory and practice* (pp. 121-46). New York: Routledge.

Coleman, R. E. (2000). *The master plan of evangelism and discipleship.* Spokane, WA: Prince Press.

Cooper-White, P. (2011). *Braided selves: Collected essays on multiplicity, God and persons.* Eugene, OR: Cascade Books.

Cox, H. (1995). *Fire from heaven: The rise of Pentecostal spirituality and the reshaping of religion in the twenty-first century.* Reading, MA: Addison-Wesley.

Crittenden, P. M. (1995). Attachment and psychopathology. In S. Goldberg, R. Muir & J. Kerr (Eds.), *John Bowlby's attachment theory: Historical, clinical, and social significance* (pp. 367-406). New York: Analytic Press.

Crittenden, P. M. (2008). *Raising parents: Attachment, parenting, and child safety.* Collumpton, UK: Willan Publishing.

Crittenden, P. M., & Landini, A. (2011). *Assessing adult attachment: A dynamic-maturational approach to discourse analysis.* New York: W. W. Norton.

Cushman, P. (1995). *Constructing the self, constructing America: A cultural history of psychotherapy.* Reading, MA: Addison Wesley.

Damasio, A. (2005). *Descartes' error: Emotion, reason, and the human brain.* New York: Penguin.

Davies, J. (1996). Linking the "pre-analytic" with the post-classical: Integration, dissociation and the multiplicity of unconscious process. *Contemporary Psychoanalysis, 32,* 553-76.

Davies, J. (2004). Whose bad objects are we anyway? Repetition and our elusive love affair with evil. *Psychoanalytic Dialogues, 14,* 711-32.

Davies, J., & Frawley, M. (1994). *Treating the adult survivor of childhood sexual abuse: A psychoanalytic perspective.* New York: Basic Books.

Dayton, D. W. (1987). *Theological roots of Pentecostalism.* Metuchen, NJ: Scarecrow Press.

DeForest, I. (1954). *The leaven of love.* New York: Harper.

Dickens, C. (2005). *Hard times.* Seattle: Madison Park Press.

Dicks, H. V. (1967). *Marital tensions: Clinical studies towards a psychoanalytic theory of interaction.* London: Routledge & Kegan Paul.

Dobbs, T. (2009). *Faith, theology, and psychoanalysis: The life and thought of Harry S. Guntrip.* London: James Clarke.

Doherty, W. J. (1995). *Soul searching: Why psychotherapy must promote moral responsibility.* New York: Basic Books.

Drozek, R. (2010). Intersubjectivity theory and the dilemma of intersubjective motivation. *Psychoanalytic Dialogues, 20,* 540-60.

Dueck, A., & Parsons, T. D. (2007). Ethics, alterity, and psychotherapy: A Levinasian perspective. *Pastoral Psychology, 55,* 271-82. doi:10.1007/s11089-006-0045-y.

Dueck, A., & Reimer, K. (2009). *A peaceable psychology: Christian therapy in a world of many cultures.* Grand Rapids, MI: Brazos.

Dupont, J. (Ed.). (1988). *The clinical diary of Sandor Ferenczi.* Cambridge, MA: Harvard University Press.

Eagle, M. N. (2013). *Attachment and psychoanalysis: Theory, research and clinical implications.* New York: Guilford Press.

Egeland, B., & Carlson, E. A. (2004). Attachment and psychopathology. In L. Atkinson & S. Goldberg (Eds.), *Attachment issues in psychopathology and intervention* (pp. 27-48). Mahwah, NJ: LEA.

Ehrenberg, D. (1992). *The intimate edge.* New York: Norton.

Eigen, M. (1981). The area of faith in Winnicott, Lacan, and Bion. *International Journal of Psychoanalysis, 62,* 413-33.

Eigen, M. (1998). *The psychoanalytic mystic.* London & New York: Free Association Books.

Epstein, M. (1995). *Thoughts without a thinker: Psychotherapy from a Buddhist perspective.* New York: Basic Books.

Epstein, M. (1998). *Going to pieces without falling apart: A Buddhist perspective on wholeness.* New York: Broadway Books.

Epstein, M. (2001). *Going on being: Buddhism and the way of change.* New York: Broadway Books.

Faculty of the Anderson University School of Theology (2007). *We Believe.* Retrieved from www.chog.org/sites/default/files/documents/WeBelieve .pdf.

Fairbairn, W. R. D. (1952). *Psychoanalytic studies of the personality.* London: Tavistock.

Fayek, A. (2004). Islam and its effect on my practice of psychoanalysis. *Psychoanalytic Psychology, 21,* 452-57.

Feld, B. (2004). Holding and facilitating interactive regulation in couples with trauma histories. *Psychoanalytic Inquiry, 24,* 420-37.

Ferenczi, S. (1995). *The clinical diary of Sandor Ferenczi,* J. Dupont (Ed.), M. Balint and N. Z. Jackson (Trans.). Cambridge, MA: Harvard University Press.

Finkelstein, L. (1988). Psychoanalysis, marital therapy, and object-relations theory. *Journal of the American Psychoanalytic Association, 36,* 905-31.

Finn, M. G., & Gartner, J. (1992). *Object relations theory and religion: Clinical applications.* Westport, CT: Praeger.

Fisher, J. V. (1999). *The uninvited guest: Emerging from narcissism towards marriage.* London: Karnac Books.

Fonagy, P. (2001). *Attachment and psychoanalysis.* New York: Other Press.

Fonagy, P., Gergely, G., Jurist, E. J., & Target, M. (2002). *Affect regulation, mentalization, and the development of the self.* New York: Other Press.

Fonagy, P., Steele, H., & Steele, M. (1991). Maternal representations of attachment during pregnancy predict the organization of infant-mother attachment at one year of age. *Child Development, 62,* 891-905.

Fosha, D. (2000). *The transforming power of affect: A model for accelerated change*. New York: Basic Books.

Fosha, D. (2009). *Emotion and recognition at work: Energy, vitality, pleasure, truth, desire, and the emergent phenomenology of transformational experience*. In D. Fosha, D. J. Siegel & M. F. Solomon (Eds.), *The healing power of emotion: Affective neuroscience, development & clinical practice* (pp. 172-203). New York: W. W. Norton.

Fosha, D., Siegel, M. F., & Solomon, M. F. (Eds.). (2009). *The healing power of emotion: Affective neuroscience, development and clinical practice*. New York: W. W. Norton.

Fosshage, J. L. (1997a). Listening/experiencing perspectives and the quest for a facilitating responsiveness. *Progress in Self Psychology*, 13, 33-55.

Fosshage, J. L. (1997b). "Compensatory" or "primary": An alternative view. Discussion of Marian Tolpin's "compensatory structures: paths to the restoration of the self." *Progress in Self Psychology*, 13, 21-27.

Fosshage, J. L. (1998). Self psychology and its contributions to psychoanalysis: An overview. *Psychoanalytic Social Work*, 5, 1-17.

Fosshage, J. L. (2005). The explicit and implicit domains in psychoanalytic change. *Psychoanalytic Inquiry*, 25, 516-39.

Fosshage, J. L. (2011). How do we "know" what we "know"? And change what we "know"? *Psychoanalytic Dialogues*, 21, 55-74.

Fosshage, J. L. (2012, October). Forming and transforming self experience. Paper presented at the meeting of the Annual Self Psychology Conference, Washington, DC.

Fosshage, J., Lachmann, F., & Lichtenberg, J. (1992). *Self and motivational systems: Toward a theory of technique*. Hillsdale, NJ: Analytic Press.

Fosshage, J., Lachmann, F., & Lichtenberg, J. (1996). *The clinical exchange: Techniques derived from self and motivational systems*. Hillsdale, NJ: Analytic Press.

Foster, R. J. (1998). *Streams of living water: Celebrating the great traditions of the Christian faith*. New York: HarperCollins.

Fowler, J. W. (1981). *Stages of faith: The psychology of human development and the quest for meaning*. New York: HarperCollins.

Freud, A. (1936). *The ego and the mechanisms of defense: The writings of Anna Freud*. New York: International Universities Press.

Freud, S. (1913). *Totem and taboo*. London: Norton.

Freud, S. (1914). On narcissism. In J. Strachey (Ed.), *The standard edition of the complete psychological works of Sigmund Freud* (Vol. 14, pp. 67-102). London: Norton.

Freud, S. (1920). *Beyond the pleasure principle*. London: Norton.

Freud, S. (1923). *The ego and the id*. London: Norton.

Freud, S. (1926). The question of lay analysis. In J. Strachey (Ed.), *The standard edition of the complete psychological works of Sigmund Freud* (Vol. 10, pp. 177-258). London: Norton.

Freud, S. (1913/1950). *Totem and taboo*. London: Norton.

Freud, S. (1927/1961). *The future of an illusion*. London: Norton.

Freud, S. (1989). *An outline of psychoanalysis* (J. Strachey, Ed. & Trans.). New York: W. W. Norton. (Original work published 1940.)

Freud, S. (2001). Obsessive actions and religious practices. In E. Capps (Ed.), *Freud and Freudians on religion: A reader* (pp. 17-24). New Haven, CT: Yale University Press.

Gabbard, G. O. (2010). *Long-term psychodynamic psychotherapy: A basic text* (2nd ed.). Washington, DC: American Psychiatric Publishing.

Gallese, V. (2009). Mirror neurons, embodied simulation, and the neural basis of social identification. *Psychoanalytic Dialogues, 19*, 519-36.

Gardner, J. R. (2000). Using self psychology in brief psychotherapy. *Progress in Self Psychology, 16*, 219-48.

Gay, P. (1987). *A godless Jew: Freud, atheism, and the making of psychoanalysis*. New Haven, CT: Yale University Press.

Gay, P. (1988). *Freud: A life for our time*. New York: Norton.

Geist, R. A. (2007). Who are you, who am I, and where are we going: Sustained empathic immersion in the opening phase of psychoanalytic treatment. *International Journal of Psychoanalytic Self Psychology, 2*, 1-26.

Geist, R. A. (2008). Connectedness, permeable boundaries, and the development of the self: Therapeutic implications. *International Journal of Psychoanalytic Self Psychology, 3*, 129-52.

Geist, R. A. (2011). The forward edge, connectedness, and the therapeutic process. *International Journal of Psychoanalytic Self Psychology, 6*, 235-51.

Geist, R. A. (2013). How the empathic process heals: A microprocess perspective. *International Journal of Psychoanalytic Self Psychology, 8*, 265-81.

George, C., Kaplan, N., & Main, M. (1996). *Adult attachment interview protocol*

(3rd ed.) (Unpublished manuscript). University of California at Berkeley.

Gerson, M. J. (2001). The ritual of couples therapy: The subversion of autonomy. *Contemporary Psychoanalysis, 37,* 453-70.

Ghent, E. (1990). Masochism, submission, surrender: Masochism as a perversion of surrender. *Contemporary Psychoanalysis, 26,* 108-36.

Gill, M. (1982). *Analysis of transference: Vol. 1. Theory and technique.* New York: International Universities Press.

Goldberg, A. (1988). Changing psychic structure through treatment: From empathy to self-reflection. *Journal of the American Psychoanalytic Association, 36,* 211-24.

Goldberg, A. (1990). *The prison house of psychoanalysis.* Hillsdale, NJ: Analytic Press.

Goldberg, A. (2002). Self psychology since Kohut. *Progress in Self Psychology, 18,* 1-13.

Goldberg, A. (2011). The enduring presence of Heinz Kohut: Empathy and its vicissitudes. *Journal of the American Psychoanalytic Association, 59,* 289-311.

Goldberger, M. (1995). The couch as defense and as potential for enactment. *Psychoanalytic Quarterly, 64*(1), 23-42.

Goodman, D. M. (2012). *The demanded self: Levinasian ethics and identity in psychology.* Pittsburgh, PA: Duquesne University Press.

Goodman, D. M., & Grover, S. F. (2008). Hineni and transference: The remembering and forgetting of the other. *Pastoral Psychology, 56,* 561-71. doi:10.1007/s11089-008-0143-0.

Goodrick, E. W., & Kohlenberger, J. R. (2004). *The strongest NIV exhaustive concordance* (Rev. ed.). Grand Rapids, MI: Zondervan.

Gottman, J. M. (1999). *The marriage clinic: A scientifically based marital therapy.* New York: W. W. Norton.

Gray, P. (2005). *The ego and analysis of defense* (2nd ed.). Lanham, MD: Jason Aronson.

Greenbaum, H. (1983). On the nature of marriage and marriage therapy. *The Journal of the American Academy of Psychoanalysis and Dynamic Psychiatry, 11,* 283-97.

Greenberg, J. R., & Mitchell, S. A. (1983). *Object relations in psychoanalytic theory.* Cambridge, MA: Harvard University Press.

Greenson, R. (1967). *The technique and practice of psychoanalysis.* New York: International Universities Press.

Gregersen, N. H. (2006). Emergence: What is at stake for religious reflection? In P. Clayton & P. Davies (Eds.), *The re-emergence of emergence: The emergentist hypothesis from science to religion* (pp. 279-302). New York: Oxford University Press.

Greggo, S. P., & Sisemore, T. A. (Eds.). (2012). *Counseling and Christianity: Five approaches.* Downers Grove, IL: IVP Academic.

Grenz, S. J. (2001). *The social God and the relational self: A trinitarian theology of the imago Dei.* Louisville, KY: Westminster John Knox Press.

Grenz, S. J., & Franke, J. R. (2001). *Beyond foundationalism: Shaping theology in a postmodern context.* Louisville, KY: Westminster John Knox Press.

Grossmann, K. E., Grossmann, K., & Waters, E. (Eds.). (2005). *Attachment from infancy to adulthood: The major longitudinal studies.* New York: Guilford Press.

Gunter, W. S., Jones, S. T., Campbell, T. A., Miles, R. L., & Maddox, R. L. (1997). *Wesley and the quadrilateral: Renewing the conversation.* Nashville: Abingdon Press.

Gunton, C. (1998). *The triune creator: A historical and systematic study.* Grand Rapids, MI: Eerdmans.

Guntrip, H. (1949/1971). *Psychology for ministers and social workers* (3rd ed.). London: George Allen & Unwin.

Guntrip, H. (1969a). Religion in relation to personal integration. *British Journal of Medical Psychology, 42*, 323-33.

Guntrip, H. (1969b). *Schizoid phenomena object-relations and the self.* Madison, CT: International Universities Press.

Guntrip, H. (1971). *Psychoanalytic theory, therapy, and the self: A basic guide to the human personality in Freud, Erikson, Klein, Sullivan, Fairbairn, Hartman, Jacobson, & Winnicott.* New York: Basic Books.

Hall, D. J. (1986). *Imaging God: Dominion as stewardship.* Grand Rapids: Eerdmans.

Hall, T. W., & Brokaw, B. F. (1995). The relationship of spiritual maturity to level of object relations and God image. *Pastoral Psychology, 43*, 373-91.

Hall, T. W., Fujikawa, A., Halcrow, S., Hill, P. C., & Delaney, H. (2009). Attachment to God and implicit spirituality: Clarifying correspondence and compensation models. *Journal of Psychology and Theology, 37*, 227-42.

Happel, S. (2002). The soul and neuroscience: The empirical conditions for human agency and divine action. In R. J. Russell, N. Murphy, T. C. Meyering & M. A. Arbib (Eds.), *Neuroscience and the person: Scientific perspectives on divine action* (pp. 281-304). Vatican City State: Vatican Observatory Publications.

Harris, A. (2006). *Gender as soft assembly*. Hillsdale, NJ: Analytic Press.

Hartmann, H. (1939). *Ego psychology and the problem of adaptation*. New York: International University Press.

Haynal, A. (2002). *Disappearing and reviving: Sandor Ferenczi in the history of psychoanalysis*. London: Karnac.

Hazan, C., & Shaver, P. R. (1987). Romantic love conceptualized as an attachment process. *Journal of Personality and Social Psychology, 52*, 511-24.

Hedges, L. E. (1991). *Listening perspectives in psychotherapy*. New York: Aronson.

Hoffman, I. Z. (1983/1999). The patient as interpreter of the analyst's experience. *Contemporary Psychoanalysis, 19*, 389-422.

Hoffman, I. Z. (1998). *Ritual and spontaneity in the psychoanalytic process*. Hillsdale, NJ: Analytic Press.

Hoffman, L. W., & Strawn, B. D. (2009). Normative thoughts, normative feelings, normative actions: A Protestant, relational psychoanalytic reply to E. Christian Brugger and the faculty of IPS. *Journal of Psychology & Theology, 37*(2), 126-33.

Hoffman, L. W., & Strawn, B. D. (Eds.). (2010). Relational psychodynamic integration [Special Issue]. *Journal of Psychology and Christianity, 29*(2).

Hoffman, M., & Strawn, B. D. (Eds.) (2008). Transformation: Psychoanalysis and religion in dialogue. *Psychoanalytic Inquiry, 28*(5), 529-639.

Hoffman, M. T. (2004). From enemy combatant to strange bedfellow: The role of religious narratives in the work of W. R. D. Fairbairn and D. W. Winnicott. *Psychoanalytic Dialogues, 14*, 769-804.

Hoffman, M. T. (2011). *Toward mutual recognition: Relational psychoanalysis and the Christian narrative*. New York: Routledge.

Holliman, P. J. (2002). Religious experience as selfobject experience. *Progress in Self Psychology, 18*, 193-206.

Holmes, J. (1993). *John Bowlby and attachment theory*. New York: Brunner-Routledge.

Holmes, S. R. (2012). *The quest for the Trinity*. Downers Grove, IL: IVP Academic.

Horner, A. J. (1991). *Psychoanalytic object relations therapy*. Northvale, NJ: Jason Aronson.

Horowitz, M., Marmar, C., Krupnick, J., Wilner, N., Kaltreider, N., & Wallerstein, R. (1997). *Personality Styles and Brief Psychotherapy*. Northvale, NJ: Jason Aronson.

Hughes, J. M. (1990). *Reshaping the psychoanalytic domain: The work of Melanie Klein, W. R. D. Fairbairn, and D. W. Winnicott*. Berkeley: University of California Press.

Jacobs, L. (2010). Truth or what matters: Commentary on paper by Philip A. Ringstrom. *Psychoanalytic Dialogues, 20,* 224-30.

Jacobsen, D. (2003). *Thinking in the Spirit: Theologies of the early Pentecostal movement*. Bloomington: Indiana University Press.

Jacobsen, D., & Jacobsen, R. H. (2004). *Scholarship and Christian faith: Enlarging the conversation*. New York: Oxford University Press.

Jacobson, E. (1964). *The self and the object world*. New York: International Universities Press.

Jeeves, M., & Brown, W. S. (2009). *Neuroscience psychology and religion: Illusions, delusions, and realities about human nature*. West Conshohocken, PA: Templeton Foundation Press.

Johnson, E. L. (2007). *Foundations for soul care: A Christian psychology proposal*. Downers Grove, IL: IVP Academic.

Johnson, E. L. (Ed.). (2010). *Psychology & Christianity: Five views* (2nd ed.). Downers Grove, IL: IVP Academic.

Johnson, S. M. (2004). *The practice of emotionally focused couple therapy: Creating connection* (2nd ed.). New York: Brunner-Routledge.

Jones, J. W. (1991). *Contemporary psychoanalysis and religion: Transference and transcendence*. New Haven, CT: Yale University Press.

Jones, J. W. (1996). *Religion and psychology: Psychoanalysis, feminism, and theology*. New Haven, CT: Yale University Press.

Jones, J. W. (2007). The return of the repressed: Narcissism, religion, and the ferment in psychoanalysis. *The Annual of Psychoanalysis, 35,* 47-60.

Jones, S. L. (1994). A constructive relationship for religion with the science and profession of psychology: Perhaps the boldest model yet. *American Psychologist, 49,* 184-99.

Jones, S. L., & Butman, R. E. (1991). *Modern psychotherapies: A comprehensive Christian appraisal*. Downers Grove, IL: InterVarsity Press.

Jones, S. L., & Butman, R. E. (2011). *Modern psychotherapies: A comprehensive Christian appraisal* (2nd ed.). Downers Grove, IL: InterVarsity Press.

Karen, R. (1998). *Becoming attached: First relationships and how they shape our capacity to love*. New York: Oxford University Press.

Kinzer, M. (2000). *The nature of Messianic Judaism: Judaism as genus, Messianic as species*. West Hartford, CT: Hashivenu Archives.

Kinzer, M., & Juster, D. (2002). *Defining Messianic Judaism*. Retrieved May 24, 2004, from http://www.s221757179.onlinehome.us/LevHashem/docs/Defining_Messianic_Judaism.pdf.

Kirsner, D. (2001). The future of psychoanalytic institutes. *Psychoanalytic Psychology, 18*, 195-212.

Kirsner, D. (2004). Psychoanalysis and its discontents. *Psychoanalytic Psychology, 21*, 339-52.

Koch, C. (2004). *The quest for consciousness: A neurobiological approach*. Englewood, CO: Roberts and Company.

Koenig, H., King, D., & Carson, V. B. (2012). *Handbook of religion and health*. New York: Oxford University Press.

Kohut, H. (1959). Introspection, empathy, and psychoanalysis: An examination of the relationship between mode of observation and theory. *Journal of the American Psychoanalytic Association, 7*, 459-83.

Kohut, H. (1966). Forms and transformations of narcissism. *Journal of the American Psychoanalytic Association, 14*, 243-72.

Kohut, H. (1968). The psychoanalytic treatment of narcissistic personality disorders: Outline of a systemic approach. *The Psychoanalytic Study of the Child, 23*, 86-113.

Kohut, H. (1970). On courage. In C. B. Stozier (Ed.), *Self psychology and the humanities* (pp. 5-50). New York: W. W. Norton.

Kohut, H. (1971). *The analysis of the self*. Madison, CT: International Universities Press.

Kohut, H. (1975). The psychoanalyst in the community of scholars. *The Annual of Psychoanalysis, 3*, 341-70.

Kohut, H. (1977). *The restoration of the self*. Madison, CT: International Universities Press.

Kohut, H. (1984). *How does analysis cure?* Chicago: University of Chicago Press.

Kohut, H. (1985). Religion, ethics, values. In C. B. Stozier (Ed.), *Self psychology and the humanities: Reflections on a new psychoanalytic approach* (pp. 261-62). New York: W. W. Norton.

Kohut, H., & Wolf, E. S. (1978). The disorders of the self and their treatment: An outline. *The International Journal of Psychoanalysis, 59*, 413-25.

Kreeft, P. J. (2001). *Catholic Christianity: A complete catechism of Catholic beliefs based on the Catechism of the Catholic Church.* San Francisco: Ignatius Press.

Küng, H. (1979). *Freud and the problem of God.* New York: Doubleday.

Lachmann, F. M. (2008). *Transforming narcissism: Reflections on empathy, humor, and expectations.* New York: Analytic Press.

Lavner, J. A., & Bradbury, T. N. (2012). Why do even satisfied newlyweds eventually go on to divorce? *Journal of Family Psychology, 26*, 1-10.

Lawrence, R. T. (1997). Measuring the image of God: The God Image Inventory and the God Image Scales. *Journal of Psychology and Theology, 25*, 214-26.

Lee, R. R., & Martin, J. C. (1991). *Psychotherapy after Kohut: A textbook of self psychology.* New York: Routledge.

Lee, R. R., Roundtree, A., & McMahon, S. (2009). *Five Kohutian postulates: Psychotherapy theory from an empathic perspective.* Lanham, MD: Aronson.

Leichsenring, F., & Rabung, S. (2008). Effectiveness of long-term psychodynamic psychotherapy: A meta-analysis. *Journal of the American Medical Association, 300*, 1551-65.

Leone, C. (2008). Couple therapy from the perspective of self psychology and intersubjective theory. *Psychoanalytic Psychology, 25*, 79-98.

Leupp, R. T. (2008). *The renewal of trinitarian theology: Themes, patterns and explorations.* Downers Grove, IL: InterVarsity Press.

Levenson, H. (2010). *Brief dynamic therapy.* Washington, DC: American Psychological Association.

Levinas, E. (1969). *Totality and infinity* (A. Lingis, Trans.). Pittsburgh: Duquesne University Press.

Levinas, E. (1989). *The Levinas reader.* Sean Hand (Ed.). Oxford: Basil Blackwell.

Levy, S. T. (1985). Empathy and psychoanalytic technique. *Journal of the American Psychoanalytic Association, 33*, 353-78.

Lewis, C. S. (1952). *Mere Christianity.* San Francisco: HarperCollins.

Lewis, C. S. (1980). *The weight of glory and other addresses.* New York: Macmillan.

Lichtenberg, J. D. (1989). *Psychoanalysis and motivation.* Hillsdale, NJ: Analytic Press.

Lichtenberg, J. D., Lachmann, F. M., & Fosshage, J. L. (2011). *Psychoanalysis and motivational systems: A new look*. New York: Routledge.

Lieberman, A. E., & Van Horn, P. (2008). *Psychotherapy with infants and young children: Repairing the effects of stress and trauma on early attachment*. New York: Guilford Press.

Lindquist, K. A., Wager, T. D., Kober, H., Bliss-Moreau, E., & Barrett, L. F. (2012). The brain basis of emotion: A meta-analytic review. *Behavioral and Brian Sciences, 35*, 121-202.

Livingston, M. S. (2007). Sustained empathic focus, intersubjectivity, and intimacy in the treatment of couples. *International Journal of Psychoanalytic Self Psychology, 2*, 315-38.

Lodahl, M. (1997). The cosmological basis for John Wesley's "gradualism." *Wesleyan Theological Journal, 32*(1), 17-32.

Lodahl, M. (2004). *All things necessary to our salvation: The hermeneutical and theological implications of the article on the holy Scriptures in the manual of the church of the Nazarene*. San Diego: Point Loma Press.

Loewald, H. (1980). On motivation and instinct theory. In H. Loewald (Ed.), *Papers on psychoanalysis* (pp. 102-37). New Haven, CT: Yale University Press.

Longino, H. E. (1990). *Science as social knowledge: Values and objectivity in scientific inquiry*. Princeton, NJ: Princeton University Press.

Lothane, Z. (1998). The feud between Freud and Ferenczi over love. *The American Journal of Psychoanalysis, 58*, 21-39.

Luyten, P., & Blatt, S. J. (2013). Interpersonal relatedness and self-definition in normal and disrupted personality development: Retrospect and prospect. *American Psychologist, 68*, 172-83.

Lyons-Ruth, K. (1999). The two-person unconscious: Intersubjective dialogue, enactive relational representation, and the emergence of new forms of relational organization. *Psychoanalytic Inquiry, 19*, 576-617.

Lyons-Ruth, K. (2006). The interface between attachment and intersubjectivity: Perspective from the longitudinal study of disorganized attachment. *Psychoanalytic Inquiry, 26*, 595-616.

MacIntyre, A. (1964). Freud as moralist. *New York Review of Books, 2*(1), 14-15.

MacIntyre, A. (1984). *After virtue: A study in moral theory* (2nd ed.). Notre Dame, IN: University of Notre Dame Press.

MacIntyre, A. (2007). *After virtue: A study in moral theory* (3rd ed.). Notre Dame, IN: University of Notre Dame Press.

Maddox, R. L. (1994). *Responsible grace: John Wesley's practical theology.* Nashville: Kingswood Books.

Maddox, R. L. (2010). Wesleyan theology and moral psychology precedents for continuing engagement. In M. K. Armistead, B. D. Strawn, & R. W. Wright (Eds.), *Wesleyan theology and social science: The dance of practical divinity and discovery* (pp. 7-19). Newcastle upon Tyne, UK: Cambridge Scholars.

Mahler, M. S., Pine, F., & Bergman, A. (1975). *The psychological birth of the human infant: Symbiosis and individuation.* New York: Basic Books.

Main, M. (1991). Metacognitive knowledge, metacognitive monitoring, and singular (coherent) vs. multiple (incoherent) models of attachment: Findings and directions for future research. In P. Harris, J. Stevenson-Hinde & C. Parkes (Eds.), *Attachment across the lifecycle* (pp. 127-59). New York: Routledge.

Main, M., Goldwyn, R., & Hesse, E. (2003). *Adult attachment scoring and classification systems* (Unpublished manuscript). University of California, Berkeley.

Main, M., Kaplan, N., & Cassidy, J. (1985). Security in infancy, childhood, and adulthood: A move to the level of representation. In I. Bretherton & E. Waters (Eds.), *Growing points in attachment theory and research,* (pp. 66-104) Monographs of the Society for Research in Child Development.

Main, M., & Solomon, J. (1986). Procedures for identifying infants as disorganized/disoriented during the Ainsworth Strange Situation. In M. T. Greenberg, D. Ciccheti & E. M. Cummings (Eds.), *Attachment in the preschool years: Theory, research, and intervention* (pp. 121-60). Chicago: University of Chicago Press.

Mangis, M. W. (1999). An alien horizon: The psychoanalytic contribution to a Christian hermeneutic of humility and confidence. *Christian Scholar's Review, 28*(3), 411-31.

Mangis, M. W. (2008). *Signature sins: Taming our wayward hearts.* Downers Grove, IL: InterVarsity Press.

Mann, J. (1973). *Time-limited psychotherapy.* Cambridge, MA: Harvard University Press.

Marcus, P. (2003). *Ancient religious wisdom, spirituality, and psychoanalysis.* Westport, CT: Praeger.

Maroda, K. (1999). *Seduction, surrender and transformation.* Hillsdale, NJ: Analytic Press.

Maroda, K. (2004). *The power of countertransference.* Northvale, NJ: Aronson.

Maroda, K. (2009). *Psychodynamic technique: Working with emotions in the therapeutic relationship.* New York: Guilford Press.

McAdams, D. P. (2001). The psychology of life stories. *Review of General Psychology, 5*, 100-122.

McAdams, D. P. (2011). Life narratives. In K. L. Fingerman, C. Berg, J. Smith & T. C. Antonucci (Eds.), *Handbook of life-span development* (pp. 589-610). New York: Springer.

McAdoo, H. R. (1965). *The spirit of Anglicanism.* New York: Charles Scribner's.

McDargh, J. (1983). *Psychoanalytic object relations theory and the study of religion: On faith and the imaging of God.* Lanham, MD: University Press of America.

McGrath, A. (1995). *Evangelicalism and the future of Christianity.* Downers Grove, IL: InterVarsity Press.

McGrath, A. (Ed.). (2001a). *Christian literature: An anthology.* Oxford, UK: Blackwell.

McGrath, A. (Ed.). (2001b). *The Christian theology reader* (2nd ed.). Oxford, UK: Blackwell.

McGrath, A. (2011). *Christian theology: An introduction* (5th ed.). Oxford, UK: John Wiley.

McWilliams, N. (1994). Psychoanalytic diagnosis: Understanding personality structure in the clinical process. New York: Guilford Press.

McWilliams, N. (1999). *Psychoanalytic case formulation.* New York: Guilford Press.

McWilliams, N. (2004). *Psychoanalytic psychotherapy: A practitioner's guide.* New York: Guilford Press.

Meissner, W. W. (1984). *Psychoanalysis and religious experience.* New Haven, CT: Yale University Press.

Meissner, W. W. (1992). *What is effective in psychoanalytic therapy: The move from interpretation to relation.* Northvale, NJ: Jason Aronson.

Middlemore, M. P. (1941). *The nursing couple.* London: Hamish Hamilton, Medical Books.

Mikulincer, M., & Shaver, P. R. (2007). *Attachment in adulthood: Structure, dynamics, and change.* New York: Guilford Press.

Miller, L. J. (Ed.). (2012). *The Oxford handbook of psychology and spirituality.* New York: Oxford University Press.

Mitchell, S. A. (1988). *Relational concepts in psychoanalysis: An integration.*

Cambridge, MA: Harvard University Press.

Mitchell, S. A. (1991). Contemporary perspectives on self: Toward an integration. *Psychoanalytic Dialogues, 1*, 121-47.

Mitchell, S. A. (1993). *Hope and dread in psychoanalysis.* New York: Basic Books.

Mitchell, S. A. (1997). *Influence and autonomy in psychoanalysis.* Hillsdale, NJ: Analytic Press.

Mitchell, S. A. (1998). The analyst's knowledge and authority. *Psychoanalytic Quarterly, 67*, 1-31.

Mitchell, S. A. (2000). *Relationality: From attachment to intersubjectivity.* Hillsdale, NJ: Analytic Press.

Mitchell, S., & Aron, L. (Eds.). (1999). *Relational psychoanalysis: The emergence of a tradition.* Hillsdale, NJ: Analytic Press.

Mitchell, S. A., & Black, M. J. (1995). *Freud and beyond: A history of modern psychoanalytic thought.* New York: Basic Books.

Murphy, N. (1996). *Beyond liberalism and fundamentalism: How modern and postmodern philosophy set the theological agenda.* Harrisburg, PA: Trinity Press International.

Murphy, N. (1997). *Anglo-American postmodernity: Philosophical perspectives on science, religion, and ethics.* Boulder, CO: Westview Press.

Murphy, N. (2005a). Philosophical resources for integration. In A. Dueck & C. Lee (Eds.), *Why psychology needs theology: A Radical-Reformation perspective* (pp. 3-27). Grand Rapids, MI: Eerdmans.

Murphy, N. (2005b). Theological resources for integration. In A. Dueck & C. Lee (Eds.), *Why psychology needs theology: A Radical-Reformation perspective* (pp. 28-52). Grand Rapids, MI: Eerdmans.

Nagel, T. (2012). *Mind & cosmos: Why the materialist neo-Darwinian conception of nature is almost certainly false.* New York: Oxford University Press.

Nordling, B., & Scrofani, P. (2009). Implications of a Catholic anthropology for developing a Catholic approach to psychotherapy. *Edification, 3*(1), 76-79.

Ogden, T. (1982). *Projective identification and psychotherapeutic technique.* New York: Jason Aronson.

Ogden, T. (1994). *Subject of analysis.* Northvale, NJ: Jason Aronson.

Oliver, K. (2001). *Witnessing beyond recognition.* Minneapolis: University of Minnesota Press.

Olthuis, J. H. (2001). *The beautiful risk: A new psychology of loving and being loved.* Grand Rapids, MI: Zondervan.

Oord, T. J. (2004). *Science of love: The wisdom of well-being.* Philadelphia: Templeton Foundation Press.

Oord, T. J. (2010). *The nature of love: A theology.* St. Louis: Chalice Press.

Oord, T. J., & Lodahl, M. (2005). *Relational holiness: Responding to the call of love.* Kansas City: Beacon Hill Press.

Orange, D. M. (1995). *Emotional understanding: Studies in psychoanalytic epistemology.* New York: Guildford Press.

Orange, D. M. (2009). Psychoanalysis in a phenomenological spirit. *International Journal of Psychoanalytic Self Psychology, 4,* 119-21. doi:10.1080/15551020802527845.

Orange, D. M. (2010a). Recognition as: Intersubjective vulnerability in the psychoanalytic dialogue. *International Journal of Psychoanalytic Self Psychology, 5,* 227-43. doi:10.1080/15551024.2010.491719.

Orange, D. M. (2010b). *Thinking for clinicians: Philosophical resources for contemporary psychoanalysis and the humanistic psychotherapies.* New York: Routledge.

Orange, D. M. (2011). *The suffering stranger: Hermeneutics for everyday clinical practice.* New York: Routledge.

Orange, D. M. (2012). Book review, M. Hoffman, Toward mutual recognition: Relational psychoanalysis and the Christian narrative. *Psychoanalytic Psychology, 29,* 112-18.

Orange, D. M., Atwood, G. E., & Stolorow, R. D. (1997). *Working intersubjectively: Contextualism in psychoanalytic practice.* New York: Routledge.

Ornstein, A. (1974). The dread to repeat and the new beginning: A contribution to the psychoanalysis of the narcissistic personality disorders. *Annual of Psychoanalysis, 2,* 231-48.

Ornstein, A. (1991). The dread to repeat: Comments on the working-through process in psychoanalysis. *Journal of the American Psychoanalytic Association, 39,* 377-98.

Ornstein, P. H. (1995). Critical reflections on a comparative analysis of "Self Psychology and Intersubjectivity Theory." *Progress in Self Psychology, 11,* 47-77.

Ornstein, P. H. (2008). Heinz Kohut's self psychology—and ours: Transformations of psychoanalysis. *International Journal of Psychoanalytic Self Psychology, 3,* 195-214.

Ornstein, P., & Ornstein, A. (1997, November). *Brief but deep: Finding the focus in "focal psychotherapy."* Paper presented at the meeting of the 20th Annual International Conference on the Psychology of the Self, Chicago.

Ornstein, P. H., Ornstein, A., Zaleznik, A., & Schwaber, E. (1977). On the continuing evolution of psychoanalytic psychotherapy: Reflections and predictions. *Annual of Psychoanalysis, 5,* 329-70.

Ornston, D. (1982). Strachey's influence: A preliminary report. *The International Journal of Psychoanalysis, 63,* 409-26.

Ornston, D. (1985). Freud's conception is different from Strachey's. *Journal of the American Psychoanalytic Association, 33,* 379-412.

Outler, A. C. (1985). The Wesleyan quadrilateral in Wesley. *Wesleyan Theological Journal, 20*(1), 7-18.

Panksepp, J. (2009). Brain emotional systems and qualities of mental life: From animal models of affect to implications for psychotherapeutics. In D. Fosha, D. J. Siegel & M. Solomon (Eds.), *The healing power of emotion: Affective neuroscience, development & clinical practice* (pp. 1-26). New York: W. W. Norton.

Pappenheim, H., & Papiasvili, E. D. (Eds.). (2010). Contemporary perspectives on the Oedipus complex. *Psychoanalytic Inquiry, 30*(2).

Parker, S. E. (2012). *Winnicott and religion.* Northvale, NJ: Jason Aronson.

PDM Task Force. (2006). *Psychodynamic diagnostic manual.* Silver Springs, MD: Alliance of Psychoanalytic Organizations.

Peacocke, A. (2006). Emergence, mind, and divine action: The hierarchy of the sciences in relation to the human mind-brain-body. In P. Clayton & P. Davies (Eds.), *The re-emergence of emergence: An emergentist hypothesis from science to religion* (pp. 257-78). New York: Oxford University Press.

Peacocke, A. (2007). *All that is: A naturalistic faith for the twenty-first century.* Minneapolis: Fortress Press.

Phillips, A. (1989). *Winnicott.* Cambridge, MA: Harvard University Press.

Phillips, A. (1995). *Terror and experts.* Cambridge, MA: Harvard University Press.

Phillips, A. (1998). *The beast in the nursery: On curiosity and other appetites.* New York: Pantheon.

Pine, F. (1998). *Diversity and direction in psychoanalytic technique.* New Haven, CT: Yale University Press.

Pinker, S. (1997). *How the mind works.* New York: W. W. Norton.

Pinnock, C. H. (2001). *Most moved mover: A theology of God's openness.* Grand Rapids, MI: Baker.

Pizer, B. (2008). The heart of the matter in matters of the heart: Power and intimacy in analytic and couples relationships. *International journal of Psychoanalytic Self Psychology, 3,* 304-19.

Pizer, S. (1998). *Building bridges: The negotiation of paradox in psychoanalysis.* Hillsdale, NJ: Analytic Press.

Plantinga, A. (2011). *Where the conflict really lies: Science, religion, and naturalism.* New York: Oxford University Press.

Polanyi, M. (1958). *Personal knowledge: Towards a post-critical philosophy.* Chicago: University of Chicago Press.

Polkinghorne, J. (2004). *Science and the Trinity: The Christian encounter with reality.* New Haven, CT: Yale University Press.

Polkinghorne, J. (2009). *Theology in the context of science.* New Haven, CT: Yale University Press.

Porges, S. W. (2009). Reciprocal influences between body and brain in the perception and expression of affect: A polyvagal perspective. In D. Fosha, D. J. Siegel & M. F. Solomon (Eds.), *The healing power of emotion: Affective neuroscience, development and clinical practice* (pp. 27-54). New York: W. W. Norton.

Powell, S. M., & Lodahl, M. E. (Eds.). (1999). *Embodied holiness: Toward a corporate theology of spiritual growth.* Downers Grove, IL: InterVarsity Press.

Process of Change Study Group (1998). Non-interpretive mechanisms in psychoanalytic therapy: The "something more" than interpretation. *International Journal of Psycho-Analysis, 79,* 903-21.

Rachman, A. (1997). *Sandor Ferenczi: The psychotherapist of tenderness and passion.* Northvale, NJ: Jason Aronson.

Ramzy, I. (1983). The place of values in psycho-analysis. *Psychoanalytic Inquiry, 3,* 551-72.

Rangell, L. (2004). *My life in theory.* New York: Other Press.

Rayner, E. (1991). *The independent mind in British psychoanalysis.* Northvale, NJ: Jason Aronson.

Reimer, K., & Dueck, A. (2006). Inviting Soheil: Narrative and embrace in Christian caregiving. *Christian Scholar's Review, 35,* 205-20.

Reis, B. (2009). We: Commentary on papers by Trevarthen, Ammaniti & Trentini and Gallese. *Psychoanalytic Dialogues, 19,* 565-29.

Reis, B. (2010). All roads do not lead to Rome. *Psychoanalytic Dialogues, 20,* 231-35.

Renik, O. (1993). Analytic interaction: Conceptualizing technique in light of the analyst's irreducible subjectivity. *Psychoanalytic Quarterly, 62,* 553-71.

Renik, O. (2006). *Practical psychoanalysis for therapist and patient.* New York: Other Press.

Rholes, W. S., & Simpson, J. A. (2004). Attachment theory: Basic concepts and contemporary questions. In W. S. Rholes & J. A. Simpson (Eds.), *Adult attachment: Theory, research, and clinical implications* (pp. 3-14). New York: Guilford Press.

Rieff, P. (1966). *The triumph of the therapeutic: Uses of faith after Freud.* Chicago: University of Chicago Press.

Riker, J. H. (2010). *Why is it good to be good: Ethics, Kohut's self psychology, and modern society.* New York: Aronson.

Ringstrom, P. (2010a). Meeting Mitchell's challenge: A comparison of relational psychoanalysis and intersubjective systems theory. *Psychoanalytic Dialogues, 20,* 196-218.

Ringstrom, P. (2010b). Reply to commentaries. *Psychoanalytic Dialogues, 20,* 236-50.

Ringstrom, P. A. (1994). An intersubjective approach to conjoint therapy. In A. Goldberg (Ed.), *Progress in self psychology* (Vol. 10, pp. 159-82). Hillsdale, NJ: The Analytic Press.

Ringstrom, P. A. (2012). A relational intersubjective approach to conjoint treatment. *International Journal of Psychoanalytic Self Psychology, 7,* 85-111.

Rizzuto, A. (1979). *The birth of the living god: A psychoanalytic study.* Chicago: University of Chicago Press.

Rizzuto, A. M. (1998). *Why did Freud reject God? A psychodynamic interpretation.* New Haven, CT: Yale University Press.

Rizzuto, A. M. (2004). Roman Catholic background and psychoanalysis. *Psychoanalytic Psychology, 21,* 436-41.

Roberts, R. C. (1997). Parameters of a Christian psychology. In R. C. Roberts & M. R. Talbot (Eds.), *Limning the psyche: Explorations in Christian psychology* (pp. 74-101). Grand Rapids, MI: Eerdmans.

Roberts, R. C., & Wood, W. J. (2007). *Intellectual virtues: An essay in regulative epistemology.* Oxford, England: Clarendon Press.

Rochat, P. (2003). Five levels of self-awareness as they unfold in life. *Consciousness and Cognition, 12,* 717-31.

Rubin, J. B. (1997). Psychoanalysis is self-centered. In C. Spezzano & G. J. Gariulo (Eds.), *Soul on the couch: Spirituality religion and morality in contemporary psychoanalysis* (pp. 79-108). Hillsdale, NJ: Analytic Press.

Rubin, J. B. (1998). *A psychoanalysis for our time: Exploring the blindness of the seeing I.* New York: New York University Press.

Rudnytsky, P., Bokay, A., & Giampieri-Deutsch, P. (Eds.). (1996). *Ferenczi's turn in psychoanalysis.* New York: New York University Press.

Runyon, R. (1998). *The new creation: John Wesley's theology today.* Nashville: Abingdon Press.

Russell, R. J., Murphy, N., & Stoeger, W. R. (Eds.). (2008). *Scientific perspectives on divine action: Twenty years of challenge and progress* (Vol. 6). Berkley, CA: Center for Theology and Natural Sciences.

Safran, J. D. (2002). Brief relational psychoanalytic treatment. *Psychoanalytic Dialogues, 12,* 171-95.

Safran, J. D. (Ed.). (2003). *Psychoanalysis and Buddhism: An unfolding dialogue.* Boston: Wisdom Publications.

Safran, J. D. (2009). Interview with Lewis Aron. *Psychoanalytic Psychology, 26,* 99-116.

Scharff, D. E., & Scharff, J. S. (1991). *Object relations couples therapy.* Lanham, MD: Jason Aronson.

Schiffman, M. (1992). *Return of the remnant: The rebirth of Messianic Judaism.* Baltimore: Lederer.

Schore, A. N. (2003). *Affect dysregulation and disorders of the self.* New York: Norton.

Schore, A. N. (2009). Right brain affect regulation: An essential mechanism of development, trauma, dissociation, and psychotherapy. In D. Fosha, D. J. Siegel & M. Solomon (Eds.), *The healing power of emotions: Affective neuroscience, development & clinical practice* (pp. 112-44). New York: W. W. Norton.

Schore, A. N. (2011). The right brain implicit self lies at the core of psychoanalysis. *Psychoanalytic Dialogues, 21,* 75-100.

Searle, J. R. (2008). *Philosophy in a new century: Selected essays.* Cambridge: Cambridge University Press.

Seligman, S. (2003). The developmental perspective in relational psychoanalysis. *Contemporary Psychoanalysis, 39,* 477-508.

Sells, J. N., & Yarhouse, M. A. (2011). *Counseling couples in conflict: A rela-*

tional restoration model. Downers Grove, IL: IVP Academic.

Shabad, P. (2001). *Despair and the return of hope: Echoes of mourning in psychotherapy.* Northvale, NJ: Jason Aronson.

Shaddock, D. (2000). *Contexts and connections.* New York: Basic Books.

Shedler, J. (2006). That was then, this is now: An introduction to contemporary psychodynamic therapy. Retrieved from www.psychsystems.net/Publications/Shedler.

Shedler, J. (2010). The efficacy of psychodynamic psychotherapy. *American Psychologist, 65*(2), 98-109.

Shelley, B. L. (1995). *Church history in plain language* (2nd ed.). Nashville: Thomas Nelson.

Shults, F. L. (2003). *Reforming theological anthropology: After the philosophical turn to relationality.* Grand Rapids, MI: Eerdmans.

Shults, F. L., & Sandage, S. J. (2003). *The faces of forgiveness: Searching for wholeness and salvation.* Grand Rapids, MI: Baker Academic.

Shults, F. L., & Sandage, S. J. (2006). *Transforming spirituality: Integrating theology and psychology.* Grand Rapids, MI: Baker Academic.

Siegel, A. M. (1996). *Heinz Kohut and the psychology of the self.* New York: Routledge.

Siegel, D. J. (2012). *The developing mind: How relationships and the brain interact to shape who we are* (2nd ed.). New York: Guilford Press.

Silberstein, M. (2006). In defense of ontological emergence and mental causation. In P. Clayton & P. Davies (Eds.), *The re-emergence of emergence: The emergentist hypothesis from science to religion* (pp. 203-26). Oxford, UK: Oxford University Press.

Sisemore, T. A. (2011). An introduction to the Christian psychology special issue. *Journal of Psychology and Christianity, 30,* 271-73.

Slochower, J. (1996). *Holding and psychoanalysis: A relational perspective.* Hillsdale, NJ: Analytic Press.

Slochower, J. (2006). *Psychoanalytic collisions.* Mahwah, NJ: Analytic Press.

Smith, G. D. (Ed.). (1955). *The teaching of the Catholic Church* (Vols. 1-2). New York: Macmillan.

Socarides, D. D., & Stolorow, R. D. (1984/1985). Affects and selfobjects. *The Annual of Psychoanalysis, 12/13,* 105-19. Madison, CT: International Universities Press.

Sorenson, R. L. (2004a). *Minding spirituality.* Hillsdale, NJ: Analytic Press.

Sorenson, R. L. (2004b). Kenosis and alterity in Christian spirituality. *Psychoanalytic Psychology*, 21, 458-62.

Spezzano, C. (1993). *Affect in psychoanalysis*. Hillsdale, NJ: Analytic Press.

Spezzano, C., & Gargiulo, G. (Eds.). (1997). *Soul on the couch: Spirituality, religion and morality in contemporary psychoanalysis*. Hillsdale, NJ: Analytic Press.

Spittler, R. P. (1999). Corinthian spirituality: How a flawed anthropology imperils authentic Christian existence. In E. L. Blumhofer, R. P. Spittler, & G. A. Wacker (Eds.), *Pentecostal currents in American Protestantism* (pp. 3-22). Urbana: University of Illinois Press.

Sroufe, A. (2002). Attachment in developmental perspective. *Journal of Infant, Child, and Adolescent Psychotherapy*, 2, 19-25.

Sroufe, L. A. (2005). Attachment and development: A prospective, longitudinal study from birth to adulthood. *Attachment & Human Development*, 4, 349-67.

Sroufe, L.A., & Waters, E. (1977). Attachment as an organizational construct. *Child Development*, 48, 1184-99.

Stanton, M. (1991). *Sandor Ferenczi: Reconsidering active intervention*. Northvale, NJ: Jason Aronson.

Stanton, M., & Welsh, R. (2012). Systemic thinking in couple and family psychology research and practice. *Couple and Family Psychology: Research and Practice*, 1, 14-30.

Stark, M. (1999). *Modes of therapeutic action*. Northvale, NJ: Jason Aronson.

Starr, K. (2008). *Repair of the soul: Metaphors of transformation in Jewish mysticism and psychoanalysis*. New York: Routledge.

Stepansky, P. E. (2009). *Psychoanalysis at the margins*. New York: Other Press.

Stern, D. B. (1992). Commentary on constructivism in clinical practice. *Psychoanalytic Dialogues*, 2, 331-63.

Stern, D. B. (1997). *Unformulated experience: From dissociation to imagination in psychoanalysis*. Hillsdale, NJ: Analytic Press.

Stern, D. B. (2010). *Partners in thought: Working with unformulated experience, dissociation and enactment*. New York: Routledge.

Stern, D. N. (1985). *The interpersonal world of the infant: A view from psychoanalysis and developmental theory*. New York: Basic Books.

Stern, D. N., Sander, L. W., Nahum, J. P., Harrison, A. M., Lyons-Ruth, K., Morgan, A. C., & Tronick, E. Z. (1998). Non-interpretive mechanisms in psychoanalytic therapy: The "something more" than interpretation. *The*

International Journal of Psychoanalysis, 97, 903-21.

Stolorow, R. D. (1994a). Kohut, Gill, and the new psychoanalytic paradigm. *Progress in Self Psychology, 10,* 221-26.

Stolorow, R. D. (1994b). Converting psychotherapy to psychoanalysis. In R. D. Stolorow, G. E. Atwood & B. Brandchaft (Eds.), *The intersubjective perspective* (pp. 145-56). New Jersey: Jason Aronson.

Stolorow, R. D. (2002). From drive to affectivity: Contextualizing psychological life. *Psychoanalytic Inquiry, 22,* 678-85. doi:10.1080/07351692209349012.

Stolorow, R. D. (2007). *Trauma and human existence: Autobiographical, psychoanalytic, and philosophical reflections.* New York: Analytic Press.

Stolorow, R. D., & Atwood, G. E. (1979). *Faces in a cloud: Subjectivity in personality theory.* New York: Aronson.

Stolorow, R. D., & Atwood, G. E. (1984). Psychoanalytic phenomenology: Toward a science of human experience. *Psychoanalytic Inquiry, 4,* 87-105. doi:10.1080/07351698409533532.

Stolorow, R. D., & Atwood, G. E. (1992). *Contexts of being: The intersubjective foundations of psychological life.* Hillsdale, NJ: Analytic Press.

Stolorow, R. D., & Atwood, G. E. (2002). *Contexts of being: Intersubjective foundations of psychological life.* New York: Routledge.

Stolorow, R. D., & Brandchaft, B. (1987). Developmental failure and psychic conflict. *Psychoanalytic Psychology, 4,* 241-53.

Stolorow, R., Brandchaft, B., & Atwood, G. (1987). *Psychoanalytic treatment, an intersubjective approach.* Hillsdale, NJ: Analytic Press.

Stolorow, R. D., Brandchaft, B., & Atwood, G. E. (1995). *Psychoanalytic treatment: An intersubjective approach.* New York: Routledge.

Stolorow, R., Orange, D., & Atwood, G. (2002). *Worlds of experience: Interweaving philosophical and clinical dimensions in psychoanalysis.* New York: Basic Books.

Stone, B. P., & Oord, T. J. (Eds.). (2001). *Thy nature and thy name is love: Wesleyan and process theologies in dialogue.* Nashville: Kingswood.

Stozier, C. B. (2001). *Heinz Kohut: The making of a psychoanalyst.* New York: Farrar, Straus & Giroux.

Strawn, B. D. (2004). Restoring moral affections of heart: How does psychotherapy heal? *Journal of Psychology and Christianity, 23*(2), 140-48.

Strawn, B. D. (Ed.). (2004). Psychology and Wesleyan theology [Special issue]. *Journal of Psychology and Christianity, 23,* 99-188.

Strawn, B. D. (Ed.). (2007). Psychoanalytic psychotherapy and religion: A case study approach [Special Issue]. *Journal of Psychology & Theology, 35*(1).

Strawn, B. D., & Leffel, G. M. (2001). John Wesley's orthokardia and Harry Guntrip's "heart of the personal": Convergent aims and complementary practices in psychotherapy and spiritual formation. *Journal of Psychology and Christianity, 20*(4), 351-59.

Strupp, H. H., & Binder, J. L. (1985). *Psychotherapy in a new key: A guide to time-limited dynamic psychotherapy.* New York: Basic Books.

Suchet, M., Aron, L., & Harris, A. (Eds.). (2007). *Relational Psychoanalysis: Volume 3: New voices.* New York: Routledge.

Sulloway, F. J. (1979). *Freud, biologist of the mind: Beyond the psychoanalytic legend.* New York: Basic Books.

Summers, F. (1994). *Object relations theories and psychopathology: A comprehensive text.* Hillsdale, NJ: Analytic Press.

Summers, F. (1996). Self psychology and its place among contemporary psychoanalytic theories. *Annual of Psychoanalysis, 24,* 157-71.

Summers, F. (1999). *Transcending the self: An object relations model of psychoanalytic therapy.* New York: Routledge.

Summers, F. (2013). *The psychoanalytic vision: The experiencing subject, transcendence, and the therapeutic process.* New York: Routledge.

Sutherland, J. D. (1989). *Fairbairn's journey into the interior.* London: Free Association Books.

Suttie, I. (1935). *The origins of love and hate.* London: Free Association Books.

Sweeney, D. A. (2005). *The American evangelical story: A history of the movement.* Grand Rapids, MI: Baker.

Symington, N. (1994). *Emotion and spirit: Questioning the claims of psychoanalysis and religion.* New York: St. Martin's Press.

Tan, S. Y. (2011). *Counseling and psychotherapy: A Christian perspective.* Grand Rapids, MI: Baker Academic.

Taylor, C. (1989). *Sources of the self: The making of the modern identity.* Cambridge, MA: Harvard University Press.

Taylor, C. (2007). *A secular age.* Cambridge, MA: Belknap Press.

Taylor, C. (2011). *Dilemmas and connections.* Cambridge, MA: Belknap Press.

Teicholz, J. G. (2000). The analyst's empathy, subjectivity, and authenticity: Affect as the common denominator. *Progress in Self Psychology, 16,* 33-53.

Teicholz, J. G. (2006). Qualities of engagement and the analyst's theory. *In-*

ternational Journal of Psychoanalytic Self Psychology, 1, 47-77.

Thelen, E., & Smith, L. B. (1994). *A dynamic systems approach to the development of cognition and action.* Cambridge, MA: MIT Press.

Thompson, C. (2010). *Anatomy of the soul: Surprising connections between neuroscience and spiritual practices that can transform your life and relationships.* Carol Stream, IL: Tyndale House.

Tisdale, T. C. (1998). A comparison of Jewish, Muslim, and Protestant faith groups on the relationship between level of object relations development and experience of God and self. *Dissertation Abstracts International: Section B: The Sciences & Engineering, 58,* 9-B, p. 5144.

Tisdale, T. C., Key, T. L., Edwards, K. J., Brokaw, B. F., Kemperman, S. R., Cloud, H., . . . Okamoto, T. (1997). Impact of treatment on God image and personal adjustment, and correlations of God image to personal adjustment and object relations development. *Journal of Psychology & Theology, 25,* pp. 227-39.

Tolpin, M. (1971). On the beginnings of a cohesive self: An application of the concept of transmuting internalizations to the study of the transitional object and signal anxiety. *The Psychoanalytic Study of the Child, 26,* 316-54.

Tolpin, M. (1986). The self and its selfobjects: A different baby. *Progress in Self Psychology, 2,* 115-28.

Tolpin, M. (1997). Compensatory structures: Paths to the restoration of the self. *Progress in Self Psychology, 13,* 3-19.

Tolpin, M. (2002). Doing psychoanalysis of normal development: Forward edge transferences. *Progress in Self Psychology, 18,* 167-90.

Toulmin, S. (1990). *Cosmopolis: The hidden agenda of modernity.* Chicago: University of Chicago Press.

Trader, A. (2012). Patristic embroidery on a cognitive pattern and other uses of the Fathers' yarn: Introducing the evidence of early Christian texts into therapeutic practice. *Edification, 6,* 85-96.

Trevarthen, C. (1979). Communication and cooperation in early infancy: A description of primary intersubjectivity. In M. Bullowa (Ed.), *Before speech: The beginnings of human communication* (pp. 321-47). London: Cambridge University Press.

Trevarthen, C. (2009). The intersubjective psychobiology of human meaning: Learning of culture depends on interest for co-operative practical work—and affection for the joyful art of good company. *Psychoanalytic Dialogues, 19,* 507-18.

Tronick, E. (2007). The neurobehavioral and social-emotional development of infants and children. New York: Norton.

Tronick, E., & Beeghly, M. (2011). Infants' meaning-making and the development of mental health problems. *American Psychologist, 66,* 107-19.

Tronick, E. Z., Brushweiller-Stern, N., Harrison, A. M., Lyons-Ruth, K., Morgan, A. C., Nahum, J. P., . . . Stern, D. N. (1998). Dyadically expanded states of consciousness and the process of therapeutic change. *Infant Mental Health Journal, 19,* 290-99.

Trop, G. S., Burke, M. L., & Trop, J. L. (2002). Chapter 9: Thinking dynamically in psychoanalytic theory and practice: A review of intersubjectivity theory. *Progress in Self Psychology, 18,* 129-47.

Trop, J. L. (1994). Conjoint therapy: An intersubjective approach. *Progress in Self Psychology, 10,* 147-58.

Tyson, P. L., & Tyson, R. L. (1990). *Psychoanalytic theories of development: An integration.* New Haven, CT: Yale University Press.

Uttal, W. R. (2011). *Mind and brain: A critical appraisal of cognitive neuroscience.* Cambridge, MA: The MIT Press.

Vande Kemp, H. (1996). Historical perspective: Religion and clinical psychology in America. In E. P. Shafranske (Ed.), *Religion and the clinical practice of psychology* (pp. 71-112). Washington, DC: American Psychological Association.

Vitz, P. C. (1993). *Sigmund Freud's Christian unconscious.* Grand Rapids, MI: Eerdmans.

Vitz, P. C., & Felch, S. (2006). *The self: Beyond the postmodern crisis.* Wilmington, DE: Intercollegiate Studies Institute.

Volf, M. (1998). *After our likeness: The church as the image of the Trinity.* Grand Rapids, MI: Eerdmans.

Wachtel, P. (1997). *Psychoanalysis, behavior therapy and the relational world.* Washington, DC: American Psychological Association.

Wachtel, P. L. (2008). *Relational theory and the practice of psychotherapy.* New York: Guilford Press.

Wachtel, P. L. (2010). One-person and two-person conceptions of attachment and their implications for psychoanalytic thought. *The International Journal of Psychoanalysis, 91,* 561-81.

Wacker, G. A. (1999). Travail of a broken family: Radical evangelical responses to the emergence of Pentecostalism in America, 1906-16. In E. L. Blumhofer, R. P. Spittler, & G. A. Wacker (Eds.), *Pentecostal currents in*

American Protestantism (pp. 23-49). Urbana: University of Illinois Press.

Wallin, D. J. (2007). *Attachment in psychotherapy.* New York: Guilford Press.

Warrington, K. (2008). *Pentecostal theology: A theology of encounter.* London: T & T Clark.

Webb, T. L., Miles, E., & Sheeran, P. (2012). Dealing with feeling: A meta-analysis of the effectiveness of strategies derived from the process model of emotion regulation. *Psychological Bulletin, 128,* 775-808.

Webber, R. (1999). *Ancient-future faith: Rethinking evangelicalism for a post-modern world.* Grand Rapids, MI: Baker.

Wegter-McNelly, K. (2011). *The entangled God: Divine relationality and quantum physics.* New York: Routledge.

Westermann, C. (1974). *Genesis 1-11: A commentary.* Minneapolis: Augsburg Publishing.

Wheelis, A. (1973). *How people change.* New York: HarperPerennial.

Willard, D. (1998). *The divine conspiracy: Rediscovering our hidden life in God.* New York: HarperSanFrancisco.

Willard, D. (2002). *Renovation of the heart.* Colorado Springs, CO: NavPress.

Wilson, T. D. (2002). *Strangers to ourselves: Discovering the adaptive unconscious.* Cambridge, MA: Belknap Press.

Winnicott, D. W. (1942). The nursing couple: By Merell Middlemore. *The International Journal of Psychoanalysis, 23,* 179-81.

Winnicott, D. W. (1953). Transitional objects and transitional phenomena: A study of the first not-me possession. *The International Journal of Psychoanalysis, 34,* 89-97.

Winnicott, D. (1960). *The theory of parent-infant relationship.* In *The maturational process and the facilitating environment.* New York: International Universities Press.

Winnicott, D. (1961). *The family and individual development.* London: Tavistock.

Winnicott, D. (1965). *The maturational processes and the facilitating environment.* New York: International Universities Press.

Winnicott, D. W. (1971). *Playing and reality.* London: Tavistock.

Winnicott, D. W. (1975). *Through paediatrics to psycho-analysis: Collected papers.* New York: Basic Books.

Wolf, E. S. (1988). *Treating the self: Elements of clinical self psychology.* New York: Guilford Press.

Worthington, E. L. (2010). *Coming to peace with psychology: What Christians can learn from the psychological sciences.* Downers Grove, IL: IVP Academic.

Wright, N. T. (1999). *The challenge of Jesus: Rediscovering who Jesus was and is.* Downers Grove, IL: InterVarsity Press.

Wright, R. (2010). Serving the cause of Christ: Wesley's "experimental religion" and psychology. In K. Armistead, B. Strawn, & R. Wright (Eds.), *Wesleyan theology and social science: The dance of practical divinity and discovery.* Cambridge: Cambridge Scholars Publishing.

Wright, R., & Strawn, B. D. (2010). Grief, hope and prophetic imagination: Psychoanalysis and Christian tradition in dialogue. *Journal of Psychology and Christianity, 29*(2), 149-57.

Wynkoop, M. B. (1967). *Foundations of Wesleyan-Arminian theology.* Kansas City: Beacon Hill Press.

Wynkoop, M. B. (1972). *A theology of love: The dynamic of Wesleyanism.* Kansas City: Beacon Hill.

Yangarber-Hicks, N. (2005). Messianic believers: Reflections on identity of a largely misunderstood group. *Journal of Psychology and Theology, 33*, 127-39.

Yangarber-Hicks, N., & Hicks, M. W. (2005). Messianic believers: Exploratory examination of cultural identity and psychotherapy experiences. *Journal of Psychology and Christianity, 24*, 219-32.

Yarhouse, M. A., & Sells, J. N. (2008). *Family therapies: A comprehensive Christian appraisal.* Downers Grove, IL: IVP Academic.

Zeitner, R. M. (2012). *Self within marriage: The foundation for lasting relationships.* New York: Routledge.

Zimmermann, J. (2013). *Incarnational humanism: A philosophy of culture for the church in the world.* Downers Grove, IL: IVP Academic.

List of Contributors

Earl D. Bland, PsyD, is a licensed psychologist, professor of psychology, and dean of the School of Behavioral Sciences and Counseling at MidAmerica Nazarene University. In addition, he teaches at the Greater Kansas City Psychoanalytic Institute and the Brookhaven Institute for Psychoanalysis and Christian Theology. Earl writes and presents in the areas of psychoanalytic treatment, spiritual formation and the integration of psychology and Christianity. He maintains a private practice where he treats individuals and couples.

Todd W. Hall, PhD, is a licensed psychologist, and serves at Rosemead School of Psychology, Biola University as professor of psychology, editor-in-chief of the *Journal of Psychology and Theology* and director of the Institute for Research on Psychology and Spirituality. He is the coauthor (with John Coe) of *Psychology in the Spirit: Contours of a Transformational Psychology* (IVP Academic).

Dr. Mitchell Hicks is a licensed clinical psychologist and earned his PhD in clinical psychology from the University of Cincinnati in 2003. He is a graduate of the Adult Psychoanalytic Psychotherapy Program at the Chicago Institute for Psychoanalysis and is a member of the full-time faculty in the Walden University School of Psychology's Clinical PhD program where he teaches classes in advanced psychopathology, ethics, religious and spiritual issues in psychotherapy, and practicum and internship seminars. He maintains a private practice in Arlington Heights, Illinois. Although he considers himself a generalist in working with adults and older adults, he has a particular interest in psychoanalytic psychotherapy, the psychology of men and masculinity, problems with pornography and sexual compulsivity, religious and spiritual material in therapy, and clinical supervision.

Lowell W. Hoffman, PhD, is a clinical psychologist in full-time practice at Brookhaven Center in Fogelsville, Pennsylvania. His certification as a psychoanalyst is from the New York University post-doctoral program in psychotherapy and psychoanalysis. He is a founding board member of the Society for Exploration of Psychoanalytic Therapies and Theology (SEPTT), faculty, supervisor, and codirector with Marie T. Hoffman, PhD, at Brookhaven Institute for Psychoanalysis and Christian Theology (BIPACT), and author of psychoanalytically integrative journal articles and book chapters.

Paul C. Jones, PhD, is a licensed psychologist and the director of the graduate programs in counseling at Southern Nazarene University. He served for four years as the executive director of Life Counseling Center, Southern Nazarene University's training and community mental health clinic, and is currently in private practice. He is the author of *Traditioning as Integration: Rationally Justifying the Practice of Relational Psychoanalysis in Social Trinitarian Theology* (2008).

Lauren E. Maltby, PhD, is a licensed psychologist specializing in child maltreatment and parent-child relationships. She is a program manager at For The Child, a child abuse prevention and treatment agency, and supervises at Harbor-UCLA Medical Center in the Child Trauma Clinic. She maintains a small private practice in Southern California.

Michael Mangis, PhD, is professor of psychology at Wheaton College, where he has taught master's and doctoral courses since 1989. In addition to numerous articles and book chapters, he is author of *Signature Sins: Taming Our Wayward Hearts* (InterVarsity Press, 2008). He is also a licensed clinical psychologist and licensed clinical professional counselor. For eleven years he was executive director of Heartland Counseling in Elburn, the training clinic for the Center for Rural Psychology, the non-profit Dr. Mangis founded in 2000. At Heartland, he supervised graduate interns as well as maintained his own clinical practice. Survivor of a stroke in 2008, his professional interests include traumatic brain injury, rural psychology, integration of psychology and Christianity, native American issues, ethics of professional counseling, and psychodynamic psychology.

Brad D. Strawn, PhD, is a licensed psychologist and the Evelyn and Frank Freed Professor of the Integration of Psychology and Theology at the Graduate School of Psychology, Fuller Theological Seminary. He has post-doctoral training in psychoanalysis, publishes regularly in integrative journals and most recently coauthored *The Physical Nature of Christian Life: Neuroscience, Psychology & the Church* (with Warren W. Brown, 2012). He is a faculty member of the Brookhaven Institute for Psychoanalysis and Christian Theology (BIPACT) and is an ordained elder in the Church of the Nazarene.

Theresa Clement Tisdale is a licensed clinical psychologist and professor of graduate psychology at Azusa Pacific University where she teaches psychodynamic psychotherapy as well as the integration of spirituality and spiritual formation with psychotherapy. She is currently a third year candidate at Newport Psychoanalytic Institute and maintains an independent practice in Glendora, California. Her academic, clinical and research specialties are psychodynamic psychotherapy, spirituality and spiritual formation, and the integration of spirituality/religion in clinical practice; she presents and publishes on each of these topics. She is also on the preaching team of Christ Our King Anglican Church in Azusa, California.

Ron Wright is professor and chair of the department of psychology and counseling at Southern Nazarene University. He attended Fuller Theological Seminary where he received a PhD in clinical psychology and a MA in theology. His research interests include the integration of relational psychoanalysis and Wesleyan theology, the philosophical and moral assumptions embedded within psychological theory and how those relate to theological perspectives, the relationship of attachment states of mind to spiritual development (including image of God), and mixed methods (qualitative and quantitative) approaches for examining cross-cultural perspectives on psychological well-being.

Index

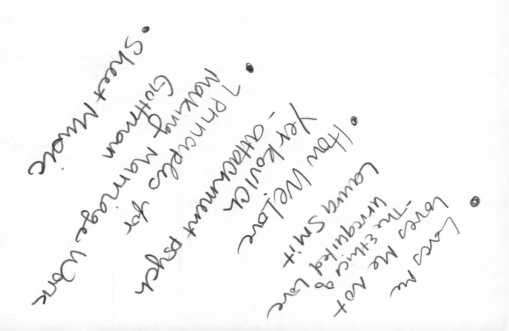